growing the

SOUTHWEST

garden

growing the SOUTHWEST garden

JUDITH PHILLIPS

Timber Press
Portland, Oregon

Frontispiece: The opportunity to visit places—to see what they're about, what they can support, what they want to be, and who will use them—and then to design gardens for those places, is a lifelong learning endeavor.

Photo credits appear on page 307.

Published in 2015 by Timber Press, Inc.

The Haseltine Building
133 S.W. Second Avenue, Suite 450
Portland, Oregon 97204-3527
timberpress.com

Printed in China
Text and series design by Jane Jeszeck

Library of Congress Cataloging-in-Publication Data

Phillips, Judith, 1949- author.
  Growing the Southwest garden/Judith Phillips. — First edition.
    pages cm
  Includes index.
  ISBN 978-1-60469-522-9 — ISBN 978-1-60469-521-2
  1. Gardening—Southwestern States. I. Title.
  SB453.2.A165P48 2015
  635.0979—dc23
                                   2014042914

A catalog record for this book is also available from the British Library.

*To the generous trees
that shade our gardens*

Contents

INTRODUCTION

The Changing Southwest

The arid Southwest has always been a place of extremes. We are home to some of the oldest continuously occupied human communities in the world and to the first commercial venture to launch civilians into space. We love extreme sports: snowboarding, white-water rafting, climbing 14,000-ft. peaks, and spelunking deep into subterranean caverns. And we are masters of an extreme sport we don't need to leave home to enjoy: gardening.

The edges of the garden are wrapped inside a wall, yet visibly connected to the low desert beyond. Ocotillo, acacia, and palo verde, native in the surrounding area, add color, fragrance, form, and texture, and are a prickly security barrier.

National Weather Service maps often show record daytime high temperatures in Phoenix, Arizona, while Alamosa, Colorado (scarcely 450 miles to the northeast as the crow flies), boasts the national nighttime low. Both are very dry; Phoenix in large measure due to the extreme heat, Alamosa because of its position in the rain shadow of the high peaks that surround it. While the positions of these places haven't changed in countless human lifetimes, the number of people who live in them or visit to enjoy their natural wonders has increased dramatically.

In many ways, Phoenix and Alamosa represent the changing Southwest, always a rugged landscape visited by adventurers and settled by hardy souls who saw the potential and were enticed by living on the edge. Urbanization has buffered some of the extremes and amplified others. While we live in air-conditioned comfort and turn on the tap when we're thirsty, the acres of hard surfaces—streets, parking lots, rooftops, and driveways that absorb heat and repel rainwater—have created heat islands in an already parched landscape. On the northern edge of the Chihuahuan Desert, where I've spent much of my life, climate extremes are leaving their mark. Our average 6 in. of rainfall has decreased by half some years, while hotter summers have increased the rate at which moisture evaporates. Like the meander of a phantom stream, dryness ripples through this place. The soil is parched deep below the surface and some plants now live rainfall to rainfall, as insecure a lifestyle as a family living paycheck to paycheck.

Shifts in the plant community and the wildlife it supports have been palpable for some time now, but change seems to be accelerating and intensifying: desert grass remains winter gray through several summers, awaiting rain that, like the kiss of Prince Charming, would bring it to life again. It's no fairy

In drought, desert grassland and the distant mesas are brown. Irrigated farmland runs like a ribbon of green through the parched landscape.

tale for the thousands of songbirds who rely on those grasses, consuming 50,000 seeds per bird per day, all winter. Grasslands gray instead of green; silence where there once was birdsong; sunbaked sidewalks and dying street trees—the question is, what can and should we do about it? Individually and as communities we can do plenty. We can garden with new attention to the place we live, the plants we choose to grow, and the way we care for those places and plants. This requires no sacrifice in the quality of the landscapes we create. In fact, we'll be more successful at growing beautiful gardens that are a joy to live in, harbor songbirds and butterflies, and don't break the water budget.

A PERSONAL JOURNEY

Change becomes real to people at different times and for different reasons. For me, the wake-up call came in early February of 2011, when across the Southwest there were a few nights of extremely low temperatures, well below zero in many places, -21°F in my garden. That brief episode had a profound effect on some of the plants that had been thriving here for years, and while the deep freeze was a shock, the rest of the growing season was worse. Very cold nights lingered through spring, while the days waxed from warm to hot. New shoots on plants turned black from frost, new buds opened green and then frosted black again before heat finally prevailed. In early May, high desert pre-dawns still hovered near freezing and the daytime temperatures spiked to 101°F. The only constants seemed to be months of Saharan-fine dust storms; smoke from enormous wildfires in Arizona, New Mexico, and Texas; and desert plants underfoot, dried crunchy as cornflakes. When rain finally came, it was a torrent that washed across the powdery soil, very little of the moisture penetrating to plant roots.

Flash floods are not a new phenomenon in the desert. As long as I've lived here, summer torrents have swept our arroyo every few years, causing no damage, bringing a surge of growth and blooms to the desert willows, Apache plume, and bush penstemon rooted in the usually dry streambed. Only in the last decade have floods significantly altered the arroyo's depth and meander and washed away many of the plants that once anchored the soil. The nearby bosque, the woodland along the Rio Grande, has been engulfed in flames at least once each spring and summer, as the mercury in the thermometer crept upward. The bosque doesn't spontaneously combust—people unaware of the brittle drought conditions have been the cause every time.

In the past decade, we've experienced a 10 percent increase in the number of days above 100 degrees, while gardeners in El Paso and Tucson marvel at our having so few blistering days. Clearly the extremes are growing more extreme and we need to find ways to cope with the new normal.

Being a gardener and garden designer, I look to nature for patterns that I can use to make spaces look and feel good for the plants and the people with whom I work. Many people in the Southwest are transplants from greener pastures (literally), and since our concept of beauty is formed early in our lives, we have a verdant ideal of the landscape— one that is very much at odds with the reality of this place. Even local natives who grew up in small towns kept green by acequias (community irrigation ditches), or were children of the early sprinkler age, when water was nearly free and lawns were considered a civic duty, have been using an unusually wet period as their norm. After the last severe drought, the 1930s through the mid-1960s, there was an abnormal wet stretch until the late 1990s, wetter than any other time in the last 2000 years.

Most of us enjoy viewing the stark drama of the desert at a safe distance, but we don't want to be poked by its sharp edges. I'm a transplant who arrived here from the soggy shore of Lake Erie, curious about the plants that native people relied on for food and fiber. I quickly rooted into the desert sand (remember, it was an unusually wet time, when the soil stayed moist a few inches below the surface), in love with the beautiful plants that surrounded me. Why wouldn't a garden of softly fragrant sages, vibrant wildflowers, and spectacular succulents draw people outdoors to connect with nature? In order to find ways to cope with the new extremes, we need to make that connection, learn

TOP Super storm cells move slowly across dry desert and dump unbelievable amounts of water on small areas, leaving the surrounding desert aching for just a few drops. BOTTOM Slow-moving torrential rains pound desert soil that is so dry, it repels the water. The dust picked up by the rain flows in sheets across the desert and fills arroyos with powerful, churning mud.

how dryland plants adapt to this climate, and use their adaptive savvy to guide our future gardening choices.

CHANGE IS GLOBAL

Deserts are places of extremes, so living here it's easy to assume that the new extremes are local and only temporary, but in recent years our whole planet has been undergoing some of the hottest, coldest, wettest, and driest weather worldwide since such data has been recorded. Technology allows images and ideas to spread, compressing both time and space. We can see polar bears faced with miles of open sea, where once they made their living on ice. Farmers in Indiana and Michigan turn what drought-shriveled crops they can to silage one year, the next year forced to delay planting because the soil is too soggy to till. In 2011, North America was walloped by winter storms. In 2012, it was Europe and North Africa's turn to shiver while much of the core of our continent enjoyed spring flowers a month before they normally bloom. 2013 brought abundant late-winter moisture and powerful community-flattening tornados to the middle of North America. The shifting climate has intensified the tornados that splinter lives, and has produced fierce winds called derechos. Such winds topple century-old trees and tear down power lines, leaving hundreds of thousands of people without lights or air-conditioning, while temperatures spike in the storm-ravaged areas. Summer firestorms and flooding—the yin and yang of calamity—have swept Australia with devastating power that we in the American West find all too familiar.

We are all affected by ice melting at the poles, even if it is in ways that seem abstract and convoluted. How can Arctic warming make southwestern winters colder? According to the Southwest Climate Change Network, ice melting in the Arctic exposes more of the dark-colored seawater, allowing it to absorb and release heat, in turn melting more ice. A warmer Arctic is weakening the temperature gradient from the North Pole southward to middle latitudes, causing the jet stream to dip and dive like a tango diva, letting frigid air pour into southern latitudes. In the United States, as the jet stream loops back north, it sweeps warm, moist air across the continent, dumping record snows on Northeast cities ill-equipped to manage such excess—while the Southwest remains drought stricken. This is equal-opportunity instability; throw a dart at the world map, and although the immediate causes differ, the effects are increasingly difficult to manage and costly to repair.

Individual weird weather events can be attributed to a perplexing number of interrelated contributing factors, but there's little doubt among people who work and play outdoors that change is indeed in the wind. Not only is the change measurable, we now have the tools to monitor it, and since there are many more people on the planet affected by it, we have strong impetus to learn how to cope. Desert plants are straightforward in dealing with stress, so they are excellent models for learning to cope with the changes here. They cut their losses in times of scarcity and burst out in blooms when rain finally comes. Those of us living in the arid Southwest—west Texas, New Mexico, Arizona, southeastern Nevada, southern Utah, and southwestern Colorado—are surrounded by an amazing array of plants known to be resilient and adaptable. Many have already made the move into cultivation, adopted by gardeners largely because they are beautiful. We are in the best possible time and place to learn how desert plants cope, and to recognize the winning strategies at work in plants from similar environments.

Our best response to the erratic nature of desert rain is to capture rainwater from rooftops to create blooming oases.

THE NEW NORMAL

In the desert, gardening has always been somewhat unpredictable; now we find ourselves facing hotter, drier summers with rain coming less frequently to cool and refresh the landscape. The new warming is only mildly discomfiting. We can adjust by adopting plants from slightly warmer ecosystems, better suited to the increasing heat. We can harvest rainwater to make better use of it when it comes. But higher high temperatures are only part of the change. The truly chilling projection is the probability of colder winter temperatures. Worse still, winters are likely to be erratically colder. Daily daytime temperatures in winter are likely to continue to grow milder, especially in urban areas where the oceans of asphalt create heat islands consistently 5 to 10 degrees warmer than temperatures in nearby rural areas. Then, as the wobbly jet stream allows

frigid Arctic air to plunge south, temperatures will drop precipitously for one or a series of nights, as occurred in February 2011. Plants are trapped in an oven turned icebox.

Higher summer temperatures would make heat-loving plants the obvious choice for adjusting our planting schemes, but surviving the occasional bitter cold events (in otherwise warmer winters) requires plants to be adapted to a greater degree of cold as well. In parts of the Southwest, the need to adapt to both near-zero and triple-digit temperatures is of great concern, because plants rarely do both. In low desert areas, the high temperatures are inching from scorching to broiling, while the low temperatures, which historically seldom dropped below freezing, are flirting with frost more often. A consequence of the new extremes could be greater plant loss with fewer alternatives able to survive the stress, unless we manage space and water with a goal of tempering heat and buffering cold.

Where greater extremes equal loss of biodiversity, our best bet might be to think in terms of garden ecology. Just as preserving ecosystem diversity on a global scale is a first line of defense in slowing the impact of climate change, harboring diversity is a way of coping with the new extremes in our gardens. A large gene pool of adaptive plants begets new plants that are even better suited to local conditions. We are fortunate that the extremes in elevation and precipitation make western North America one of the most biologically diverse areas anywhere on earth. If plants are to adapt to changing environments quickly (and there is evidence that in just three generations a plant can be significantly different than its parentage), they need the richest gene pool possible to make the leap. The more genetic variability available, the greater the rate of adaptation possible.

Conventional horticulture and agriculture have focused on specific goals; breeders select for desirable qualities such as larger flowers, new and unusual bloom colors and forms, prolonged blooming, uniform growth habits, and uniform ripening time. Nature places survival and regeneration at the top of her list of selection priorities. In nature, the plants best adapted to their current circumstances are the ones that reproduce successfully. The poorly adapted wither and die, taking with them the genes that made them less suited to the place. The time, water, and chemicals consumed by lawn

TOP Extreme winter cold damages plants and takes time to repair. MIDDLE Extreme summer heat also damages plants and takes time to repair. BOTTOM Diversity is nature's way of dealing with calamity. Ecosystem stability depends on it.

monocultures are only one example of the high price we pay in disease and insect susceptibility and resource consumption, when diversity is sacrificed for an ideal of uniformity. Ecological balances falter when diversity declines, whether in nature or in our gardens. Including layers of well-adapted plants in our landscapes helps reverse the trend toward homogeneity. Every garden has an impact; a community of gardens much more so. A nation of gardens that harbor local diversity is a giant step toward ecological stability.

YOUR PLACE, YOUR GARDEN

Understanding the place where you garden is the first step toward a planting that thrives. Plants respond to place with alacrity. Some are generalists, able to inhabit a broad range of landscape niches. Others have more specific needs and adaptations. Some tolerate extreme heat and/or drought. Some adapt to extreme cold, while others tolerate only limited degrees of cold. Desert plants endure rapid shifts in temperature, while Mediterranean natives prefer more consistency day to night and season to season. Riparian plants tolerate periodic flooding, adapting to saline soils and growing quickly when water is available.

Some plants respond to warm days and nights while others grow more rapidly while temperatures are cool. Many arid-adapted plants reseed prolifically, competing aggressively for resources. Most are resilient in wind because they have limber stems and/or strong wood. Plants native to harsh environments have developed several of these adaptations that combine to give them an edge. Through natural selection, plants continuously diversify in order to better adapt to changing growing conditions. If within three generations plants can become better suited to their altered environment, in as little

as three or four years many wildflowers and native grasses will genetically adapt to new extremes. Gardeners can learn to foster resilience. How we treat the plants in our gardens can either nudge them toward being better suited to the extremes—or make them dependent on a steady input of resources (the drip, drip, drip of irrigation) to survive.

Nature embraces change, employs it to spur greater resilience. To survive the changing climate, we'll need to choose plants with the extremes in mind, bumping resilience to the top of the list of priorities in our nursery shopping cart. Understanding how plants adapt, what they need to quickly establish and stay healthy, is as handy as a well-sharpened spade.

The big picture

The first part of this book, "The Wisdom of Place" outlines the great span of the southwestern deserts, how geography and our place on the map influence conditions in our gardens. While gardening in arid places is not a sport for wimps and the prospect of greater climatic extremes is daunting, we desert gardeners and our resilient xeric plants are up to the challenge. We dig and weed, haul mulch and prune, all the while thinking about how and where plants fit into the plan. We look at the lay of the land, see the way rain and wind flow across it, and the response of plants to their situations. We grow with our gardens.

Because gardens are processes, not end products, they are open-ended efforts to make spaces comfortable and beautiful. Whether you are faced with a blank slate where you want to make a garden or are just intermittently replacing plants that have been severely damaged or killed by weird weather events, the first order of business is to envision the spaces in which you want to live. What kinds of surfaces are needed for the ways you want to use

Local biomes are rich plant communities that can add resilience to our gardens.

A high desert garden on the edge of wild land mirrors and expands on the native plants that surround it, blending seamlessly and enriching wildlife habitat.

different areas? Do the spaces available for planting suit the plants you want to grow? To plant lovers, this may seem backwards, but more often than not, choosing and placing plants is an exercise in mediation. Consider where you have or want a patio, and if a tree might shade it. Factor in the rainwater that could flood in from nearby roof gutters, as well as what will run off the patio pavement. Then search for the tree or trees that might thrive under the given conditions. Larger trees need both more canopy space and more rooting area. To accommodate a shade tree, you may need to adjust the placement of a building addition or the size or shape of a patio. Perhaps smaller trees with deeper roots might fit the space and require no architectural changes.

Understanding how a space works—where rainwater enters, wind howls, cold air or water pools and persists; where heat accumulates, light is most intense, and shade is deepest; where soil is compacted, and people and pets make paths and linger—reveals cues to the potential of the place. This knowledge helps determine which areas will be planted, and leads to ideas for plants that might thrive in them.

Planning with flexibility

"Taming the Elements with Design," the book's second part, discusses how to reconcile the various ways you want to use space with the ambient conditions in place. A design gallery of images offers a range of solutions to many design challenges that are typical of southwestern gardens: buffering harsh conditions with walls or fences, shade covers draped with vines, patios for living outdoors, harvested rainwater feeding cool tree-shaded spaces, dramatic desert plant vignettes. You can imagine how the pictured gardens might translate to your spaces, weigh your options, consider the merits of each, and start putting together a plan of action.

Matching plants and places

Plants in the landscape are interdependent. A tree or vine canopy affects the light available to nearby plants; the roots compete for space, water, and nutrients. The moisture required by a large shade tree determines the water budget for everything within its rooting area. Many southwestern gardeners use what are really large shrubs as their shade canopy, surrounded by compatible smaller shrubs, cacti, and other succulents, as well as seasonal annual and perennial flowers and grasses to carpet the soil. In the book's third part, "Planting for Southwest Success," you'll find a palette of plants I've found to be well-suited to the extreme conditions Southwest gardeners encounter, along with informative descriptions.

Managing your Southwest garden

When the purposes served by the plants in the garden are understood, appropriate maintenance can follow and this chicken and egg relationship is explored in "Good Southwest Gardening Practices,"

the fourth part of this book. The sometimes atypical soil preferences of desert plants are discussed here, as well as ways to manage water needs and usage efficiently. The threat of regional pests and diseases is also covered, as well as the cleanup and maintenance measures that are essential to a healthy southwestern garden.

We live in a time of rapid change. Creating landscapes that respond successfully to ongoing shifts is one of the most compelling challenges of our era. What I offer here are suggestions for coping with and adapting to the new extremes in southwestern gardens. Much of this advice comes from the years I've spent learning from plants that are masters of resilience, from observing how they respond to stress, and how what might be considered poor growing conditions are nearly ideal from a desert plant's perspective. We can make our own lives and gardens small islands of ecological equity in a turbulent sea, by adopting the carpe diem attitude of the plants around us. Collectively aiding and abetting garden resiliency, playing in the dirt, smelling the rosewoods, can make refuges of the places we live. To me, that's a small step in a good direction.

THE WISDOM OF PLACE

The ecology and wisdom of the arid Southwest is complex; gardening here can be challenging—but it is never boring. How a garden settles into its surroundings determines how it feels to spend time there, as well as how much effort it will take to maintain. Dudley Patterson, a White Mountain Apache elder, described the strong influence that landscape features have on his people: "Wisdom sits in places." Understanding the peculiarities, the wisdom of a place, can make it much more rewarding to garden there. While there are few shortcuts to this knowledge, there are many paths to understanding.

Beavertail prickly pear cactus (*Opuntia basilaris*) knows its place. In hot desert it orients its pads to avoid scorching sun; in cold desert it orients to capture warmth.

Satellite images allow us to travel across the Southwest and gain an appreciation for the grand and diverse places we garden. The major rivers are highlighted: higher elevation communities draw water directly from mountain streams fed by snowmelt, while most desert cities cluster near the rivers that are fed by all the small mountain streams.

UNDERSTANDING THE EXTREMES

The screen of your laptop gives you an enticing window on the world, a bird's-eye view of the high mountains and desert basins, as well as the watersheds that connect them. By satellite, you can tour the entire Southwest in minutes, 100 miles above the earth. Zoom in to view your watershed and your community from 25 miles overhead. Zoom in again to 7500 ft. for a closer look at your neighborhood and your garden.

You can see exactly how many degrees north of the equator you are, which directly affects the angle of the sun on your space at different times of the year. From the date on the satellite image you can see the slanted shadows—angled strongly northward if the image was made in December. The further south you are, the stronger the shadows are angled to the south in June or July. This is a paradigm shift if you move to the Southwest from Chicago or Spokane, and think of the north sides of buildings as being persistently shady. In fact, the northwest side of your garden can be very hot and sunny in summer if it bakes in the sun through the hottest part of the day; much cooler if shaded by a few well-placed trees.

THE LAY OF THE LAND: INFLUENCE OF REGIONAL GEOGRAPHY

From 100 miles up, the Southwest is a rumpled canvas. The great brown sweeps of desert or grassland erupt into darker-shaded mountains and canyons. Shadows mark barely distinct watersheds. Large urban areas are faint geometry imposed on the land. From this lofty position, you witness the impact of intercontinental position, mountain and basin topography, and urban heat islands on the distribution of rainfall. From 10 miles above the earth, urban grids lie in stark contrast to the undulations of the earth. Spaces between the mountains and mesas look empty. This is deceptive, as is the perception of the rigid flatness of the urban grids. Across the Southwest, there is great variation in both the contours of the land and the diverse plants that grow there. From 25,000 ft. you retain the sense of the expansiveness, but you can also trace the source of your drinking water, from the closest peaks to the basin nearest you. Like looking at a photo of an ancestor, you glimpse the source of the life within you.

When you descend to 7500 ft., forms become more distinct. Relative sizes can be deceptive and you see that the shadows are actually shades of green. Peaks 14,000 ft. high rise up and seem to almost touch the camera as you drift past. Where water runs through it, the landscape is obviously more vibrantly green. You can discern dominant

For landscape design, native plants that transition gracefully from wildlands to gardens come from the middle ground, niches between 2500 ft. and 7500 ft. in elevation.

A satellite image with the watersheds that flow through Albuquerque, New Mexico, highlighted helps us understand how complex and tenuous water is in the Southwest. The only perennial stream is the highly manipulated Rio Grande in the center of the image.

plant types: pointy mountaintop conifers, round-crowned ponderosa pines and oaks, charred burn scars from recent infernos, shrubby growth a decade after fire, and remnants of dense, stream-side forests called bosques. The sparser forests on mesa tops and east- and north-facing slopes are junipers, pinyons, and possibly oaks. Dark dots spaced just close enough to be in shouting range of each other might be junipers. Further south the dots are more likely to be mesquite or creosote bushes. Cities are either oases, their urban forests

Become a watershed tourist and travel to the top of the mountains nearest you to survey the immensity of the Southwest and witness water as the source of life.

supplemented by irrigation and rainwater harvested from the impervious surfaces, or they are hard edged and harsh.

At 7500 ft., the impact of water on the land and plants is clear. Glistening ribbons, muddy flows, and rippling pools trace the flow of water across the landscape. You can begin to discern soil types: barely weathered rocky foothills; sweeping skirts of alluvial fans; older, eroded, fine-grained open plains; ancient clays of the floodplains; active dune sand; arroyo corridors swept by periodic floods and

persistent winds. In the vast, undeveloped spaces surrounding the places we live, in the diversity or in the lack of vegetation, the patterns of water and the human footprint on the land loom large.

Although a drop in temperature of 3½ degrees usually accompanies a 1000-ft. rise in elevation, plant migrations are not just upslope to escape heat. Cool air is denser than warm and pools in low pockets, so temperatures in upland canyons and valleys can be 15 degrees cooler than on surrounding slopes exposed to sun and wind.

Northeast-facing exposures are consistently cooler, especially from autumn through the middle of spring, when they receive less direct sunlight. Because they are cooler, their soils retain more moisture. As conifer forests die out, the few survivors are likely to be found near the toe of northeast-facing slopes where extra moisture accumulates and evaporates more slowly. Spongy limestone outcroppings and moisture-retaining deposits of volcanic rock will also harbor plants in places that would otherwise be too dry. South and west exposures are hotter and drier, heat up earlier in spring, and may push the limits of poorly adapted plants in summer—keeping them actively growing later in fall, or nudging them out of dormancy sooner in late winter—unless water is withheld to prevent freeze damage. These details we learn best by experiencing them, by being out on the land, hearing the crunch of dry soil underfoot. Catching a whiff of sage, juniper, or creosote bush, or the sweet scent of moisture, a gardener absorbs the wisdom of place like a thirsty dryland shrub eager to root more deeply.

SEASONS: HOTTER/COLDER, RAINIER/DRIER

Seasonal pulses of heat and cold, wet and dry are normal in arid ecosystems—our temperatures and rainfall usually yo-yo compared with places having more cloud cover and abundant moisture. Average temperatures and rainfall are almost meaningless numbers from a practical gardening standpoint. In this place of extremes, average is the middle ground we swing past on our way from the highs to the lows, the wet to the dry. In the Southwest, daytime temperatures creep steadily upward, with acres upon acres of sunbaked paving and walls absorbing heat during the day, adding up to 6 degrees to the ambient temperature in urban areas. Like embers in a fireplace, they continue to heat the surrounding air

long after the sun sets. The lack of moisture, low humidity, and clear skies at night used to guarantee a cooling respite. Now in large cities, nighttime temperatures remain unnaturally warm. An increase of 6 to 22 degrees is possible, depending on the space. Even if rainfall amounts stay nearly the same, higher temperatures raise evapotranspiration (moisture loss) rates, so the net result is less available water. Yet there is potential advantage to all the hard surfaces if they are utilized to capture rainwater and divert it to plants, especially to trees that in return will buffer the heat.

Miles from urban heat islands, up on the high ridges of the southern Rockies, even in rare years with deep accumulations of snow, downslope reservoirs now capture less than in the past. Wind storms in the desert thousands of feet below loft fine dust particles high into the atmosphere. The dust settles on the snow, turning the surface dark and heating it enough to slowly melt into the soil or vaporize into the air. Less snow accumulates, until warming spring temperatures begin a thaw that fills streams, snowmelt rushing downslope to fill reservoirs stored for agriculture and urban use. Unseasonably warm winds are more likely to sublimate the frozen moisture into the atmosphere before it melts. Precious moisture goes from solid ice and snow to dissipated vapor before roots can absorb it. Forest trees live storm to storm, with little moisture reserved in the soil.

There's no joy in Mudville if there's no mud in Mudville. Less water stored in reservoirs is also less water available for human use. Still, the mountaintops receive two to three times the precipitation of the desert below. One of the frustrations of desert gardeners is watching virga, clouds that drift overhead trailing curtains of rain that evaporate 1000 ft. overhead. Sometimes you can smell the rain as it floats by to drop on the nearest mountain ridges.

Reciprocity makes the survival of trees and human comfort possible in the desert.

The drier the land becomes, the wetter the clouds must be to break the drought and rain on the lowlands. In response to ecological change, wildlife and native plants adapt or migrate. Most people, having built livelihoods in concrete oases, must do the same. Learning to capture rainwater from rooftops and pavement can help offset the changes. As carbon builds up in the atmosphere, many plants are expected to grow faster and larger, but at lower elevations, increasing warmth and the corresponding decrease in available moisture becomes an even greater limitation to growth.

Watersheds are born in the high mountains. In cold desert areas, snow on the mountains in winter makes farmers optimistic. In the low desert, clouds collecting in the highlands generate hope, even if they often bring no moisture.

The Southwest area covered in this book includes four general climate regions that sometimes play outside the lines. An island of Cold/Semi-Arid Foothills climate can be found around Flagstaff, whose larger surrounding area is mostly Cool/High Desert. Likewise, the area around Ruidoso is an outpost of Cool/High Desert in the middle of Warm/Intermediate Desert. So goes the Southwest. These are not hard and fast climate boundaries; some years this map might look very different. But I have tried to provide general designations to help gardeners in their planning.

DESERT CLIMATES AND MICROCLIMATES

The Southwest area covered in this book includes four general climate regions that sometimes play outside the lines. An island of Cold/Semi-Arid Foothills climate can be found around Flagstaff, whose larger surrounding area is mostly Cool/High Desert. Likewise, the area around Ruidoso is an outpost of Cool/High Desert in the middle of Warm/Intermediate Desert. So goes the Southwest. These are not hard and fast climate boundaries; some years this map might look very different. But I have tried to provide general designations to help gardeners in their planning.

Hot/Low Desert

While it may seem redundant to label an area hot desert—like calling fire "hot"—in terms of garden climate, it is very appropriate to distinguish between the hot deserts, the more temperate warm deserts, and the cold deserts of the Southwest. The differences in ideal planting and pruning times, when pests are likely to proliferate, and when and how much to water can vary by a month or more as temperatures rise and fall with the elevation. Hot or low desert is primarily the Lower Colorado Basin in western and southern Arizona, including Phoenix and Yuma. Here, in the hottest and most arid of the deserts, where summer nights may remain above 90°F, constant heat and drought are the challenges. Planting is done in fall, as winter is the best season for establishing new plants and renewing growth of existing ones. Pruning for shape and to remove any dieback from rare but damaging frost is done in spring, and done lightly to prevent sunscald. Some cleanup pruning is done in autumn to remove heat damage and prepare for new growth. Late autumn through midspring are ideal outdoor living times. Summer is the reason air-conditioning was invented.

Deserts that inspire our gardens are the beautiful, resilient, water-thrifty plant communities that dominate the Southwest.

Warm/Intermediate Desert

The warm or intermediate desert covers Tucson and Sedona, Arizona; Roswell and Las Cruces in southern New Mexico; El Paso and Midland-Odessa in southwest Texas; St. George, Utah; and Las Vegas, Nevada. Spikes of extreme heat are tempered by periods of summer temperatures in the 90s. Winter temperatures may drop below freezing at night any time between mid-November and mid-March, but quickly rebound. Planting may be done in fall to establish larger plants, but in intermediate areas, planting is also done in spring once the coldest nights have passed. Pruning for shape and to repair damage from occasional and more severe deep freezes than experienced in low desert is done in spring—lightly, to prevent sunscald. Light cleanup pruning may be done at the end of summer to repair heat damage.

The great diversity of Southwest microclimates creates a dazzling mosaic of garden possibilities and pitfalls.

Cool/High Desert

The cool or high desert covers the Colorado Plateau from the Mogollon Rim to the foothills of the southern Rockies, and the short-grass prairie east of the mountains, including Prescott, Arizona;Albuquerque, Ruidoso, and Farmington, New Mexico; Lubbock and Amarillo, Texas; and Grand Junction, Colorado. The coolest of the deserts, these areas drop below freezing most nights in winter, and spike to 100°F or higher in summer, interrupted by periods of high 80s to mid-90s. Even in urban areas, night temperatures cool to the 60s and 70s. Planting of temperate climate plants is done in fall, as a prolonged cold period is best for establishing them. Planting of heat-adapted plants is done in spring, when the soil has warmed enough to stimulate rooting. Pruning to remove any damage from severe frost is done late in spring, to avoid removing more growth than necessary, and as in the other deserts, done lightly to prevent sunscald.

Cold/Semi-Arid Foothills

The cold and semi-arid foothills at around 7500 ft. elevation include the communities of Flagstaff, Arizona; Durango, Colorado Springs, and Pueblo, Colorado; Santa Fe and Taos, New Mexico. While some degree of drought permeates the entire Southwest, these places are cool enough in summer—typically in the high 80s, rarely spiking near triple digits, with clouds that are more likely to bring actual relief to the highlands. Lofted high into the atmosphere by heat reflected from the soil in low deserts, moisture in the mountain foothills is cool enough to condense as rain. Soils here retain moisture, likely to have more organic matter from decomposing leaves and

roots. Planting is done in late spring, as winter is too cold for root development; late spring and summer are the best seasons for establishing new plants and renewing growth in existing ones. Pruning times are similar to the high desert, and mulch is added in autumn to protect tender plants.

Each of these regions has many subtle variations on the theme of how climate shapes the garden. Each city has microclimates that beg for further finesse, and as cities grow they shift in climate, becoming warmer and more arid.

Even in a small garden, the variations of how air and water flow though the landscape can create distinct microclimates that can be used to great advantage. Windbreaks increase the nutrient-holding capacity of a space, and tender plants can be sheltered from extremes by hardier trees and shrubs, walls, and overhangs. Citrus trees growing among mesquites and palo verdes suffer less dieback than those growing out in the open, where the wobbly jet stream can allow polar air to sweep into the desert. Active growth of some species is possible whenever the median temperature is 40°F for at least two weeks. Cool season species may initiate new growth when day temperatures are 50°F and nights hover near freezing, while warm season species

TOP Depending on where you live, spring in the desert can be ablaze with annual wildflowers or soft green with new grasses and yucca blooms. BOTTOM South and west exposures are hotter and drier, heat up earlier in spring, and may push the limits of poorly adapted plants in the extremes of summer heat and winter cold.

rarely initiate growth until nighttime temperatures are consistently 50°F or higher. The air calmed by enclosures keeps the temperature warmer, as walls and paving absorb heat during the day. The enclosed space may stay several degrees warmer overnight. This can protect plants from routine cold, but make them softer and more vulnerable in extreme cold events. Managing water carefully in winter, being quite miserly once plants are well rooted, allows plants to harden off and helps to minimize frost damage. The planting and pruning times and watering suggestions given in this book are optimal, producing less stress on the plants and on the people tending them. Real life and successful gardens happen while we're planning other options.

RAIN ON ME: THE DESERT PLANTS' REFRAIN

Learning the commonalities and peculiarities of a place is a wise move on the part of the Southwest gardener. Moisture is not distributed evenly throughout the year or the region. Summer rainfall in much of Arizona amounts to about half the year's moisture, but in Prescott it is often less than 50 percent of average annual precipitation. In Texas and New Mexico, east of the central mountains, summer rainfall is 75 percent of average annual precipitation, while in central and western New Mexico, summer rainfall can be as much as 90 percent of average annual precipitation. Alamosa, Colorado, at 7400 ft. elevation, defies the old Rocky Mountain paradigm of deep snowpack. Winter and spring are Alamosa's driest seasons and snow depth isn't a good indication of moisture, as 30 in. of snow might yield just

A courtyard oasis protected by walls can be lusher than the surrounding landscape, without breaking the water budget.

over an inch of water. In the rain shadow of high peaks, Alamosa receives half the precipitation of other places of comparable elevation.

Across the region, most summer rain comes as violent downpours that turn dry arroyos into raging rivers, while winter moisture is often a light drizzle that lasts for a few days and soaks into the soil. Though varying in degree, limited rainfall, warm temperatures, and high solar radiation can create evapotranspiration accounting for moisture loss equivalent to two to three times the average rainfall. This results in prolonged periods of plant somnolence or dormancy. Scant rainfall results in soils low in organic matter and high in mineral salts, sometimes forming caliche, an impervious layer of calcium carbonate that limits the path of water and roots through the soil. Since regionally native plants are already adapted to these climate extremes, it seems prudent to rely on them for the framework of the garden.

Because there is such a wide sweep of elevation, moisture, and temperature ranges in the Southwest, and some plants adapt to a large portion of the range, notes on the mature size of plants in their descriptions can be confusing. Wide variations in size that read like typos are due to similarly wild variations in available moisture and ultimate heat and cold. Broadly adapted plants are likely to grow much larger where ample water is available, and conversely remain compact where drought is constantly extreme. The length of the growing season has a cumulative impact on size. Up to a point, as temperatures remain warm longer, plants continue to grow. A shrub in Tucson may have a month longer of active growth than it does in Albuquerque. The heat in Phoenix may suppress growth during the summer, just as cold suppresses growth in Taos in winter—so the number of frost-free nights isn't the

Low desert plants are best adapted to persistent heat and drought, but have little tolerance of extreme cold.

LEFT Intermediate desert seasons can change abruptly—for example, an unexpected snowstorm and the return of mild temperatures, sometimes on the same day. Moisture is always welcome. RIGHT High desert at the edge of woodland is the most temperate climate, but conifer die-off indicates drier conditions have become persistent.

only indication of how plants will perform. The number of consecutive days with temperatures above 100°F also limits annual growth, as can light intensity and exposure. Plants growing in light shade in an enclosed space will generally grow larger (given the same amount of water) because they can use more of the water for growth. Extreme sunlight and wind both increase evapotranspiration and create the compact plant forms that are characteristic of arid places.

Climate and supplemental moisture needs

How often plants need supplemental water changes seasonally, varying with the type of plants and how well-rooted they are. The extreme cold of higher elevations calls for a drastic reduction or suspension of watering from late August through mid-March. This will cause plants to go dormant as days shorten,

By early summer, the lowlands are waiting for rain. Clouds not quite wet enough to rain trail virga, curtains of moisture that dry before they hit the ground.

and stay dormant until the temperatures moderate in spring. Rain and snow are sufficient moisture for most deciduous plants, except in extremely dry winters. Conifers may be watered every six weeks to limit bark beetle infestation due to low sap pressure. In hot desert areas where frosts are rare, the return of cooler temperatures spurs growth in many plants; they may need added moisture to support new foliage and flowers. Regardless of where you garden, it is prudent to water only enough to keep plants healthy, as erratic cold events are possible in all areas from mid-December through February. Moisture-filled plants are more vulnerable to cold, whether the thermometer reads 25°F or -25°F.

We as gardeners can become attuned to the pulses of wet and dry, cold and hot, wise to the ways of this beautifully extreme place.

ALL ABOUT EXTREMES

In order to grow, plants need space both above and below ground. One of the dilemmas of desert gardening is knowing when to stop—finding a balance between shading the soil to keep it cooler, but not crowding plants so their shapes become indistinguishable. The plant density of nearby undeveloped areas can offer some insight into what is sustainable. Another balance peculiar to southwestern gardening is learning to water so that plants are healthy, but not so lush that they lure every pest looking for a free lunch. Once plants are well-rooted, applying water in infrequent, soaking pulses akin to and in lieu of natural rainfall patterns keeps desert plants healthier than maintaining consistently damp soil. The colder the winters are likely to be, the more gardeners should encourage fall dormancy by withholding water at the end of summer. Being slow to respond to the onset of budding in spring not only saves water, but also helps reduce freeze damage. Arid-adapted plants are truly marvelous—extremely resource efficient because they have to be. *Leucophyllum* was known among early settlers as barometer bush or rain sage because the buildup of moisture in the air that leads to summer monsoons is enough to cause plants to bud, and they are quick to bloom when rain comes.

OPPOSITE TOP **Natural springs and the oases of plants they support are rare and precious in the Southwest.**
OPPOSITE BOTTOM **The young orchard at the Rio Grande Botanic Garden demonstrates both traditional acequias and modern bubbler irrigation.**

PLANTS ADAPTING TO EXTREMES

Adaptation to cold, heat, and dryness defines a plant's suitability to the desert landscape. The American West is warming more rapidly than many other parts of the continental United States. Fortunately, we live surrounded by rich islands of diversity, where native plant populations are making incremental adjustments to local shifts in heat and cold and increasing dryness.

Because of the varied topography of mountain ranges and the lowlands between them, there are tens of thousands of warmer and cooler, wetter and drier niches. In many places, entire forests and grasslands are thinning or disappearing, replaced by more heat- and drought-resistant shrubs. We can apply observations of how and where plants adapt in nature to our gardens, learning which plants tolerate the greatest extremes and which plants need a buffer. Because microclimates can span two or more hardiness zones within the same garden, many of the plant descriptions in this book give the ultimate temperature range within which each plant is known to have grown well. The more familiar you are with the microclimates in your garden, the better you will know the cold sinks and hot spots and can judge what is best suited where.

Plants that have a wide native range can be quite genetically distinct in terms of the degree of heat, cold, and drought to which they are best suited. Creosote bush, native near super-hot Phoenix, may freeze to the ground or even die in cooler Albuquerque, while plants grown from seeds collected near Socorro hardly show any tip damage. *Salvia greggii* may be quite long-lived and bloom most of the summer in cooler Santa Fe or Lubbock, but suffer several stress-related maladies in hotter Tucson, and be hardly worth planting in Yuma. Ideally, we could choose plants that are locally grown under similar climatic conditions from seeds harvested nearby, but profit margins dictate that large wholesale nurseries cluster where the growing season is longer, so they do their customers a great service when they document their seed sources. Extreme gardeners should look for plants grown from stock adapted to their region under conditions as similar as possible to where they will be expected to live, whenever possible patronizing local growers.

A fernbush leaf. Note the fine dissection that dissipates heat, and soft hairs that shade the surface and reduce evapotranspiration.

ADAPTING TO COLD

Cold induces dormancy, a restorative rest period that prolongs the lifespan of plants adapted to it. Cold also stimulates hormonal changes that make plants more fruitful—apples, pears, plums, peaches, and apricots all require some chilling to be productive. Many alpine plants require a prescribed number of cold hours, as well as exposure to intense ultraviolet light in order to set viable seed. These plants may grow outside their adaptive ranges but they will only reproduce where they are very well suited, the ultimate sign of health and well-being in the natural world. Tropical plants may be long-lived perennials in their native range, but they act as frost-tender annuals in climates with hot summers and cold winters. Mediterranean plants are typically heat and drought tolerant and some are much more cold tolerant than they need to be where they are native, but in Mediterranean climates, there is relatively little temperature change day to night and season to season. Jupiter's beard, thyme, and culinary sage as well as some cultivars of rosemary, oregano, and rock rose tolerate southwestern extremes with grace. Other Mediterranean plants are not as well adapted.

Roots are key agents of resilience, increasing the plant's ability to absorb moisture and to store energy. Buffered by soil, cold usually has much less impact on roots than it does on the top growth, so roots are likely to be less cold tolerant than the top growth. In places where winter temperatures fluctuate widely and wildly, plants in raised beds or pots need extra protection from the extremes. Raised beds might be built of insulating material, such as stone or solid block, or be relatively shallow—12 to 16 in. high—so that plants can root deeper than the bed. Raised beds can also be built large enough so roots along the edges can burn or freeze off, while plants maintain enough root mass for them to remain viable. Plants in pots can be moved to cooler, shaded spots during the hottest summer months in the low desert, moved to warmer spaces in cold winter areas, or planted with annuals that are replaced seasonally.

Low desert plants tolerate more extreme heat but less cold. Many are vulnerable to temperatures below 20°F. Cold desert plants evolved to survive heat and cold and rapid shifts between the two extremes, but prolonged exposure to extreme heat may weaken and finally kill them. The beauty of diversity is having access to plants that are well suited to a broad range of extremes. The U.S. Department of Agriculture's Plant Hardiness Zone Map is the most widely accepted resource for figuring out hardiness zones, and their updated map reflects the changes in climate regionally (search the Internet for "USDA Hardiness Zones," or visit planthardiness.ars.usda.gov to find your exact zone by entering your zip code). But the mosaic of elevation, exposure, and urban heating in the West make trial-and-error experimentation a fact of life—the fun and sometimes the frustration of playing in the southwestern garden.

ADAPTING TO HEAT AND ARIDITY

Drought and heat are inextricably linked. Any way you measure it, even in periods that exceed average rainfall in the desert Southwest, drought is a given. The demand for water consistently exceeds precipitation, the severity of drought varying from year to year and place to place. Supply is managed by channeling flows and mining groundwater. While recognizing cold damage seems fairly straightforward, constantly exceeded heat tolerance sets off a cascade of enzymatic changes within the plant that

A group of Sonora Desert plants exhibit many drought adaptations. The wildflowers bloom early, avoiding drought. Yucca stores moisture in its leaves and stem. Ocotillo leaves persist only until heat and drought intensify, then the stems assume the role of food production, as do the stems of the palo verde. Many of the plants have small leaves, reducing evaporative surface, and dissipating heat.

can be intensified by drought, but are difficult to distinguish from the symptoms of lack of water. During prolonged cold periods, as cold-dormant plants transpire significantly less water, withholding water is a fairly simple matter. As temperatures soar, our instinct is to add more water—not always the best response to heat-related plant stress. Many indicators of heat stress are similar to those of drought stress, including dieback of buds, stunted growth, and discolored leaves. When humidity is low, the evapotranspiration rates of temperate-climate foliage may exceed the ability of the roots to pull moisture from the soil. Leaves scorch even when the soil is saturated. Climate change is raising the severity of drought beyond the point where poorly adapted plants can grow well. Not only is there less water per household to lavish on perennially stressed plants, the plants themselves languish and sometimes die, despite heroic efforts to keep them alive.

Plants respond to lack of moisture by wilting, which reduces the leaf surface exposed to full sun. Wilting occurs in stages. Incipient wilting occurs when leaves and stems lose moisture to a degree that is technically measurable but observable only by subtle change in leaf color—a slight dulling and graying of the leaves, which is a sign that plants are lightly stressed. Temporary wilting occurs when plants obviously lose turgor during the day, like zucchini leaves midday in July. The amount of moisture transpired exceeds the amount absorbed, but there is enough moisture in the soil that plants can recover overnight when temperatures cool down. Plants vary greatly in their tolerances. Heat-loving species are adapted to frequent temperature spikes above 100°F. Permanent wilting occurs when the soil becomes so dry that plants cannot recover unless water is added to the soil. Permanent wilting may become fatal if dry conditions persist.

The region-wide die-off of pines and junipers in places they have dominated for centuries is evidence of persistent, heat-related drought. Ongoing research is demonstrating just how differently these two arid-adapted conifers respond to heat and drought. Pinyons close their stomata and try to wait out the onslaught of dry heat. When extreme conditions prove long term, they die of carbon starvation. Junipers keep leaf pores open and sacrifice whole limbs trying to wait out the stress, dying of thirst if relief is too long in coming. The scientific consensus is that due to the combined impact of warmer temperatures and reduced soil moisture, the extensive conifer forests of the West will be a memory within two human generations. Because trees take generations to mature, what you plant in your garden today must be able to adapt to ongoing change to survive the new extremes. Desert plants have evolved ways to survive; they make the most of times when water is more abundant and wait out periods of shortfall. Some avoid heat and drought. Others endure the extremes by developing much greater seasonal root mass. Employing an extensive kit of survival tools enables the best-adapted plants to absorb whatever moisture is available and use it conservatively, despite intense sunlight and heat, low humidity, and moisture-stealing wind.

Drought evasion strategies: avoiding extremes

Plants termed ephemerals—seasonal annuals that germinate when temperature and moisture allow—avoid harsh conditions by employing short growth cycles. These are the wildflowers that seem to appear overnight, blanketing great sweeps of ground after sufficiently wet winters. They disappear just as abruptly when the moisture is exhausted. Mexican gold poppy, desert bluebells, and blue bonnets

(*Lupinus* species) are among these early-blooming harbingers of spring that rush to seed as temperatures climb. There are also summer ephemerals, monsoon-dependent annuals that sprout after the first soaking rain with evocative names like trailing windmills (*Allionia choisyi*), love-lies-bleeding (*Amaranthus*), and devil's claw (*Proboscidea*), as well as the brilliantly green, edible, succulent weed purslane, and its comely cousin moss rose (*Portulaca* species).

Winter annuals are the early color explosion of the low desert, while summer annuals are likely to have thick stems and leaves that resist heat and are more prevalent at middle elevations. Biennials like desert marigold and wild asters (*Machaeranthera* species) may germinate anytime temperatures are warm enough in soil that is moist, but bloom only after their rosettes of leaves have weathered enough cold to stimulate budding. Bulbs often prefer inhospitable, thin soils, but avoid inauspicious climatic conditions, storing energy below ground and remaining dormant until they can capitalize on seasonal moisture either in spring or summer.

Most plants adapted to extremes begin and end their lives as very well-protected seeds. Saltbush and Indian rice grass have chemical inhibitors of various strengths in the seeds that extend sprouting over a prolonged time, reserving a portion of the seeds for times when conditions will allow the seedlings to survive. Other arid-land plants, including creosote bush, sumacs, mesquite, and soapberry, have hard, impervious seedcoats that gradually break down by abrasion, freezing, and thawing, before the embryos can respond to moisture and warmth. As climate conditions grow hotter and drier, only the most resilient seedlings survive, so each generation either becomes better adapted to the new extremes, or ceases to exist. Avoidance will only take plants so far when coping with extremes. There are many more endurance mechanisms than avoidance strategies. Roots, stems, and leaves all have several visible characteristics that buffer heat and drought, as well as chemical means of resisting heat that are observable mostly in the net effect of plant resilience. Some plants even adapt to fire as a means of rejuvenation and regeneration.

Drought endurance strategies

Root adaptations Chilean poet Pablo Neruda asked why trees conceal the splendor of their roots. Good question, indeed—in arid climates, roots often make up more than 75 percent of the plant mass,

The extreme endurance of this bristlecone pine started when its roots began to inch their way through seams in the rock.

Young gayfeather roots store moisture and food to sustain growth, eventually pushing deep into the soil.

At night, roots transfer water from moist to dry areas of the soil, keeping more of the roots functional and more of the plant canopy supplied with moisture, better able to withstand the coming day's heat.

a great reservoir of resiliency. Plants protect their roots to survive extremes. When trying to make a living where extremes are the norm, the more root support a plant has in the wind and the more water absorption in the heat, the better life will be. Buried in the soil, roots remain cooler in summer and warmer when temperatures plummet. Unseen yet essential, tiny root hairs host microorganisms that assist in absorbing water and the elements vital for growth, while above ground, plant stems transport water to the leaves, where sunlight is converted to food. Leaves are recyclable; if left to decompose where they fall, they enrich the soil, closing the circle and creating niches increasingly hospitable to plant growth. A basic difference between trees and shrubs is that trees store much of the energy needed for growth in their canopies (which are exposed to heat and cold, drying wind, and abrasive dust), while shrubs keep more of their reserves hidden in the soil.

By virtue of size alone, trees need more water than other plants, with the exception of lawns. In arid climates, a large tree with a canopy spread of 20

ft. or more, shading 400 sq. ft. of soil, is estimated to need between 2000 and 3000 gallons of water per year to thrive. By comparison, 400 sq. ft. of fescue or bluegrass lawn needs a minimum of 6000 gallons of water per year to survive (assuming that the soil has been amended to retain moisture and an efficient sprinkler system is used on a conservative schedule during the coolest time of day). Under less careful management, a lawn can take three times the water of a tree per square foot of coverage, and five times or more what an arid-adapted small tree will need. Trees offer a cool spot to linger on a summer afternoon. A sod blanket might offer shade of a sort, but most people aren't in any hurry to take advantage of that amenity.

Roots are the most protected part of plants, and plant vigor depends on maximizing the supporting and absorbing root system, developing a large root-to-shoot ratio. Taproots aid the establishment of new plants, but become redundant or limited in overall importance as plants mature. In order to have access to necessary oxygen, most roots are concentrated in the top 2 to 3 ft. of soil, and under good conditions extend far beyond the branch canopy. Deeper roots add drought resilience where shallow groundwater or subsurface reservoirs of harvested rainwater are available. Soil compaction in urban spaces can severely limit plants' ability to root extensively enough to thrive. Given the limitations, the soil preparation before planting, the choice of tree species, and where trees are planted on a site, the companion plantings that will share the space and the resources available are all critical to trees' success in arid climates.

Small desert trees are trees in name only. Like shrubs, they have large root-to-shoot ratios and store much of the energy needed for growth in their roots rather than in the canopy. Many xeric plants retain as little as 5 percent of their root mass as woody structural roots; 75 percent or more are finer roots and root hairs that dry up as the soil dries and revive or regenerate when moisture is available. The dainty yet durable flame flower is an example. Under the most extreme conditions, many desert plants produce short, thick roots without root hairs in order to maintain turgor when soil is too dry for normal root function, an adaptation termed "drought rhizogenesis." Roots also form reciprocal relationships with soil microbes. The microbes help roots absorb water and nutrients in exchange for a share of the carbohydrates the plants are then able to produce more abundantly. The microorganisms associated with fine root hairs respond to rain in a few hours, while woody roots may take several days to become fully functional; their symbiosis makes the most of scattered showers and torrential downpours.

Bush morning glory (*Ipomoea leptocaulis*), desert four o'clock, and dotted gayfeather are herbaceous plants that develop massive, starchy roots extending several feet below ground. The top growth dies back from extreme drought, heat, or cold, but the energy stored in the roots guarantees a resurrection when conditions improve. Desert willows, broom dalea, and bush penstemon have a layer of spongy tissue sheathing their roots, leather-like when dry, but soft and highly absorbent when the soil is moist. All desert-adapted plants root far and wide, tapping available moisture from light rains on the surface and from shallow groundwater when present.

Stem adaptations While roots are the foundation of plant health, stems and leaves are where the work of photosynthesis is done. Temperate climate plants have the luxury of relying on the leaves to manufacture food, but xeric plants sometimes cut their evaporative losses by photosynthesizing in their stems, reducing or eliminating reliance on leaves. These plants are often called brooms, like Spanish broom (*Spartium*) and Scotch broom (*Cytissus*). Joint firs are ancient plants of botanical interest because they are a link between conifers and flowering plants. Their slender blue or green stems add evergreen interest in desert gardens. The palo verde, with its vibrant golden-green bark, is one of the most beautiful warm desert trees. Most succulents photosynthesize over the entire surface of their plant bodies, while ocotillo can make food in the stems when moisture is scant, but burst forth a flourish of foliage after a soaking rain.

Other stem adaptations, such as stems growing in dense clusters, are seen in many arid-land natives, from *Echinocereus* cactus to shrubs such as Apache plume, daleas, turpentine bush, lavenders, and damianita. This growth form breaks up the flow of heavy rainfall, allows more water to be absorbed, and allows stems to harvest dew sometimes for a week or longer after the storm. Sotol, nolina, and yucca with semi-succulent, caudiciform stems go one better in actually storing water in their stems. Prickly pears orient their succulent stems parallel to the sun's rays to reduce heat load at lower elevations; at higher elevations, they orient perpendicular to the sun's rays to capture heat. Stem structure also plays a conserving role. Artemisia stems have layers of cork between growth rings of xylem, and

saltbushes, greasewood (*Sarcobatus*), and winterfat (*Krascheninnikovia*) have concentric rings and arcs of cambium within their xylem and phloem that buffer the stems from cold and drought.

Leaf adaptations Leaves are wonderfully diverse in the strategies they employ to curb evaporative loss and resist blistering heat. Akin to the stem orientation of prickly pear, cottonwoods angle their leaf surfaces away from the sun's rays to reduce moisture loss. The softly hairy, fuzzy, and scaly coatings on leaves that lend a silver cast to foliage shade their surfaces from ultraviolet radiation, deflect wind, and reduce evapotranspiration. Waxy coatings on leaves resist evaporation as well. The small, narrow leaves of legumes such as mesquite, palo verde, and dalea dissipate heat and lose less moisture than broad leaves do, while artemisias, saltbushes, creosote bushes, and buddlejas produce two types of leaves: larger leaves when moisture is available, and a smaller set of leaves that transpire more efficiently during drought. In cold desert areas, the smaller leaves often remain on the plant in winter.

Many warm desert plants are evergreen and can photosynthesize whenever conditions are favorable, without using stored energy to produce new biomass. But in desert areas with cold winters, drying winds and persistently freezing nighttime temperatures make foliage a seasonal liability, and fewer plants retain their leaves from December through February. Many desert plants also shed leaves in summer to reduce evapotranspiration when heat and drought are severe. Plants that have succulent leaves store moisture within tissue often doubly protected by waxy or scaly leaf coatings. All of these are obvious features when you recognize the purpose they serve, and they give plant communities designed for extremes a paradoxical character.

Creosote bush leaves are small and resinous; roots are deep and seeds are well protected in woody capsules.

Plants adapted to aridity are either airily insubstantial or boldly dramatic. But there are also familiar plants that employ defensive tactics that are nearly impossible to discern outside a lab. Rosemary, Aleppo pine, pistache, and some hollies have leaves with fewer stomata (the tiny leaf pores that regulate evaporative loss), or their stomata are sunken deep into leaf tissue so that wind causes less moisture loss, or they have stomata that close at the onset of drought to reduce moisture loss. Most desert plants employ several of these strategies, and many also rely on chemistry to survive.

Chemical adaptations Allelopathy—the ability to produce biochemicals that can suppress the growth or reproduction of nearby plants, or suppress the growth of the plant itself to limit competition for water and nutrients—is not limited to desert plants. Ponderosa pine, tree of heaven (*Ailanthus altissima*), ragweed (*Bassia scoparia*), and black walnut (*Juglans nigra*) all compete more effectively for resources with the help of terpenes and other growth inhibitors they exude. These inhibitors allow the roots of the plant producing them to access more soil and moisture, a handy tool when resources are scarce. A much more widespread phenomenon is the ability of plants to photosynthesize with closed stomata during the day, avoiding moisture loss in a process named crassulacean acid metabolism (CAM). Carbon dioxide (CO_2) is absorbed at night when evaporation rates are significantly lower. CAM plants store CO_2 as malic acid for use during daylight hours. During severe drought, they recycle CO_2 with stomata closed day and night, but when moisture is plentiful, CAM plants open stomata during the day like other plants. There is a danger in this adaptation however. When stomata stay closed due to prolonged extremes of heat and drought, plants may never recover, slowly dying of carbon starvation while trying to weather the extremes. There are limits of endurance for even the most xeric succulents.

Many heat-adapted plants are classified as having C4, carbon 4 metabolism. Most temperate climate, cool season plants are C3 metabolizers, which require fully open stomata to move CO_2 during photosynthesis. Most western warm season grasses, as well as food crops such as maize, sorghum, and amaranth are C4 plants that have two areas for CO_2 absorption and use malic acid to build up CO_2 reserves. C4 plants can shut their stomata partially during the heat of the day to reduce moisture loss

without affecting photosynthesis, and can tolerate solar radiation levels higher than C3 plants. Most arid-adapted C3 plants rely on winter precipitation and are common at higher elevations. C4 plants are dependent upon summer rainfall. During periods of prolonged drought, individual plants will only produce a few green shoots, enough to make food with the little moisture left in the soil. From a distance, miles of desert grassland may look winter brown in the middle of July, but up close you can see that life goes quietly on. If rainfall patterns shift later in the season, from July and August to September and October, some grasses may not survive. Grasslands may be replaced by desert shrubs that can use the moisture whenever it comes.

Desert soils accumulate mineral salts because there is little rain to leach them from the soil, making salt tolerance another important adaptation. Extremely saline soil draws the moisture out of plant tissues by osmosis, causing plants to wilt even when the soil appears moist enough to sustain growth. Halophytes (salt-tolerant plants) can maintain high osmotic pressure within their cells, resisting the pull of soil salts. Some halophytes include saltbush, picklebush (*Allenrolfia*), alkali sacaton, and saltgrasses *Distichlis* and *Puccinellia*. Extreme salinity may also induce CAM response in plants that only employ that pathway when stressed sufficiently. Harsh conditions call for all the means available to survive. While this may seem a bit more information than is necessary for the average gardener, we witness the result of these adaptations in the survival of some plants and the failure of others. It's good to know beauty is more than skin deep.

ADAPTING TO FIRE

Fast, patchy, relatively low-temperature fires have always been part of the natural system. Fire clears debris and restores nutrients; roots and seeds less than an inch below the surface usually survive, some are even stimulated to sprout.

But increasing heat and drought have made wildfire much more common in the ecology of the Southwest, and have allowed intense conflagrations to kill everything in their path, including the soil microorganisms and seeds that are essential for recovery. Without fire in nature, trees and shrubs overtake grasses where there is enough moisture to sustain them. In desert grasslands, fire occurs every ten or more years, as enough fuel accumulates to burn; much less frequently than in the wetter plains grasslands where fuels accumulate more rapidly and fire may be an annual event. Summer forest fires are usually more damaging than fires that occur when plants are dormant, and larger trees with thicker bark are less vulnerable, whether the tree is a mesquite in central Texas, with a 2-in. trunk diameter, or a ponderosa pine above 7500 ft. in elevation, with a 2-ft. trunk diameter. Deciduous plants tend to be more fire resistant than evergreens. Frequent fires increase stands of mesquite and undermine snakeweed (*Gutierrezia*), to the advantage of chamisa (*Ericameria*) at lower elevations and creeping mahonia further upslope. Saltbush, salvia, yarrow, penstemon and French lavender are all fire-resistant species.

Public land fire managers are becoming much more adept at minimizing damage, and when possible, using fire for ecological good. Unfortunately, the frequency and ferocity of fires has been giving

TOP **CAM plants include most cacti, agaves, euphorbias, succulents such as iceplants, flame flower and sedums, and some milkweed and pine species.** BOTTOM **Cells of salt-tolerant plants maintain high osmotic pressure, resisting soil salts.**

When gardening, we are more likely to water too much than not enough, and pampering plants that need to weather extremes is doing them a disservice.

Desert seeds are well protected. Tumbled through gravel along a flooding arroyo or rubbed between sheets of sandpaper, the abrasion breaks the thick seedcoats to allow in moisture and oxygen.

them plenty of experience. While forest fires get the most media attention, almost all southwestern ecosystems have lightning-sparked fires as part of their ecology.

Quick-moving, low-intensity fires restore nutrients to the soil and burn away thatch while vegetation is dormant, making desert grasslands turn vibrant green with the next soaking rain. The invasion of African buffelgrass (*Pennisetum ciliare*) has become a serious threat in warm desert ecosystems, sucking up moisture, burning destructively hot in plant communities poorly adapted to fire, and destroying saguaro and other cactus. There are unintended consequences when introducing species that are *too* well-adapted to play well with native plants already stressed by climate change. In plant communities where fire is a regular part of the natural system, the ultimate heat adaptation is seed germination stimulated by fire, such as with manzanita and ceanothus.

REPRODUCTIVE ADAPTATIONS TO EXTREMES

Growers of plants adapted to arid places know that it is sometimes very difficult to get seeds to germinate with any consistency. All seeds have a preferred set of conditions under which they sprout best; exposure to light or darkness, a range of temperatures and moisture. Plants from colder climates often need a period of cold in moist soil to germinate. Tropical plants have relatively few inhibitors and plants that have been cultivated for a long time often have the inhibitors bred out of them. There are manuals available that detail these preferences. Arid-adapted plants have evolved a few added impediments that cause seeds to become exposed to ideal conditions unevenly. They keep a reserve of protected seeds in case erratic heat or cold strikes when the seedlings are still too tender to survive. Saltbushes, creosote bush, mesquite, sumacs, and soapberry have impervious seedcoats that prevent germination until significant weathering or abrasion erodes the protection. Penstemon, ricegrass, mariola, and some salvia are among the plants that have a seed dormancy induced by chemical inhibitors, which must break down before seeds can sprout. Again, the response is uneven so some seeds are kept in reserve. "Just in case" is a cultural imperative among desert plants.

In nature, wind-pollinated plants may respond more quickly to changes in their environment than insect- or bird-pollinated species, because pollens from a greater number of plants mix together—allowing greater opportunity to fine-tune adaptations to local conditions. When the species are dominant in a place—as oaks, artemisias, saltbushes, and grasses typically are—they have an edge in responding to change rapidly. While this process is very important in wildlands, it may seem more esoteric when it comes to our gardens—except that lessons can be drawn from natural selection. If we take native seed that is well adapted to extreme growing conditions and pamper their seedlings with more water, the surviving progeny of those plants will be less resilient to extremes.

Athletes push themselves to perform well under stress; the most successful find the balance between effort and injury. Another analogy is good parenting, which involves both nurturing and fostering independence. Arid-land gardening is similar. We want our plants to grow up resilient and become self-sustaining, even though we don't want them to leave home.

TAMING THE ELEMENTS
WITH DESIGN

Good design reconciles how the space will be used, how it should look and feel with how the hard surfaces can serve the future planting, and how the plants complete the built space. The Southwest is a place rich in mythology, where the origin stories of native peoples offer timeless life lessons linked to places in the landscape. Gardeners transplanted from wetter climates often labor under gardening myths that are neither timely nor valid here. The misconception that deserts are barren wastelands—as well as the opposite notion that if you try hard enough and pour enough water on it anything can grow here—thwart our efforts to live comfortably in this arid climate.

An informed blend of smart plant choices, integrated hardscaping, irrigation considerations, and appropriate mulches adds up to good desert garden design.

DESIGNING WITH PLANTS

This is a place of remarkable variety in plants and microclimates. Some plants are suited to specific niches, while others are so adaptable that they will grow in nearly the entire region. It is impossible to represent an area so diverse with only a few hundred plants, yet when you consider individual spaces, there are often only a handful of plants that fit really well—so we can narrow the field quite a bit.

Just as space within the garden limits the number and kinds of plants that are well suited, space within the pages of this book limits the number of plants covered to those most valuable in surviving and buffering the extremes. There is no merit in forcing plants that yearn for greener pastures to survive here. The most resilient, adaptable, and beautiful plants are the ones that are indispensable when designing gardens, able to field the extremes of heat as it inches to new highs and occasional cold events that plummet to numbing depths.

Gardens are journeys that fortunately for the garden lover never end. Knowing the most direct route between destinations, the best planting options, and most successful caretaking strategies makes the best use of time and resources. Trees, shrubs, and, in the low desert, architectural succulents, dominate the plant palette, cover the most ground, and have the most impact on how a space looks and feels. These plants are in effect structural

Small sculptural trees like *Forestiera*, along with compatible companion plants, create focus.

and look and grow best when coordinated with soil contours, walls, and paving—the architecture of space. Within the built garden, the larger plants complement the walls and trellises, shade covers, and paving. Vines drape over arbors, trees shade paths and patios, walls create privacy and are backdrops for plant silhouettes.

TREES, DIVAS OF DESIGN

Trees as garden art and architecture are shaped both by genetics and by forces in their environment. Intense sunlight, strong winds, heat and cold, drought and flood, and the plants sharing space and resources affect each other's eventual size and shape. In arid ecosystems, fewer trees are spread across a larger area, clustered where more moisture is available. Thick trunks or multiple short stems store energy and provide trees greater wind resistance; their broad, rounded canopies balance food production and storage with evaporative loss. In the hottest, driest desert ecosystems, trees are only found along perennial streams or in arroyos where groundwater is shallow. Even in those sweet spots, smaller trees dominate, as few large trees are

Look to natural patterns for ways to contour soil to collect rainwater, and for a sense of how many trees to plant.

The rock-lined *rambla* (a Spanish reference to natural rainwater streambeds) at Santa Fe Botanical Gardens can carry a flood of water through the gardens during summer thunderstorms.

**Trees are pivotal, the anchors of space;
the rest of the garden serves as a complement.**

able to thrive. Temperatures moderate with a rise in elevation, and even if there is only slightly more rain, lower evapotranspiration rates allow an increase in size and number of trees and shrubs. These natural patterns are well worth considering when deciding how many trees a garden can sustain and where they might grow best. The spaces surrounding buildings are the most seen and used, and also the shortest distance for directing rainwater to plants—ideal places to plant trees.

Trees offer shade, and their network of roots keeps the soil from eroding as they shelter and feed wildlife, sequester carbon dioxide, and oxygenate the air. Urban trees also reduce the need for air conditioning, as moisture transpired from their leaves cools the air. Trees improve air quality by absorbing pollution through leaf pores and collecting fine particulates on their surfaces. Depending on growth rate and ultimate size, a tree can sequester from 35 to 800 pounds of carbon dioxide per year. Two trees 25 to 30 ft. tall can fulfill the oxygen needs of the average person. Trees help create more temperate spaces beneath their outspread branches, sheltering tender plants, preventing damage from intense sun and heat, and buffering hard frost. They share resources, especially moisture, with everything within rooting range. It makes good sense, then, to invest water in trees—especially in desert cities where rainwater captured from all the hard surfaces could provide much of the moisture the trees need. Indeed, rainwater harvesting from pavement is an opportunity to create urban oases.

Loosening compaction and making soils pervious improves the conditions for the roots of trees. In most cases, returning soil to its natural porosity

and permeability is much more beneficial than creating a humus-rich growing medium foreign to arid climates.

Keep in mind that although trees are potentially the longest-lived plants in the landscape, they begin to decline when their wood exceeds their stored energy and potential to produce more growth. Greater size is a disadvantage in arid climates because it increases evaporative surfaces and exposes trees to greater extremes. While plants within several feet of the ground in our gardens may be protected by walls and other plants, a leafy canopy 20 or 30 ft. above ground endures blazing sun, blistering heat, desiccating wind, and bitter cold—sometimes within the same week.

Trees in plant communities

Plants in landscapes form a community. Tree canopies affect the quality of light beneath their branches, as well as the water available to nearby plants. Small-leaved trees have lighter canopies and use water more efficiently; desert legumes fix nitrogen and enrich the soil, easily sharing space with companion plants. Other trees survive by limiting the competition. As pines mature, they produce terpenes that suppress the growth of other vegetation, allowing the conifers a larger share of available resources. Mulberries create such dense shade and absorb water so efficiently that other plants struggle in their company. As trees mature, the shade from the canopy and accumulating mulch of leaf litter suppress the growth of ground cover plants. At the same time, the roots that the trees rely on to absorb water extend out beyond the edge of the branch canopy. Look under a mature shade tree after a rain

A Tucson streetscape anchored by trees has a sustainable variety of plants. BOTTOM Thick trunks or multiple shorter stems store energy and provide trees greater wind resistance; their broad, rounded canopies balance food production and storage with evaporative loss. Fallen leaves left as mulch reduce moisture loss from the soil.

storm and you'll see that the area closest to the trunk is relatively dry; light rain falling on leaves is diverted out toward the edge of the branches and drops to the ground along the perimeter, at the edges of the canopy, where most of the absorbing roots are likely to be.

As garden trees mature, the shaded space closest to the trunk becomes more useful to us as a patio, covered with flagstones or pavers or decking that allows air and enough moisture to penetrate, keeping structural roots alive. Pavers set in fine, crushed stone, or decomposed granite (not set in mortar) can also be lifted and reset to level if, after a decade or more of root growth, the paving heaves in places. The pavers should slope gradually away from the trunk, at least 1 in. drop per 8 ft. of run, so that the surface feels level but has enough pitch to drain any rainwater that filters through the leaf canopy toward where the absorbing roots can tap it.

Selecting the best species and specimens

What are the best trees for your garden? In the plant descriptions, look at the temperature range to which the trees are best suited, and the mature size they can attain. When size is indicated as 15 to 25 ft. tall, the assumption is that under more extreme conditions (hotter or colder, windier, drier), the plants will grow more slowly and ultimately stay smaller. Where more moisture is available and life is generally easier, plants will grow more rapidly and ultimately become larger. Using water wisely involves getting the most return for your liquid assets, so it's smart to combine as many of the features you're looking for in fewer plants: manageable size, adaptation to the light intensity and degree of heat and cold on-site, spring flowers, summer shade, edible fruit, fall color or evergreen leaves, pest resistance, and wildlife habitat. If you can have it all in a few

generous trees, you can lavish the care and reap the rewards. Less really can yield more.

The convoluted story of the development of hybrid mesquites in southwestern landscapes is illustrative. Argentine-Chilean native *Prosopis alba* has outlived the other Chilean introduction *P. chilensis*, which proved too frost sensitive to be widely usable. The characteristics that made hybridizing worthwhile were semi-evergreen foliage and greater size—to 30 ft. tall and twice as wide. An early selection, 'Colorado', is thornless and cold hardy to 15°F. More recently, 'Phoenix' ('Colorado' grafted onto velvet mesquite rootstock) has gained market share, as it is also thornless, but perhaps even more cold tolerant and wind resilient, and more deeply rooting when given thorough soakings once a month through summer. Since there is no history of the longevity of grafted mesquite, 'Phoenix' may be more of a gamble than 'Colorado'. Gardeners are left to decide whether the enhanced qualities are worth the experiment. In any case, climate adaptation is part of the agenda.

Part of the information you need to make good plant choices is exactly where the plants fit into the garden. Try to visualize mature trees in the spaces where you expect them to grow. What seems like a vast, empty space can become crowded in a few years when too many large plants are shoehorned into a too-small space. Think of trees as sculpture: large shade trees are monumental; smaller flowering trees are more human-scale works of art. There should be enough space around them to be able to admire their forms as they mature, both individually and as part of an ensemble.

Location, location, location

Ideally, shade trees—especially those that mature to 30 ft. or more in height and spread—should be

In extreme gardening, don't plant more than the conditions will support.

A young Gambel oak left branched as a large shrub has salvia and ephedra ground covers to share water as it matures.

OPPOSITE TOP When space is limited, shade can be built to create living space without blocking solar panels. OPPOSITE BOTTOM Location of solar panels determines the height of the ramada, to avoid shading that would reduce solar gain.

placed near low areas in the landscape, where run-off can be harvested to supplement irrigation and extend prime rooting real estate. Whether a tree should be planted in the catchment basin or on the edge (so the base of its trunk is never submerged when the basin fills with rainwater) depends on the permeability and water-holding capacity of the soil and the species of tree. Generally, trees that need more moisture are best adapted to periodic flooding. Also driving a tree's role in design is whether it is deciduous and loses its leaves seasonally, or evergreen and maintains its leaves year-round. Deciduous trees on eastern exposures reduce heating early in the day in summer and allow solar gain in winter; deciduous trees on southern and western exposures reduce total cumulative heat load during the day in summer and allow solar gain in winter; evergreens on northern exposures reduce heat loss in winter. Smaller trees and those with deeper roots and lower water requirements can be planted closer to walls and paving, used to shade windows and patios, and expected to keep the soil in living spaces cooler. Single-story buildings with solar panels on the roof need at least 20 ft. of clearance for trees 20 ft. in height. If taller trees are to be part of the garden, they need to be even farther away. Taller buildings can accommodate taller trees. As more and more solar arrays help power our communities, large trees on small city lots need careful siting, as they will also impact neighboring solar capacity.

Tree selection is layered in complexity, requiring thinking through space and time. Yet it is an extremely down-to-earth endeavor. Planning tree placement to allow future solar gain is relatively straightforward when designing the garden. It also avoids having to weigh the value in cooling and air

TOP LEFT Overhead power lines plus lack of rooting space and moisture doomed this sycamore within a few years of planting.
ABOVE A flagstone path drains rainwater toward plants.
BOTTOM LEFT Parking lot pavement drains rainwater to trees in sunken medians, and healthy trees shade the pavement. In residential landscapes and driveways, walkways and patios can be made to divert water to nearby plants.

Aloes used as ground cover benefit from the light shade under desert trees.

quality of a mature healthy tree against the value of solar efficiency once the tree is established. Use deciduous plants to shade windows that could provide solar gain in winter. Plant evergreens on the perimeter to buffer wind and enclose space visually. Consider that water runs downhill, that trees which drop fruit or attract birds are best not planted above patio furniture or hot tubs. Fruit trees that bloom in early spring suffer less crop loss when planted on northeast exposures, where the soil stays cooler longer in spring and budding is delayed enough to escape possible flash freezes. Heat-loving Mediterranean fruits such as figs and pomegranates, on the other hand, need all the sun they can soak up to produce well. The more you fine-tune your tree choices, the better foundation you create for the entire garden.

The success of the whole depends on the compatibility of the parts

All plants within the root zones of trees will eventually share resources with them. In order to water areas of a landscape efficiently, groups of plants clustered near each other should be similar in how often they need watering and not so thirsty that they take more than the trees can afford to share—both reasons why lawns are a poor choice as ground cover under trees. Grasses grown as a lawn compete strongly for water and may require fertilizing when it's better not to fertilize the trees. Broadleaf weed killers commonly used on lawns do not distinguish between dandelions and oaks or elms. Too many trees are poisoned to keep lawns free of weeds. Maintenance equipment also causes problems; even if used carefully, string-line trimmers repeatedly lashing the thin bark of young trees will girdle them. A typical remedy is to plant trees in the bull's eyes of a mulch circle, so the mower and edger

stay a safe distance from the plants. Design-wise, this interrupts the sweep of the lawn like the holes in Swiss cheese. As trees grow, their girth interrupts the flow of water from sprinkler heads across the lawn surface, eventually leaving dry patches in the rain shadow of the trunk and plants around it.

Grown in places that receive 40 in. or more of rainfall, lawns can be soothing green spaces, versatile in their use when not doused with chemicals. In dry climates, even with great follow-up care, carpet-like monotony is only achievable if the soil is uniformly amended with organic matter to improve its water-holding capacity, and if water is applied copiously and consistently. Anything not desired in the grass must be studiously eliminated, because the grass is less resilient than the weeds trying to replace it. Most lawn grasses are maintained best with frequent, shallow irrigations—several times per week to a depth of 8 to 12 in. in summer for fescue or bluegrass. Trees need water less often the longer they are in the garden, and should be watered more deeply, at most every two weeks in summer, to a depth of 24 to 30 in. in permeable soil. The

In a shady historic neighborhood, lawn-like ground covers replace turf. BOTTOM A labyrinth replaces a seldom-used lawn. The path pattern is fixed in the space, but the plants create a changing tapestry of color and texture.

microbes in the soil are different for grasses and trees, and without recycled leaf mulch, these associated *mycorrhiza* may not thrive, leaving the trees without important allies. In the desert, the shade of trees is a necessity; lawns are a luxury. If you're willing and able to invest in both large trees and turf, plant the trees on the perimeter, where their shade cools living space, and leave the lawn space open for efficient sprinkler performance; without it, the lawn is toast. It's easier to play bocce or soccer without trees to dodge, and lawn chair coaches can sit on the sidelines in the shade and enjoy the game.

If turf is taboo under trees, what other options do you have? There are as many answers to that question as there are gardens and people who use them. The tree species you choose to grow are the final arbiters of what will grow best beneath and beyond their branches. When you choose to grow regionally native plants as the core of your garden, you have local ecosystems for inspiration. You can create compatible planting combinations, plant communities that have been field-tested for millennia and that are continuously adapting to changing conditions here and now. Look to nature to sort out the best plants for where you garden, and embellish with plants that prefer similar conditions. The plant descriptions in this book will guide you to compatible planting options. Match heat and cold tolerance with sunlight, soils, and degree of drought resistance, and you'll find apt companions.

THE GARDEN VALUE OF SHRUBS

Shrubs dominate desert ecology; super resilient because they store most of their energy in their roots, protected from climate extremes. Along with wildflowers and grasses, shrubs weave patterns through the landscape. The joy of shrubs is in the amazing array of sizes, shapes, leaf textures,

flower colors, and scents they offer. Clusters of large shrubs can provide cooling shade in places too extreme to support trees. Evergreen shrubs provide leaf color and cover year-round, while deciduous shrubs add intense flower color seasonally—then fade to skeletons in winter, adding contrast and depth to the garden. Many large evergreens are beautiful as stand-alone specimens, but can also be clustered to make visual screens or to provide protection from the wind. While conifers like pine and juniper are rugged and aromatic, evergreen shrubs may also have brightly colored, fragrant flowers and fruits, or seedpods that add seasonal drama and bring songbirds and butterflies to the garden. Whether a shrub is evergreen or deciduous can depend on where you garden. The warmer the winters, the more likely shrubs are to hold on to their leaves, making food while the sun shines.

Worldwide, roses may be the most popular garden shrubs, in part because there are so many different species and hybrids. Gardeners almost anywhere can find roses that work for them. In arid climates, the rose family exemplifies diversity, but most arid-adapted roses don't resemble the iconic large-flowered, man-made tea rose. Desert roses include tall evergreens such as curl-leaf mountain mahogany and Arizona rosewood, which are handsome as screening and wind buffers. Mid-sized semi-evergreens such as Apache plume and fernbush add texture. The silky pink seed heads of Apache plume glow when backlit by the sun, while the soft, sage-green, finely divided leaves of fernbush subtly contrast with the bronze color of its stems and seed heads. Defying the norm of both garden roses and desert plants, none of these roses are thorny. Other plant genera with wonderful diversity in foliage and flower color include the many plants commonly called sages, including *Artemisia*, *Leucophyllum*, and

ABOVE Plants of various heights, including *Leucophyllum* 'Lynn's Legacy' in bloom, surround a buffalograss lawn, enclosing the space and shading the walls to reduce summer heat buildup.

RIGHT Mid-sized plants screen the garden from the street without blocking air circulation, and create a hospitable sense of enclosure.

OPPOSITE Mixed shrubs, succulents, and perennials separate patio spaces at this historic inn, giving guests privacy but providing each space with a long view of distant trees.

Salvia, as well as acacias, *Caesalpinia*, daleas, sumacs, and the many desert brooms.

Large deciduous shrubs can make striking stand-alone specimens. They also mix well with evergreens, together adding contrast in stem color, leaf texture, and color—from pale silver to bright emerald or deep olive. Large shrubs are at their best when they aren't crowded, placed close enough together to fill their intended role in the design, but not so close that they interfere with each other as they mature, vying for space and water. Prickly plants are useful as barriers and green security fences, but can pose maintenance problems if there's not enough space to allow routine chores like washing windows or raking up the litter they shed.

Large succulents are signature plants of the low desert, where winters are mild. Cold desert succulents are fewer in number and smaller in size, but no less interesting or prickly. Well armed to keep their water-filled tissues from being eaten by thirsty desert wildlife, even some of the thornless prickly pear varieties are protected by the small, exceedingly irritating glochids. The barbed and sword-leaved succulents need tempering in numbers and placement to avoid the appearance of a hostile takeover, as well as the physical pain of an armed confrontation. These are the exclamation points in design! Like that punctuation mark, succulents are most effective when well-placed and not overused! They are comparable to shrubs in the space they need, but are much less subtle in personality! These bold divas demand attention, yet require very little care and are best paired with other low-water, low-litter plants with showy flowers and complementary, soft textures.

Versatile mid-sized shrubs 3 to 6 ft. tall with similar spread can be used to divide spaces in the garden, control access, partially enclose a patio, screen trash and recycling bins, and, in large gardens, fill open space with color, texture, and fragrance. Small shrubs 1 to 3 ft. tall and wide can separate spaces physically without doing so visually. They can make a small space feel more generous and, as the garden matures, avoid giving garden visitors that shrinking feeling. Small shrubs add diversity to modest courtyard spaces and pockets of color in prairie plantings. They contribute flowers, fragrance, and texture. Their mounding or sprawling silhouettes add layers and depth.

Subshrubs are typically less than 30 in. tall and have woody perennial stems; the basal portion winters over, but much of the stem length is tender and green, so they are able to photosynthesize in the absence of leaves. In the desert, subshrubs often share space with desert grasses able to exploit light summer rain showers. Because subshrubs have the advantage of deep roots, they also use cool season rainfall and snowmelt, which tends to evaporate more slowly and penetrate the soil more deeply. Subshrubs play garden roles similar to small shrubs; they may border paths and mingle with flowers, grasses, and larger shrubs. Their typical mounded silhouettes add subtext to the bold accents of succulents and grasses.

In nature, plants are at the mercy of climate and topography. But in gardens, if shrubs adapted to extremes are given very modest supplemental water, they grow more consistently to their maximum size.

They bloom reliably, enclosing space, calming wind, and providing nesting, foraging, and roosting space for songbirds. It's tempting to force rapid growth with water and fertilizer, but even small amounts of fertilizer and a little too much water can cause rapid growth that is vulnerable to wind breakage. This is not only counterproductive to plant health, but also to the garden design, especially if the purpose of the shrubs is buffering wind. On large sites, repeated groupings of shrubs can establish a pleasing rhythm and create coherence and flow. Because there are so many possibilities for shrub planting, it helps to block out spaces to first develop a clear idea of the intended role of the plants in the garden. Then scan the list of shrubs to pinpoint which ones will work best in a given situation. Once the larger plants are placed, the open space around them is defined, making it easier to select the supporting cast.

LUXURIOUSLY LUSH: PERENNIALS, ANNUALS, AND BULBS

In Southwest gardens, herbaceous plants are valuable ecologically—as living mulch to keep the soil and surrounding air cooler, for seasonal color, and for adding greater depth to the landscape. They complement shrubs and grasses in color, texture, form, and mass, and share water with trees, adding a greater degree of sophistication, subtlety, and maintenance to the garden. In the cooler high desert, color comes in waves from early spring to late autumn. In the hot desert, wildflowers blast seasonal explosions of color that are first suppressed by heat and then rebound when it cools down again, if water is available. The higher in elevation and cooler the garden, the more direct sun is needed for the best show of color; in the lower and hotter garden, more shade allows wildflowers to bloom longer with less water. In all but

Eye-catching color offsets a front gate.

Gayfeather, amsonia, and salvia change color seasonally, marking the passage of time.

the coolest areas, intense summer heat interrupts flowering. Since temperatures and rainfall patterns vary so much from place to place and year to year, some perennials may bloom all growing season when moisture is available. Others ebb and flow with temperature changes and summer rains.

Plants take more water more frequently in full sun and in faster-draining soil. Perennials, annuals, and biennials often prefer a specific range of light, soil, and moisture conditions. The desert natives are for the most part suited to the most sun; lean, well-drained soil; and the least water.

To thrive, conventional garden flowers may need soil enriched with compost, shade part of the day, and frequent watering. Plant size can vary—more heat or cold and less water keeps plants smaller. Given too much water, arid-adapted plants will get big and floppy, out of shape. Drip irrigation systems can be zoned so that the plants that need water more frequently can be accommodated without overwatering more xeric species. Annuals have a one-year lifespan. Perennials are the longest lived, three to ten years or more under good conditions, depending on the species. Biennials may live two years, first as a clump of leaves, then producing a burst of flowers, then going to seed. Ecologically, annuals and biennials are pioneer plants that quickly stabilize disturbed soil. In designed landscapes, they are useful as infill while the slower-growing, more structural plantings become established. Wildflowers are often seeded directly where they will grow, and cold-adapted species may need priming (a cool, moist period followed by warmth) to germinate. Prolonged drought makes seeding riskier, but when conditions are right, seedlings' uninterrupted rooting is a huge advantage. Seeding wildflowers can be the most cost-effective way to cover large spaces.

Bulbs, corms, and tubers differ from other perennials, in that they have roots or below-ground stems that store carbohydrates and protect buds. They usually have a short season of active growth followed by a lengthy dormancy. Rhizomes also have storage facility, but often have a longer period of growth and flowering. Many perennials in this category are adapted to xeric conditions, avoiding drought by growing rapidly and flowering when conditions allow. They go dormant when conditions are unfavorable. In order for bulbs to perennialize, they must have a long enough period of active growth to store energy for future growth and flowering. Allow the leaves to feed and restore the bulbs, then slowly wither and dry. When you can pull away the dried foliage, the bulb should be fully recharged like a battery ready to produce the next show. Most bulb foliage is grassy in texture; combining bulbs with warm season ornamental grasses makes good design sense for spring-blooming bulbs, because the grasses start filling in as the bulbs are fading. Summer bulbs typically are plants that need more water, a surprise and delight in the airy shade of desert trees, when the blast of wildflower color has quite literally dried up.

GRASSES AS GROUND COVER AND ACCENT

When lawns are not part of the design, grasses can be sorted into two broad categories: those seeded either as infill ground cover or larger scale reclamation, and ornamentals transplanted in landscapes much as shrubs or perennials are used. The smaller native species are more likely to be seeded, the larger, more dramatic specimens transplanted. Native grasses grown from seed tend to root more extensively and become self-sustaining, adjusting to seasonal rhythms of growth and dormancy. Transplants often require ongoing supplemental watering to be showy on cue. Grasses are also sorted as either cool season or warm season, C3 or C4, depending on their patterns of growth and dormancy, and they germinate more consistently than most wildflowers, as long as they are sown within their preferred temperature range. As the name implies, cool season grasses grow when air and soil temperatures are cool, germinating best when nighttime temperatures are still hovering around freezing. Once daytime temperatures are consistently near 80°F, cool season seed germinates poorly and the growth of seedlings slows. Warm season species germinate well and grow when the nighttime temperatures are consistently 50°F, until persistent heat in the high 90s stifles growth. Warm season native grasses are monsoon dependent, and the brief cooling that accompanies rain, as well as the moisture, elicits a rapid response. As you might expect, warm season grasses are the mainstay of low and intermediate desert gardens while both warm and cool season types find niches in higher elevation gardens.

While a thick carpet of lawn is not sustainable in the Southwest, native grasses in masses have great habitat value; they are a dietary mainstay of

Warm season blue grama dominates the summer prairie.

Cool season needle-and-thread grass and soapweed yuccas are springtime treats.

wildlife, including the caterpillars who work so diligently to become butterflies. Sweeps of soft green leaves—some strongly vertical, others gracefully mounding—are beautiful, but it is the splendor and diversity of their seed heads, showiest from August well into winter, that earn grasses their garden space. Grasses dance in the wind, seed heads shimmering when backlit, as birds and butterflies flit; unnoticed in the lush leaves, caterpillars feed. There is so much to recommend grasses that it is wise to consider some of their drawbacks before turning the whole garden into grassland: grass pollen is airborne and can cause allergic reactions in many people; grasses are also strongly seasonal. Once the party is over, there's a major cleanup needed in cultivated spaces. Various methods for managing grasses large and small are covered in the section on garden maintenance, but all grasses are best cut back to the ground before growth resumes. Wildfire is nature's tool, but with plastic irrigation parts and the danger of a life-renewing burn becoming a conflagration, power tools and endurance are our best alternatives. There is usually a period of a month or more when the glory of grasses resembles stubble, and sexy as that may be on some men, it leaves large gaps in the garden unless balanced by plants that take the limelight when grasses rest.

A design where hard surfaces shed rainwater into planted spaces (supporting the growth of well-adapted trees and shrubs) creates a strong framework upon which to base more ephemeral plant choices.

FLOOD AND FIRE

Bioswales or rain gardens have gained popularity, an elegant solution to the problem of flooding in climates where storm water is abundant. In the Southwest, increasing warmth and more erratic rainfall have created extremely parched soils that repel rainwater when it hits suddenly and with force. Shaping the land to divert the flow to areas made more permeable, where rain will seep into the ground, restores moisture that plants can use gradually. Trees especially benefit when planted in shallow basins in low areas of the garden that capture the most water. While wetland species are the obvious choice for bioswales, plants in rainwater catchments in dry climates must be adapted to long periods of drought, interrupted by occasional inundation. Species described as oasis plants—that take more water—are the best candidates to help slow the flow, their roots opening pathways into the soil for rain to follow. In very rapidly draining soil, almost any plant will benefit from a spot that caches rainwater.

In the past, coastal chaparral was the semi-arid ecosystem that required fire planning, but in the last decade, climate change has made fire prevention a design concern throughout the Southwest. From forest to grassland, there are basic ways we can make our gardens less vulnerable. Choose fire-resistant materials for use within 30 to 50 ft. of buildings: stone for retaining walls and paving; metal for roofing; large, hardwood deciduous trees such as oak instead of resinous conifers. Irrigate plants enough to suppress burning, especially during hot, dry, windy weather when wildfires are more likely. Keep understory plants low and shrub layers clustered away from canopy plants, to avoid laddering fire from the ground cover into the trees. Employ the "less is more" strategy, the goal being to shade soil and reduce heating, but not so densely that plants compete strongly for moisture.

CATALYST FOR DESIGN

Plants are changeable. They have personalities; they are the stuff that makes outdoor space both enticing and comfortable. The following examples of real Southwest garden design solutions illustrate the many ways hardscape and planting support each other. As the garden matures, the environmental engineering is likely to disappear in the foliage. Change is inevitable, but strong design and well-adapted materials yield a garden that requires fewer outside resources as it becomes established. Climate change is making the process more uncertain, as plants are challenged by increasingly extreme conditions. Plants that are well suited to the conditions will be healthier, and healthy plants are less susceptible to insects and disease. All that is essential, but plants radiating vitality are inherently, undeniably beautiful—and isn't that why we garden?

The streambed captures rainwater, giving roots alongside it access to moist soil without flooding the plants themselves. Contemporary sculptures created by the homeowners provide nesting spaces for native bees.

Shrubs and succulents of varied sizes and shapes create a buffer from the street. Irrigation is carefully monitored. Spring demands cleanup of freeze damage (when winter is extreme), as well as leaf litter and dried flower stems left for winter interest.

DESIGN GETS REAL

Smart Desert Gardens

This gallery includes gardens from a precious few hundred square feet to acres in expanse, and that range from 1000 to 7500 ft. in elevation, yet there are consistencies in design—such as contouring to harvest rainwater, fashioning enclosures as living spaces, creating openings to take in the surrounding vistas and center the garden in its ecological context, and using native and adapted plants as the mainstays of content. These gardens are successful because they resonate with the places they occupy and with the people who occupy them. They are alive with human conversation, butterflies, birdsong, and the hum of bees. They are lived in and enjoyed.

GARDEN ONE

This desert garden is less than a mile from the Rio Grande where rainfall averages 6 in. during a good year, the terrain is flat, and the soils are clay with poor drainage, limiting the diversity of desert plants that will grow well. Cut and fill contouring creates a gently rolling surface. These contours improve drainage for plants on the raised areas, capture rainwater, and direct that moisture to trees and shrubs (whose roots have enhanced soil permeability). The garden is an ongoing creative endeavor that gives great pleasure and toned muscles to the artists who live and work here. The garden is enjoyed year-round and much time is spent collaboratively dreaming of new sculptural accents—trellises, arbors, and walking benches—and new plants that will at some point find a home here.

RIGHT Hand-made benches crafted from metal and wood recycled during home renovations have become part of the garden's history.

RIGHT The ribbon of larger stones on the left withstands the force of storm water flowing out of roof drains, and diverts it to plants surrounding the stones. Gentle contours highlight plants and make the space feel larger.

BOTTOM The contour is interrupted by a path that links two patios. White-flowered Mexican elder is balanced by evergreen curl-leaf mountain mahogany and blue ephedra. Wisteria drapes the corner patio cover, making the space cool and inviting on a hot summer afternoon.

An alfresco dining space is adjacent to the kitchen.

GARDEN TWO

There are many ways to make spaces more hospitable while conserving water. Here, living space is enclosed within walls and cooled with a light tree canopy. Pervious flagstone and fine gravel paving allow rainwater to penetrate to plant roots while the plants reduce heat.

A spring show of damianita and penstemon draws visitors toward the gate.

A pool of water in a shaded courtyard welcomes birds as well as people.

GARDEN THREE

On a western mountain slope of decomposed granite, at 5700 ft., this garden offers a series of living spaces. Here, rainfall averages 10 to 12 in. during a good year. The small street-side garden is enjoyed by the neighborhood for its seasonal colors and fragrances. A long, narrow alleyway catches the storm water from two roofs—so a French drain was excavated lengthwise through the middle of the space, allowing rainwater to penetrate quickly and planted borders to take advantage of the soil moisture.

A small street-side garden provides seasonal colors and fragrances. Purple sandpaper verbena and yellow desert zinnia are a prelude to the mass of spiky gayfeather about to bloom. Silver-leafed companions include Mojave sage and Greek germander. Escarpment live oak, creosote bush, and beargrass anchor the garden.

LEFT Concealed by the flagstone path, storm water from two roofs is collected in a French drain through the middle of the alleyway. The drain is a trench filled with cobblestones, covered with filter fabric and topped with flagstone.

BOTTOM Chocolate flowers and dwarf goldenrod are perennials with a tendency to roam, hemmed in here to curb their enthusiasm and tempt passersby with their aroma.

Garden Three, cont. Tucked between a Chinese pistache and a hackberry tree, the flagstone
patio drains into adjacent beds. Hummingbirds and butterflies are enthusiastic visitors.

GARDEN FOUR

A celebration of place, this high desert garden lies in the foothills of the southern Rockies' east slope, at nearly 7000 ft. Here, grassland meets pinyon and juniper woodland, and priceless views of worn mountaintops, canyons, and valleys seem to roll on forever. A garden almost entirely of native plants provides nectar for pollinators and food for a host of birds and other wildlife, including rattlesnakes that are warily recognized as neighbors—neighbors to be tactfully side-stepped. Paths beckon guests to wander, lingering in places to see what flits, scurries, or slithers by.

Flagstone steps separate prairie grasses from garden beds, and lead to the east portal. Aspens frame the view, thriving with sun in the morning and shade during the hottest part of the day.

An informal lawn of buffalograss and blue grama is a transition between the living space and unmowed high desert prairie.

RIGHT Grassland drops off precipitously into a deep canyon and the view from the portal includes hawks nesting on the canyon ledges and distant mountains. A pinyon jay enjoys the scene from the top of his namesake pine.

Surrounded by amazing vistas, the garden has many places to pause and savor the moment.
Autumn brings a show of gayfeather, as the grasses mellow to shades of gold.

This foothills site is at 5900 ft. elevation on a western exposure, with well-drained, decomposed granite soil. The garden's design objectives were to make it blend seamlessly into the hillside, merging with the open space and national forest land farther upslope. The lot is steeply sloped and the footprint of the resource-efficient house and a small patio occupy much of the level ground.

The top layer of decomposed granite was collected and stockpiled during construction and used as mulch after the planting was done. The first spring, the garden was awash in desert marigold from seed in the mulch.

Water harvesting is an important issue here. The cistern design accents the modern architecture, and the granite boulders (stockpiled during construction) were carefully reset to create niches for plants and to condense moisture for plant roots.

GARDEN SIX

Making the most of limited space can be a challenge to plant lovers. The patio at Zona Gardens in Tucson is an inviting example of the marriage of architecture and plants. Interesting plant groupings won't outgrow their spaces, and together, knit the garden into a synchronous mosaic.

Structure and bold color add impact to a small garden. Beaked yucca in the planter and the slender white trunks of palo blanco separate spaces without overwhelming them.

Lightly shaded by feathery palo blanco, places for people to gather are divided with compact forms of yucca and agave, blue grama, and small specimen cacti in bowls.

GARDEN SEVEN

In a historic neighborhood where lawns and large shade trees once dominated, the borders of this backyard are planted to provide privacy and buffer the wind. A mile high in elevation, but tempered by urban heating, the soil is fine, decomposed granite that drains when loosened after nearly a century of concentrated use.

Layers of plants screen one area from another and lend a sense of anticipation when exploring the garden. The space is separated into several living or work spaces, destinations that make the area seem much larger.

A boulder drilled and plumbed as a fountain houses the water reservoir below, so less moisture evaporates. The sound of gurgling water is refreshing, and the movement of the water attracts birds.

A stone bench backed with ornamental grass and warmed by a chiminea is one stop in the garden. A path also leads to a pistache-shaded work space at the bottom of the garden. RIGHT The patio adjacent to the house is an outdoor dining room and gathering place for entertaining, offering views of the garden.

GARDEN EIGHT

Santa Fe Botanical Garden shows deep understanding of and respect for the high desert that surrounds it. These are early days for the garden, and watching it grow and further define regional design will be a continuing pleasure. Visiting gardeners will come away with ideas to celebrate the high desert. It is included here because although it is a public garden, it is divided into residential-scale spaces and so, as intended, is easy to translate to home gardens in the area.

The orchard garden reflects the long agricultural history of northern New Mexico. Ramadas make shade until young trees mature and join the ranks of the sculptures that grace the garden in changing displays.

Water harvesting is a central feature of the garden, beautiful when dry and reason to celebrate when coursing with rain.

TOP Broad pathways lead directly to some areas, while narrower paths meander up and down slopes, offering a quieter experience of place. BOTTOM The cactus garden balances the water budget of the more demanding orchard and rose border, displaying cold hardy succulents as sculpture and high desert wildflowers as seasonal companions. OPPOSITE Grasses are signature plants of the high desert in autumn. Glowing in shades from purple to platinum when backlit, they dance in the breeze.

I include this green roof not as endorsement of planting gardens on southwestern rooftops, but to offer a multi-view perspective.

Where rain is abundant and gardening space limited, green roofs can be an efficient way to manage storm water, grow food, and enjoy green space. In the Southwest, where we barely have enough rain to grow plants in the ground, irrigating the roof seems extravagant. But in gardens, it seems there are always exceptions and one idea that is new to me comes from the U.S. Fish and Wildlife Service. They promote brown roofs: rainwater-dependent cover that offers the benefits of insulation and storm water absorption, plus protected nesting space for birds. If left undisturbed by the people and pets living below, brown roofs can be sustainable habitats.

GARDEN TEN

Shade in summer and wind protection in winter and spring are necessary to spend time outdoors comfortably in the Southwest. There is reciprocity between hard surfaces and plants. Roofs and paths drain rainwater to tree roots, and the trees will grow to shade the pavement, keeping temperatures more moderate in summer.

This is a garden made for outdoor living. The covered patio is a sheltered dining room for entertaining nearly year-round. Pathways lead to open areas for night sky-watching, and herb and vegetable gardening.

Garden Ten, cont. TOP Living space overflows into the garden with a flagstone patio that drains rainwater to tree basins. The apricot tree is along an east wall which buffers it from extremes, making crops more reliable; rainwater from the roof supplements drip irrigation. BOTTOM A west-facing wall provides the extra warmth Mediterranean plants prefer. Greek germander and lavender share their drip emitters with a fig tree.

GARDEN ELEVEN

Low desert plants are translucent visual barriers but very effective physical barriers in organizing space.

Plants with sculptural shapes, such as ocotillo and columnar cacti, help a short wall create an edge between garden and open desert.

PLANTING FOR SOUTHWEST SUCCESS

Of the thousands of plants that are native or cultivated in the Southwest, the suggestions that follow are the winners of the talent show, my choices for best of show in our arid gardens. The plants listed here include a wonderful array of forms, leaf colors and textures, flowers, fruits, and ornamental seed heads. But these options are more than just beautiful. Some are very broadly adapted, while others are perfect for specific places. The descriptions explain why and where they are recommended.

Chinkapin oak (*Quercus muhlenbergii*) is one of the resilent, heat- and drought-tolerant shade trees for Southwest gardens.

PLANT LISTINGS KEY

This plant key offers a shortcut to important cultural information. Most of these plants are drought tolerant; they prefer periodic deep soaks rather than frequent light watering. They are the most adaptable, taking advantage of ample rainfall when it comes and weathering drought as necessary. Drought tolerance is relative; plants growing at the hot edge of their adapted range likely need more water, while on the cold edge of their limits they'll need considerably less. The plants noted as drought loving will die out if watered too much too often, especially if the soil is poorly drained. The opposite is true of oasis plants, which are adapted to seasonal flooding and/or need more consistent moisture. Because many arid-adapted plants have aromatic foliage, the fragrant/aromatic symbol includes both flower and leaf scent. Pollinator plants are an essential part of the lives of native bees, butterflies, moths (including as larval food) and/or hummingbirds.

SUN REQUIREMENTS	MOISTURE REQUIREMENTS	SPECIAL CHARACTERISTICS
FULL SUN	**DROUGHT TOLERANT**	**NATIVE**
☀	☼(OK)	📍
PART SUN	**DROUGHT LOVING**	**SUPER HARDY**
☀	☼	🌡
SHADE	**NEEDS MORE WATER**	**WARM SEASON**
☁	💧+	☀
PART SHADE		**COOL SEASON**
◑		❄
		POLLINATOR
		🐝
		FRAGRANT / AROMATIC
		✿

A NOTE ON PLANT NAMES: Climate is not the only system undergoing rapid change. Botanical names have been changing at sometimes frustrating speed, as scientists now have the ability to explore the relationships between plants on a molecular level. The names used here are currently accepted to the best of our knowledge. In some cases, synonyms are listed. Apologies for any confusion.

TREES

Acacia aneura

Mulga

BLOOM PERIOD: Heavy in March; intermittently June through October

HEIGHT AND SPREAD: 20 ft. × 10 ft.

GROWS WELL IN: Well-drained soil in extreme heat; tolerates cold to 15° or 20°F

An adaptable, long-lived, thornless Australian native, mulga is pyramidal in shape when young, developing a rounded crown as it matures. With deep monthly watering, growth is slow to moderate so it needs little pruning for form; never prune in summer to avoid sunscald. The evergreen phyllodes vary from dull green to blue-green or silver, contrasting with the frilly yellow flower spikes and flat brown seedpods. Showy or subdued by season, mulga is a lovely small patio tree, as well as a cool backdrop for dramatic succulents and brilliant flowering shrubs.

Acacia crassifolia
syn. *Senegalia crassifolia*

Butterfly-leaf acacia

BLOOM PERIOD: March to May

HEIGHT AND SPREAD: 10 to 15 ft. × 10 to 15 ft.

GROWS WELL IN: Rocky, well-drained soil in extreme heat; cold hardy to 20°F briefly

Butterfly-leaf acacia is adorned with clusters of white puffball flowers in spring, but its rounded evergreen leaves (that resemble pairs of butterfly wings) are what set this acacia apart from all the others. Native to foothills and canyons in Mexico's Chihuahuan Desert, its naturally slow growth can be sped up by watering young plants every week or two in summer, but once well-established, butterfly-leaf acacia will thrive with deep watering every month or two. It takes minimal pruning to develop a small patio shade tree or sculptural, multi-trunked accent plant. This has been renamed *Senegalia crassifolia*, but you may still find it labeled as *Acacia*.

Mulga (*Acacia aneura*). RIGHT Butterfly-leaf acacia (*Acacia crassifolia*, syn. *Senegalia crassifolia*).

Sweet acacia

BLOOM PERIOD: January to April

HEIGHT AND SPREAD: 15 to 25 ft. tall ×
10 to 20 ft. wide

GROWS WELL IN: A wide range of soils in extreme
heat; some selections tolerate cold to the
mid-teens °F

With its cascades of fragrant yellow puffball flowers and its compact, naturally rounded canopy, sweet acacia makes a good small shade tree in places where honey bee activity, thorny branches, and seedpod litter are not a problem. Evergreen in warm winters, it thrives with water twice a month in summer, monthly or less during cooler weather. Sweet acacia is native from deserts and foothills to frost-free tropics, and until recently the synonymous *Acacia smallii* and *A. minuta* were considered distinct species, partly because of their greater cold tolerance; they are still often sold as such. Recently the name was changed to *Vachellia farnesiana*, but it will take time to find it labeled as such in nurseries.

Willow acacia

BLOOM PERIOD: Most profuse August to January,
but may flower lightly any time

HEIGHT AND SPREAD: 20 to 40 ft. × 20 ft.

GROWS WELL IN: Well-drained soil in extreme
heat; cold hardy only to 20°F

An Australian native valued as a shade or street tree, a graceful evergreen specimen, and a patio tree. Narrow gray-green phyllodes draping from slender weeping stems give willow acacia the character that sets it apart. Because of its rapid growth, dense canopy, and height, willow acacia may be vulnerable to wind-throw unless watered deeply every few weeks in summer, less often during cooler weather. Watering progressively farther from the trunk also contributes to a longer lifespan and greater stability. The tiny white or yellow puffball flowers would be easily missed except for their lightly sweet fragrance.

Willow acacia (*Acacia salicina*). LEFT Sweet acacia (*Acacia farnesiana*, syn. *Vachellia farnesiana*).

Shoestring acacia

BLOOM PERIOD: April to July

HEIGHT AND SPREAD: 25 to 30 ft. × 20 ft.

GROWS WELL IN: Well-drained soil in intense reflected heat; cold hardy only to 20°F

Shoestring acacia is a favorite street tree in Phoenix for its elegant silhouette, drooping evergreen phyllodes, and contrasting reddish bark. A thornless Australian native with clusters of pale yellow powder-puff blooms followed by long, slender, slightly constricted seedpods resembling strings of beads, shoestring acacia has a naturally graceful form that requires only light pruning to remove frost damage in spring. Its minimal litter and tolerance of reflected heat makes it a good patio tree, but it does self-sow with abandon so weeding is necessary. In large spaces, it is elegant when planted in groves.

Shoestring acacia (*Acacia stenophylla*).

Palo blanco

BLOOM PERIOD: **February to April**

HEIGHT AND SPREAD: **10 to 20 ft. × 5 to 10 ft.**

GROWS WELL IN: **Intense reflected heat; cold hardy only to 25°F**

A wisp of a tree with graceful weeping branches and a very sparse canopy of slender leaves. These leaves drop due to cold or drought, leaving evergreen phyllodes to carry on photosynthesis. The creamy white catkins are abundant in spring, but its stark silhouette and peeling white bark are palo blanco's great garden features. Native to the Sonoran Desert in Mexico, its use is limited here by cold. It is most effective as an accent in courtyards or against hot walls. Water deeply every month or two and prune to remove frost damage in spring. With a recent name change to *Mariosousa willardiana*, it will take a while to see the new name in nurseries and common usage.

Peeling bark of palo blanco.

Palo blanco (*Acacia willardiana*, syn. *Mariosousa willardiana*).

Bigtooth maple

HEIGHT AND SPREAD: 20 to 40 ft. × 10 to 20 ft.

GROWS WELL IN: High-elevation woodland and forest, especially along streams

This is a tree for gardens above 5000 ft. in elevation, where winters are distinctly cold and summers are rarely scorching hot. Bigtooth is one of the more resilient maples, better adapted to alkaline soils and low humidity than most, but still best situated in afternoon shade, where rainwater can be captured to supplement drip irrigation. Its leaves are smaller and thicker than other *Acer* species, but turn the brilliant scarlet in fall that satisfies a maple-lover's yen. Slow growing, it needs water every two weeks during the growing season, monthly or less with ample winter rain and snow.

Anacacho orchid tree

BLOOM PERIOD: March through May

HEIGHT AND SPREAD: 8 to 12 ft. × 6 to 8 ft.

GROWS WELL IN: Rocky alkaline soils in low to middle elevation desert areas; tolerates cold to 15°F when dormant.

Bauhinias give the garden a soft tropical touch with their butterfly-shaped leaves and lush clusters of satiny white flowers, sometimes suffused with pink. Anacacho orchid tree grows into a manageable small tree ideal for sunny patios. Like many arid-adapted trees, it will grow too fast and suffer wind breakage if watered too often. Water deeply every few weeks while it's blooming, monthly while days are hot, and only once or twice in late fall and winter (while nights are close to or below freezing), to encourage dormancy.

Bigtooth maple (*Acer grandidentatum*). RIGHT Anacacho orchid tree (*Bauhinia lunarioides*).

Caesalpinia cacalaco
syn. *Tara cacalaco*

Cascalote

BLOOM PERIOD: November through March

HEIGHT AND SPREAD: 10 to 20 ft. × 10 to 20 ft.

GROWS WELL IN: Hot desert areas; tolerates cold to 18°F

Cascalote is a celebration, a salsa band with roots. New growth is blushed purple; stems are thorny with bulging leaf scars, giving the trunks an interesting if prickly pattern. Sulfur-yellow flowers crown the canopy of evergreen leaves, followed by copper-colored seedpods that burst with a pop, releasing ripened seeds. Creating a multi-trunk patio tree requires light thinning of lower branches and suckers in spring. Cascalote offers welcome shade, with only deep soaking every few weeks in summer, and monthly or less when temperatures are cooler. The thornless cultivar 'Smoothie' makes a user-friendly patio tree and brilliant border plant or screen. A recent name change to *Tara cacalaco* means you may find it labeled either way.

Cascalote (*Caesalpinia cacalaco*, syn. *Tara cacalaco*).

Celtis reticulata

Netleaf hackberry

BLOOM PERIOD: Inconspicuous flowers March to May; pea-shaped fruits for songbirds August and September

HEIGHT AND SPREAD: 20 to 30 ft. × 30 ft.

GROWS WELL IN: All but hottest desert areas; weathers cold to at least -10°F

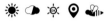

Netleaf hackberry is more a reliable workhorse than a show stopper, but I love it for its translucent spring-green foliage that darkens to deep green as temperatures climb, and for its interesting shape. Young plants look unruly with branches arching every which way. As the tree matures it develops a solid, rugged character. An excellent shade tree, it provides habitat for songbirds and butterflies. *Celtis reticulata* is adaptable to both long dry periods and flooding once well rooted, so irrigate weekly in summer to encourage growth, then water monthly or less to maintain good health. For low desert gardens, desert hackberry (*C. pallida*) is more heat tolerant, smaller, and cold hardy to 10°F.

Netleaf hackberry (*Celtis reticulata*).

'Oklahoma' redbud

BLOOM PERIOD: February and March
HEIGHT AND SPREAD: 10 ft. × 10 ft.
GROWS WELL IN: Well-drained soil in moderate heat and cold; weathers temperatures to at least -10°F

Beginning the growing season with a blaze of vibrant purple flowers cloaking the bare branches, this arid-adapted redbud then produces purple seedpods and rounded, shiny green leaves. Easily trained to a single trunk, it may also be grown as a multi-stemmed specimen. It roots deeply if compaction is remedied prior to planting, and is quite xeric by virtue of its deep roots, leathery leaves, and slow growth. Oklahoma redbud is the plant for shady spaces where a burst of seasonal color is welcome and small size is just right.

'Oklahoma' redbud (*Cercis canadensis* var. *texensis* 'Oklahoma').

Desert willow

BLOOM PERIOD: Heavy in May and June, intermittent throughout summer
HEIGHT AND SPREAD: 10 to 25 ft. × 10 to 20 ft.
GROWS WELL IN: Well-drained soil in 120°F summer heat and -20°F winter cold

Desert willow is fast growing when watered deeply every few weeks in summer, but like many xeric trees, extremely rapid growth can result in brittle branches likely to split in the wind. Not a true willow, *Chilopsis* prefers pulses of moisture rather than constantly wet soil. Lovely orchid-like blossoms are a favorite of hummingbirds and orioles. There are dozens of cultivars with white, burgundy, pink, and bicolor flowers, including several seedless clones which tend to flower longer. Chitalpa (×*Chitalpa tashkentensis*, a sterile hybrid of *Chilopsis* and *Catalpa*), is less heat tolerant, susceptible to bacterial leaf scorch, and needs more water in summer.

Desert willow (*Chilopsis linearis*).

Mexican olive

BLOOM PERIOD: January through December, with best show March to May, September, and October

HEIGHT AND SPREAD: 10 to 20 ft. × 10 to 15 ft.

GROWS WELL IN: Extreme reflected heat; suffers freeze damage near 20°F

A beautiful and stately plant for gardens seldom experiencing hard frost, its size depends in part on recovery pruning after frost, and partly on soil and moisture available. In deep soil with ample rainfall or irrigation, Mexican olive will grow to tree size, but in typical lean soil with limited water, it may only reach the 10 ft. mark after many years. It has large dark green leaves that are an excellent backdrop for its clusters of petunia-like, pure-white flowers with buttery yellow throats. The flowers are followed by golden fruits that turn juicy purple when ripe.

Mexican olive (*Cordia boissieri*).

Russian hawthorn

BLOOM PERIOD: May

HEIGHT AND SPREAD: 15 to 20 ft. × 10 to 15 ft.

GROWS WELL IN: Heat to 100°F and cold to -30°F

Russian hawthorn is the most xeric of a large group of trees that gardeners love for their show of white flowers in late spring and persistent clusters of gumball-sized, shiny red fruits in late summer and fall. The plant has the added merits of being rust resistant, having clear yellow fall color, and exfoliating golden bark that gives character to the leafless skeleton in winter. It tolerates compacted clay soils but thrives in all well-drained growing media. Water it thoroughly every two weeks while actively growing, monthly once the leaves have fallen. *Crataegus reverchonii* is a similar garden-worthy Texas native.

Russian hawthorn (*Crataegus ambigua*) in flower.

BELOW Red fruit of Russian hawthorn.

Indian rosewood

HEIGHT AND SPREAD: 30 to 50 ft. × 30 ft.

GROWS WELL IN: Extreme reflected heat; cold to 25°F once wood matures

Indian rosewood is unusual among desert legumes in not having showy flowers or conspicuous seedpods. The value of this tree is in its generous size, wonderful shade, and extensive root system. This root system contributes to its drought tolerance and its ability to prevent soil erosion in rainwater ponding areas, where its tendency to root-sprout and form groves is an asset rather than a maintenance problem. The compound leaflets are quite large, abundant, and shimmer in the breeze, giving the impression of lushness when watered every few weeks in summer and monthly the rest of the year.

Indian rosewood (*Dalbergia sissoo*).

Texas persimmon

BLOOM PERIOD: March to May

HEIGHT AND SPREAD: 15 to 20 ft. × 15 ft.

GROWS WELL IN: Endures heat spikes to 110°F+ and cold to 5°F briefly

Texas persimmon is less known outside its home state than it ought to be. It reminds me of crape myrtle both in form and in the beauty of its exfoliating bark, but its wonderfully fragrant, small white flowers are hidden in the new spring leaves. Hard-wooded and wind resilient, persimmon grows very slowly with little supplemental water, or a bit faster when watered twice a month during the growing season. A larval host for hairstreak butterflies, its sweet, black-purple fruits are relished by wildlife and the savvy gardener who shares in the late summer harvest.

Texas persimmon (*Diospyros texana*).

Texas ebony

BLOOM PERIOD: June to September
HEIGHT AND SPREAD: 15 to 30 ft. × 10 to 20 ft.
GROWS WELL IN: Well-drained soil in extreme heat; cold hardy to 10°F

Texas ebony is grown for its unusual zigzag branch pattern; dark, evergreen compound leaves; and its froth of pale yellow, fragrant flowers that are a butterfly magnet all summer long. Thick, dark brown seedpods persist on the tree though winter. Despite coastal origins, it is extremely adapted to drought, and since it is quite thorny, needs to be placed with care. Young plants are more frost-tender than established woody specimens, and dormant plants less vulnerable than ones being irrigated in winter, so it pays to protect saplings during the sudden extremes and encourage early dormancy by withholding water in fall.

Ghost gum eucalyptus

BLOOM PERIOD: May to August
HEIGHT AND SPREAD: 25 to 40 ft. × 12 to 20 ft.
GROWS WELL IN: Extreme reflected heat; cold hardy to 20°F

Ghost gum is one of the most cold-tolerant eucalyptus species, and while, like the others, it has the aromatic evergreen foliage, fast growth, and ability to grow in a wide range of soils and moisture regimes, it is noteworthy for its relative lack of litter, wind resilience, and manageable mature size. As its common name suggests, its slender white trunks, graceful drooping branches, and pale blue-gray leaves give it a ghostly aura in moonlight, but day or night it is the best eucalyptus for low desert gardens.

Ghost gum eucalyptus (*Eucalyptus papuana*). LEFT Texas ebony (*Ebenopsis ebano*, syn. *Pithecellobium flexicaule*).

Fig

HEIGHT AND SPREAD: **15 ft. × 10 ft.**

GROWS WELL IN: **Endures extreme heat; some cultivars weather cold to -10°F**

Figs are an ancient staple introduced to the Southwest by the earliest European colonists. Easily grown in most low and intermediate zones, they are coddled by gardeners near the too-hot and too-cold extremes of their practical range. As a designer, I love them for their stout stems and bold, lobed leaves which are tolerant of our low humidity. 'Chicago', 'Negronne', 'Peter's Honey', and 'Brown Turkey' are among the hardiest in the arid Southwest. Most of the *Ficus* species used as ornamentals are large tropical evergreens that freeze burn when temperatures drop below 25°F even briefly and die outright after hard freezes.

Fig (*Ficus carica*).

Desert olive

BLOOM PERIOD: **March and April**

HEIGHT AND SPREAD: **12 to 18 ft. × 12 to 15 ft.**

GROWS WELL IN: **All but the hottest desert gardens**

Desert olive has many slender, upright stems with smooth, pale gray bark and a dense canopy of small, bright green leaves that turn clear yellow in autumn. Bead-like blue fruits form on female plants in summer to the delight of many songbirds. It may be trained as an accent tree by removing all but the dominant stems, revealing their interesting crooks, or left branched to the ground for screening or wind protection. Not fussy about soils, it is most vibrant when watered thoroughly every two weeks in summer and monthly the rest of the year.

Desert olive (*Forestiera neomexicana*). BELOW Blue fruits on female plant.

115

Fragrant ash

BLOOM PERIOD: **April**

HEIGHT AND SPREAD: **12 to 20 ft. × 8 to 12 ft.**

GROWS WELL IN: **All but the hottest desert below 2000 ft., or high-elevation gardens above 8000 ft.**

Fragrant ash is rare among ash species, in having clusters of lacy, honey-scented white flowers. In nature, you'll find it on rocky canyon slopes and along occasionally flooding arroyos. In mountain gardens, plant it in a sunny spot on a boulder-strewn slope for erosion control. At lower elevations, place it in afternoon shade near a rainwater-harvesting basin. It is an excellent small shade tree watered deeply twice a month in summer, and monthly or less in cooler weather. Little leaf ash (*Fraxinus greggii*) is only cold hardy to 10°F, but adapts more easily to low desert heat.

Fragrant ash (*Fraxinus cuspidata*). RIGHT Rocky Mountain juniper (*Juniperus scopulorum*).

Rocky Mountain juniper

HEIGHT AND SPREAD: **20 to 40 ft. × 10 to 20 ft.**

GROWS WELL IN: **Cooler foothills gardens**

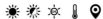

Junipers have been so overused in many urban areas that the pollen-producing males have been banned, to limit the misery of allergy sufferers—closing the barn door after the cows have escaped, since a well-grown tree can live hundreds of years. There are dozens of selections, including columnar or weeping forms; blue, green, and silver leaf color; as well as pollen-free female clones. If you garden above 6000 ft. in elevation and want soft texture, evergreen cover, wind protection, habitat value, or the possibility of making gin from the berries, explore the cultivars available. You may find just what you need.

Golden rain tree

BLOOM PERIOD: **June and July**
HEIGHT AND SPREAD: **20 to 40 ft. × 25 to 40 ft.**
GROWS WELL IN: **All areas**

The delicate apple-green leaves of golden rain tree provide wonderful filtered shade. In early summer, when heat begins to diminish the surge of spring flower color, lacy yellow blossoms crown the tree for several weeks, gradually replaced by lantern-like seed capsules. These turn rusty brown by autumn and persist into winter, providing a final season of interest. Popular as a street tree, it adapts to most soils and endures heat, cold, wind, and drought with deep watering twice monthly in summer, and monthly or less the rest of the year. Seed-eating red and black rain tree bugs sometimes occur in large numbers, but do no damage.

Goldenball leadtree

BLOOM PERIOD: **May through August**
HEIGHT AND SPREAD: **10 to 15 ft. × 8 to 12 ft.**
GROWS WELL IN: **Well-drained soil from 1000 ft. to 5000 ft. elevation range; tolerates 0°F briefly when dry**

One of the many desert legumes that deserves garden space, goldenball leadtree produces yellow puffball flowers that dangle from branches. Finely divided soft-green leaves offer light shade on patios, and for plants such as aloe that need an SPF 50+ sunscreen in summer. Basking in reflected heat from walls and paving, it takes a bit of shaping to create a nice patio tree. Protection from wind prevents damage to the brittle stems. Give a thorough soaking biweekly in summer and monthly or less the rest of the year.

Golden rain tree (*Koelreuteria paniculata*). RIGHT Goldenball leadtree (*Leucaena retusa*).

Ironwood

BLOOM PERIOD: May and June

HEIGHT AND SPREAD: 15 to 25 ft. × 15 to 20 ft.

GROWS WELL IN: Desert areas with brief episodes of cold to 20°F; persistent, prolonged cold is fatal

As the common name implies, ironwood is tough. Extreme drought and heat merely slow its growth; extreme cold is its downfall. An evergreen with sprays of tiny, pale pink flowers, it has a naturally compact, rounded shape, so pruning is done to raise the branch canopy when the plant is used as a patio tree. Since the twigs and branches are well armed with needle-sharp spines, plants should be placed and pruned to protect people from unwelcome impalement. As a visual screen barrier plant or security border, ironwood needs nothing more than infrequent deep watering once it achieves the desired size.

'Desert Museum' palo verde

BLOOM PERIOD: Intermittently July and August in response to monsoon rains

HEIGHT AND SPREAD: 10 to 25 ft. × 8 to 15 ft.

GROWS WELL IN: Well-drained soil in intense reflected heat; cold hardy to 15°F, possibly colder when dormant

A three-species cross of *Parkinsonia aculeata* with *P. florida* and *P. microphylla*, 'Desert Museum' is fast growing and free of thorns, a graceful tree with bright green stems that photosynthesize in lieu of leaves during times of extreme drought. It makes a gorgeous fountain of yellow when in bloom, and, like other palo verdes, can be short-lived when irrigated too frequently in good garden soil, but thrives in lean soil with monthly deep soaks, even in baking heat. Having no thorns makes 'Desert Museum' a great patio tree, creating shade in intense, sunlit spaces that are used frequently.

Ironwood (*Olneya tesota*). RIGHT 'Desert Museum' palo verde (*Parkinsonia* 'Desert Museum').

Blue palo verde

BLOOM PERIOD: March

HEIGHT AND SPREAD: 20 ft. × 25 ft.

GROWS WELL IN: Well-drained soil in intense reflected heat; cold hardy to 15°F, perhaps to 10°F

Blue palo verde, first to bloom in spring and the most cold tolerant of the cultivated species, has smooth, lime-green bark with a slightly blue cast, small thorns, and finely divided leaves. Young trees need shaping when used for shade in patios and other high-traffic areas. In small groves, it is showstopping in bloom, merely gorgeous the rest of the year with deep monthly watering. Littleleaf palo verde (*Parkinsonia microphylla*), slower growing to 12 ft. × 15 ft. and slightly less cold tolerant, has pale, creamy yellow flowers and the characteristic smooth, green bark that makes plants stand out in the landscape.

Blue palo verde (*Parkinsonia florida*).

Palo brea

BLOOM PERIOD: April to June

HEIGHT AND SPREAD: 20 ft. × 25 ft.

GROWS WELL IN: Well-drained soil in intense heat; cold hardy to 25°F

Similar in many ways to the other the Sonoran *Parkinsonia* species, but the least cold tolerant, palo brea is a favorite street tree in Phoenix, giving the city a vibrant feel and welcome shade in the blistering summer heat. Well adapted to heat and drought, despite 120°F summer days, palo brea can make food in its bark (like all palo verdes), giving up its leaves to conserve water and energy. Sudden freezes can kill tender new growth, so take advantage of the tree's water-wise ways and irrigate deeply but infrequently, especially in winter to avoid problems.

Palo brea (*Parkinsonia praecox*).

Bristlecone pine

HEIGHT AND SPREAD: 5 to 30 ft. × 5 to 12 ft.

GROWS WELL IN: Moderate heat and extreme cold

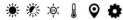

Climate extremes are taking their toll on Western forests. Rising temperatures and drier soils in the lowlands are forcing pines upslope to find more suitable conditions. Bristlecones known to be more than 2000 years old are already on the mountaintops, buffeted by freezing wind and searing drought. Pinyon pine (*Pinus edulis*) has become a poor choice in gardens below 6000 ft., while slow-growing bristlecone, with its thick, waxy needles that shed only every ten to seventeen years, grows surprisingly well in gardens several thousand feet lower than its typical range—to about 5000 ft. with generous watering every two weeks in summer and monthly in winter.

Afghan pine

HEIGHT AND SPREAD: 30 to 50 ft. × 10 to 20 ft.

GROWS WELL IN: Low desert heat with extra water; cold hardy briefly to -20°F when dormant

Native to arid Pakistan and Afghanistan, this conifer's symmetrical, narrowly conical shape and long, bright green needles are soft and cool-looking planted in small groups or offset in rows as a windbreak. Adapted to all soils (except heavy clay that is kept persistently wet), Afghan pine is a good option in desert gardens where native pines will no longer grow well. Aleppo pine (*Pinus halepensis*) grows a bit larger and is slightly less cold tolerant. Its form is more irregular but the soft green needles give it a rugged vibrancy. Use fallen needles as mulch.

Afghan pine (*Pinus eldarica*). LEFT Bristlecone pine (*Pinus aristata*).

Ponderosa pine

HEIGHT AND SPREAD: 40 to 100+ ft. × 20 ft.

GROWS WELL IN: Cool niches 6000 ft. to 8000 ft. in elevation

This is one of the conifers losing ground most quickly in southwestern forests, as heat and drought-stressed trees become targets for insects, disease, and wildfire. If you are fortunate enough to live in a healthy ponderosa forest, follow the advice of dedicated forest ecologists and reduce competition for moisture by culling any spindly trees, keeping understory brush to a minimum, and reducing needle duff to a thin layer protective of soil moisture that would burn quickly at lower temperatures in case of fire. Direct rainwater from your roof to occasionally soak the low spots between trees, so the canopy stays hydrated.

Ponderosa pine (*Pinus ponderosa*).

'Red Push' pistache

HEIGHT AND SPREAD: 25 to 40 ft. × 20 to 30 ft.

GROWS WELL IN: Extreme heat; cold hardy to 0°F

'Red Push' is an excellent shade tree with a moderate growth rate somewhat faster than Chinese pistache, with strong wind-resilient branches, and a spreading, rounded crown at maturity. Its compound leaves emerge red in spring, then open to dark green leaflets dense enough to create cooling shade all summer. Leaves turn shades of deep red, scarlet, or orange and drop after several hard freezes; since red push is seedless, fall cleanup is easy. 'Red Push' is a hybrid of *Pistacia atlantica* × *P. intergerrima*, best in low desert heat.

'Red Push' pistache (*Pistacia* 'Red Push').

Chinese pistache

BLOOM PERIOD: March to April

HEIGHT AND SPREAD: 30 ft. × 20 ft.

GROWS WELL IN: All except mountain gardens above 7000 ft.

Chinese pistache is one of the best shade trees for arid climates. It grows at a moderate pace, to proportions that yield ample filtered shade for patios, driveways, medians, and other situations where trees that are less heat- and drought-adapted suffer. Male plants produce a spike of compressed red flowers that look like little flames at the branch tips. Female plants produce clusters of baby pea–sized red fruits. Leaflets are small and dark green until fall, when they turn shades of scarlet, orange, and sometimes yellow. Once established, deep watering monthly in an area equal to the branch spread keeps this pistache healthy.

Arizona sycamore

BLOOM PERIOD: March to April

HEIGHT AND SPREAD: 50 to 70 ft. × 60 to 80 ft.

GROWS WELL IN: Moist, gravelly soil along the few perennial streams in the desert Southwest; cold hardy to -20°F

This sycamore is a majestic giant, with peeling rust and gray bark that reveals a smooth, almost white trunk and thick branches that arch—widely embracing those lucky enough to stand in its dense shade. In native groves, it stabilizes the soil and is a condo for wildlife, but it takes a healthy, productive watershed to satisfy its thirst. In designed landscapes, even when placed near low spots where rainwater collects and irrigated a few times a month in summer, it is difficult to sustain and may decline long before reaching maturity.

Arizona sycamore (*Platanus wrightii*). LEFT Chinese pistache (*Pistacia chinensis*).

Cottonwood

HEIGHT AND SPREAD: 60 to 80 ft. × 60 to 80 ft.

GROWS WELL IN: All areas where groundwater is shallow or rainwater collects

Cottonwood (*Populus deltoides* subsp. *wislizeni*).

While it is a stretch to call native cottonwood drought tolerant, it is amazingly water efficient for a tree its size, extremely adept at absorbing water and using it carefully. Cottonwoods are the hallmark tree along southwestern rivers, and provide layers of wildlife habitat. If you have the garden space and live in a river valley or have several thousand square feet of hard surface from which to harvest rainwater, consider planting a cottonwood. Its leaves dangle perpendicular to the sun to reduce evaporation, so the shade below is nicely filtered. Gold fall color is another bonus.

Honey mesquite

BLOOM PERIOD: **April and May**

HEIGHT AND SPREAD: **8 to 25 ft. × 15 to 30 ft.**

GROWS WELL IN: **Extreme heat; tolerates cold to -20°F**

☀ ☼ ◉ 🐝

Mesquite is a southwestern desert icon, resilient, well armed, and productive. Because it grows across an extended area, choose locally adapted plants whenever possible. Its small, bright green leaflets, frilly yellow flowers, and cream-speckled, purple bean pods contrast with the charcoal black bark. Watered deeply once or twice a month in summer, it will grow tall enough to shape as a patio shade tree. 'Maverick', a thornless cultivar hardy to -5°F, is more people friendly. Mesquite also makes an excellent barrier and wildlife habitat that can go without supplemental irrigation once deeply rooted. Naturally sweet flour milled from the starchy seedpods makes great muffins.

Honey mesquite in bloom. BELOW 'Maverick' honey mesquite (*Prosopis glandulosa* 'Maverick').

Velvet mesquite

BLOOM PERIOD: March and April, sometimes again after summer rain
HEIGHT AND SPREAD: 10 to 20 ft. × 15 to 30 ft.
GROWS WELL IN: Extreme heat; tolerates cold to 5°F

Similar to honey mesquite, velvet mesquite has a more western range in the Sonoran and Mohave deserts, while honey mesquite is Chihuahuan. They share the traits of thorny branches, dark, shredding bark contrasting with fine, bright green foliage, frilly flowers, and starchy seedpods, but velvet mesquite's new growth is sheathed in soft hairs, thus the common name. Landscape uses are similar, but velvet mesquite is less cold tolerant. Screwbean mesquite (*Prosopis pubescens*) is more distinctive, with tiny, gray-green leaves and a more upright form. Instead of flat, cream-colored, narrow pods several inches long, its pods are clusters of small, tightly coiled corkscrews.

Gambel oak

HEIGHT AND SPREAD: 10 to 30 ft. × 10 to 20 ft.
GROWS WELL IN: Moderate heat and cold to -30°F

This is one of the dominant oaks in the western mountains, resilient and adaptable. It may remain shrubby with many smaller trunks on drier rocky slopes, or grow to shade-tree proportions when soil is deep and moisture is plentiful. In gardens, it may be used as a screen or windbreak on the edges of the landscape, or planted in rainwater-harvesting basins as a shade tree. The deeply lobed leaves are dark green, turning rust and bronze after a hard frost. Most of the leaves persist on the branches well into winter and blend well with foliage that is blue-gray or silver.

Velvet mesquite (*Prosopis velutina*). RIGHT Gambel oak (*Quercus gambelii*).

Chinkapin oak

HEIGHT AND SPREAD: 25 to 50 ft. × 25 to 50 ft.
GROWS WELL IN: Low desert heat and higher elevation cold to -30°F

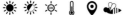

Chinkapin is one of the fast-growing oaks, valued for endurance as well as speed. It has dark green, oval leaves with wavy edges that turn subdued maroon in autumn. As the canopy matures, it broadens, and branches will sweep the ground unless pruned. Chinkapin oak needs watering every two weeks throughout the growing season in deep, well-drained soil, and monthly while dormant. Unlike many cold-adapted oaks, it rarely suffers leaf scorch in summer, even in low desert gardens, but will grow faster with afternoon shade where heat is brutal. Large acorns are produced annually to the delight of wildlife.

Chinkapin oak (*Quercus muehlenbergii*). BELOW Chinkapin oak leaves starting to turn.

Texas red oak

HEIGHT AND SPREAD: 35 ft. × 35 to 40 ft.

GROWS WELL IN: Occasional heat spikes above 100°F and cold to -20°F

Although similar in appearance to moisture- and acid-loving eastern oak species, with reddish branch tips, deeply lobed pointed leaves, and dark gray, plated bark, this red oak is adapted to alkaline soils and a more limited water budget, with moderately fast growth. Foliage is bright green, turning shades of scarlet in autumn. It grows fastest in deep, well-drained soil but will tough it out in rocky, lean soil as well, with deep watering every two weeks in summer, monthly while dormant. Leave young plants branched low to shade tender bark, gradually removing branches until the canopy is above head height.

Shrub live oak

HEIGHT AND SPREAD: 6 to 12 ft. × 6 to 12 ft.

GROWS WELL IN: Both heat and cold to at least -10°F, probably colder

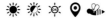

One of the smallest and most drought tolerant of the evergreen oaks, shrub live oak has small, blue-gray, holly-like leaves densely covering the many slender stems. In time, the trunk thickens and specimens can be thinned to reveal the beautiful form, or left natural to provide screening and cover for wildlife. It is adapted to crumbly granite soils and watering every few weeks in summer in any well-drained soil will produce faster growth. If you love oaks but don't have the space for one of the giants, this one will even grow well in a large pot in a wind-protected spot.

Shrub live oak (*Quercus turbinella*). LEFT Texas red oak (*Quercus texana*).

Escarpment live oak

HEIGHT AND SPREAD: **20 to 50 ft. × 20 to 30 ft.**

GROWS WELL IN: **Extreme heat and cold to -10°F**

Escarpment live oak has become one of the most popular small evergreens because of its versatility and compact size. It grows large enough to provide shade year-round in warm desert areas, while it may defoliate during extremely cold winters at higher elevations. The small, stiff, mostly smooth-margined leaves rarely heat scorch in summer, even after months of days above 100°F. Grown with deep watering once or twice a month, it stays 20 to 30 ft. tall for accent planting in smaller urban spaces, or for grouping as screening and wind protection on larger sites.

Escarpment live oak (*Quercus virginiana* var. *fusiformis*).

Mexican elder

BLOOM PERIOD: **April to July**

HEIGHT AND SPREAD: **10 to 20 ft. × 15 to 20 ft.**

GROWS WELL IN: **Moderate heat of intermediate desert; cold hardy to 0°F**

A fast-growing accent tree, it develops thick, gnarled trunks while young, adding mass and structure to new gardens. Mexican elder has ridged, tan bark; coarse, pale green leaflets; and broad, flat clusters of tiny white flowers followed by waxy, pale blue fruits that ripen dark purple. In low desert, elder tends to be green in winter but defoliates in extreme heat even if given plenty of water. In high desert gardens, it loses its leaves for a few months every winter and can die back severely during unusual cold events. Pruning is done after flowering to shape young plants and remove deadwood.

Mexican elder (*Sambucus nigra* subsp. *cerulea*).

Sapindus saponaria var. drummondii

Western soapberry

BLOOM PERIOD: May and June
HEIGHT AND SPREAD: 15 to 30 ft. × 10 to 20 ft.
GROWS WELL IN: Extreme heat; cold hardy to
-20°F, possibly colder

Soapberry is chameleon-like in the way it varies depending on its environment. In deep soil with ample water it becomes a large tree. Where roots are disturbed by flooding or soils are shallow, it root-sprouts, creating a grove of many short, slender-trunked trees. In desert gardens with deep watering every month or two, it is a nice, small, patio shade tree. Its small leaflets are bright green, turning yellow-gold in fall. Lacy clusters of tiny white flowers produce persistent waxy gold fruits the size of marbles. The waxy seed covering contains saponin, used as soap by native people.

Western soapberry (*Sapindus saponaria* var. *drummondii*).

Sophora secundiflora
syn. *Dermatophyllum secundiflorum*

Texas mountain laurel

BLOOM PERIOD: March and April
HEIGHT AND SPREAD: 10 to 25 ft. × 10 to 15 ft.
GROWS WELL IN: Well-drained, calcium-rich soil in reflected low desert heat to 5000 ft. elevation; root hardy to -10°F

Highlighted against a wall or as a centerpiece in a small courtyard, the shiny evergreen leaflets obscure shapely branches and are a cool respite in hot garden spaces. Pendulous clusters of violet-purple, pea-shaped blossoms have the unexpected scent of grape soda. Plump silver seedpods follow and the large, hard red seeds are toxic but difficult to extract from the woody capsules. It grows best when watered deeply once or twice a month when well-established. 'Silver Peso' is an elegant selection with white stems and silver foliage. Recently, the name was changed to *Dermatophyllum secundiflorum*, but it will take some time for the new label to find its way into nurseries and common usage.

Texas mountain laurel (*Sophora secundiflora*, syn. *Dermatophyllum secundiflorum*).

Scholar tree

BLOOM PERIOD: **July and August**
HEIGHT AND SPREAD: **30 to 40 ft. × 20 to 25 ft.**
GROWS WELL IN: **Intermediate and high desert areas to 7000 ft. elevation; cold hardy to -20°F**

One of the most arid-adapted shade trees, it is fast growing with an elegant vase shape, striated bark, and dense, rounded canopy of small, dark green leaflets on green branches. These filter the sun on patios and make sidewalks, parks, and parking more comfortable in summertime heat. Clusters of white, honey-scented flowers droop from the branches and are followed by small, flat, pale green seedpods that persist after the leaves drop in autumn, adding a touch of green to the dormant winter landscape. Thorough watering once or twice a month is enough to keep an established tree healthy.

Hybrid elm

HEIGHT AND SPREAD: **30 to 50 ft. × 20 to 25 ft.**
GROWS WELL IN: **Low desert heat and cold to -15°F**

In arid landscapes where shade is precious, there are relatively few trees that thrive on a limited water budget. Smaller in scale but just as stately in form as larger elms, recent hybrids of *Ulmus parvifolia* produce small, crisp leaves on arching branches. Their bark is a mosaic of bronze, gray, and rust flakes sometimes called lace bark. 'Athena' and 'Allee' are two of the finest and have proven themselves to be resistant to both disease and insects. 'Athena' is the smaller of the two, with bronze fall color, while 'Allee' matures to a full 50 ft., with rosy-gold fall color.

Scholar tree (*Styphnolobium japonicum*). RIGHT Hybrid elm (*Ulmus* hybrid).

Vitex agnus-castus

Chaste tree

BLOOM PERIOD: **May and June**
HEIGHT AND SPREAD: **10 to 25 ft. × 12 to 20 ft.**
GROWS WELL IN: **Heat in low desert; endures cold to -10°F**

☀ ☼ ☼ ✿ 🐝▸

A fast-growing, adaptable Mediterranean native, vitex is naturally sculptural, a form that is easily enhanced by removing smaller stems that obscure the dominant curving trunks. The fresh, aromatic leaves are palmate, dark green on the upper surface and silver underneath, so the plant seems to shimmer in the breeze. Long tapered spikes of small lavender-blue flowers crown the canopy and are followed by bead-like seed clusters. Pale pink and white varieties are also available. Heat intensifies flowering and thorough infrequent watering, twice a month when blooming and monthly the rest of the year, produces the strongest growth.

Zizyphus jujuba

Jujube, Chinese date

BLOOM PERIOD: **May to July**
HEIGHT AND SPREAD: **20 to 30 ft. × 10 ft.**
GROWS WELL IN: **Intense reflected heat; cold hardy to -18°F**

☀ ☼ ☼ ✿ 🐝▸

Jujube has a stiff, arching form with thorny branches that grow in a zigzag pattern, giving it an interesting winter silhouette. Unless the suckers are removed regularly, it root-sprouts and forms a grove, but otherwise needs little pruning. Shiny, bright green leaflets are refreshing relief against hot walls and the small, lacy, yellow flowers have a wonderful citrus-honey fragrance. It prefers alkaline soil with good drainage, watered once or twice a month in summer. 'Li' and 'Lang' are the most common grafted forms and are less thorny with large, date-like, bronze-colored fruit in fall—prized in Mediterranean and Asian cuisine.

Chaste tree (*Vitex agnus-castus*). RIGHT Jujube (*Zizyphus jujuba*).

PALMS

Brahea armata

Mexican blue palm, blue hesper palm

HEIGHT AND SPREAD: 15 to 45 ft. × 12 to 20 ft.

GROWS WELL IN: Extreme heat of the low to intermediate desert; cold hardy to 15°F

With occasional floods of water, slow-growing Mexican blue palm keeps its crown of beautiful blue-gray fanned leaves at eye level, where it can be used as a lush tropical-looking backdrop. With weekly watering and added nitrogen fertilizer in summer, it will grow faster to a single-trunk tree form. It is not fussy about soil as long as it drains fairly well. Old leaves can be cut off soon after they dry, making it an easy-care palm for smaller gardens.

Chamaerops humilis

Mediterranean fan palm

HEIGHT AND SPREAD: 5 to 20 ft. × 8 to 15 ft.

GROWS WELL IN: Extreme reflected heat; cold hardy to 15°F

Slow growing with evergreen fan leaves barbed on the stem margins, this palm is compact enough to cluster in groups or plant singly as an accent. Soaking twice monthly in summer nets the fastest growth. Too much water can lead to yellowing foliage. Dried leaves need to be cut off occasionally; the leaf stubs with soft hairs between them make an interesting pattern on the trunk as it grows taller. Some plants sucker profusely, creating an attractive, clustered look in a relatively small space.

Mexican blue palm (*Brahea armata*). RIGHT Mediterranean fan palm (*Chamaerops humilis*).

Phoenix dactylifera

Date palm

BLOOM PERIOD: March to April

HEIGHT AND SPREAD: 50 to 70 ft. × 20 to 40 ft.

GROWS WELL IN: Extreme reflected heat; cold hardy to 20°F

☀ ☀ ☀

This palm has been cultivated for its fruit for at least a few thousand years, and there are many cultivars available. As an ornamental, it is one of the largest palms at maturity, growing a foot or more a year to majestic size. Although it offsets shoots at the base, they are usually removed to maintain the single slender trunk. The leaves are pinnate, arching gracefully from the crown, and are extremely thorny at the base. Pruning is done carefully to avoid the wicked barbs. The root zone needs soaking thoroughly every two weeks in summer for quality fruit, only slightly less to maintain lush foliage.

Date palm (*Phoenix dactylifera*).

Sonoran palmetto

HEIGHT AND SPREAD: 20 to 25 ft. × 15 ft.
GROWS WELL IN: Well-drained soil in extreme and reflected heat; cold hardy to 15°F in dry soil

☀ ☀ ☀

Though there are green-leaved forms, the most stunning of the fan-shaped frond colors of this sabal is the pale blue. Compared with other fan palms, the leaf stem is quite long and slender, extending 5 to 8 ft. from the unbranched trunk, and the frond arches outward and downward. It is a desert species, preferring soaking twice monthly in summer, monthly the rest of the year. Typical of all palms, only dead leaves should be removed to avoid compromising the vigor of the plant.

Sonoran palmetto (*Sabal uresana*). BELOW Trunk detail of the Sonoran palmetto.

Desert fan palm

BLOOM PERIOD: March to June

HEIGHT AND SPREAD: 45 ft. × 10 to 15 ft.

GROWS WELL IN: Extreme heat; leaves die at 15°F but crown may survive rare 10°F events

The only native species and the most cold-tolerant, desert fan palm is distinct from Mexican fan palm in having a stout columnar stem and longer leaf stems, giving it a more open canopy and an interesting thatch skirt until leaves are removed. Eventually the leaf stubs fall off, leaving the trunk smooth. It hybridizes easily with *Washingtonia robusta* and some hybrids are reportedly more cold tolerant than either of the parents.

Mexican fan palm

BLOOM PERIOD: March to May

HEIGHT AND SPREAD: 60 to 75 ft. × 10 to 12 ft.

GROWS WELL IN: Extreme heat; cold hardy to 20°F

This is a fast-growing palm. Young plants watered weekly in summer can add 6 ft. a year, but once grown to specimen size, watering less results in a more manageable plant. Its stem tapers, often twice the girth at the base as at the leafy crown, and becomes smooth with age, giving it a graceful silhouette. The leafy, olive green fronds have short petioles with a filament of marginal fibers. The flowers are pink-orange and produce small black fruits that birds consume. Regular removal of dead leaves and cleanup of fruit is needed.

Desert fan palm (*Washingtonia filifera*). RIGHT Mexican fan palm (*Washingtonia robusta*).

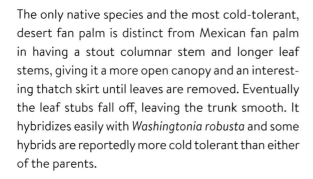

VINES

Antigonon leptopus

Queen's wreath

BLOOM PERIOD: July to October

HEIGHT AND SPREAD: 20 to 30 ft. × 4 to 6 ft.

GROWS WELL IN: Extreme reflected heat; tops die back at 22°F, roots survive to 10°F under deep mulch in dry soil

The cascade of lush, heart-shaped leaves and long clusters of intense, rose-pink to red flowers clinging to a fence, scrambling up a tree, or draping across a pergola is a great way to heat up a garden visually and cool it down physically. The stems are self-supporting with tendrils, and while it starts slowly, once well-rooted, queen's wreath covers quickly. Most vines layer new growth above the old, eventually requiring severe pruning to rejuvenate them. Where queen's wreath freezes back most winters, routine spring cleanup keeps the vine young and vigorous.

Bignonia capreolata

Cross vine

BLOOM PERIOD: March to early June

HEIGHT AND SPREAD: 30 to 50 ft. × 20 to 30 ft.

GROWS WELL IN: Intense heat, cold hardy to -10°F

A vigorous vine, somewhat controlled in its spread by our drier air and soils, it has paired leaves with a modified central leaflet that serves as a tendril for climbing. Semi-evergreen, its glossy, dark green foliage blushes purple in cold weather. Clusters of lightly fragrant, large, red-orange, trumpet-shaped flowers welcome returning hummingbirds in spring. Like most vines, a year or two of weekly watering in summer helps to develop extensive roots, then deep watering twice monthly in summer and monthly or less during cooler weather keeps plants healthy. 'Tangerine Beauty' is a popular cultivar with softer orange flower color.

Cross vine (*Bignonia capreolata*). LEFT Queen's wreath (*Antigonon leptopus*).

Bougainvillea

BLOOM PERIOD: February to June and October to December

HEIGHT AND SPREAD: 10 to 30 ft. × 8 to 20 ft.

GROWS WELL IN: Extreme reflected heat; leaves blacken at 32°F but stems tolerate frost briefly

A rambunctious, brilliantly colorful vine in frost-free areas of the low desert, bougainvillea also adapts well to large pots on the patio that can be moved to a sunny window indoors in areas with freezing winter temperatures. Cultivated worldwide, there are many cultivars available; its papery bracts range in colors from true red to magenta, coral pink, and white, surrounding tiny white flowers. Deep magenta 'Barbara Karst' is a bit more frost tolerant, but even a few hours of frost will blacken the leaves. Wait until spring to assess and clean up winter damage. The stiff stems are thorny, making pruning a job best done with care. Water twice a month in summer.

Yellow orchid vine

BLOOM PERIOD: March to July

HEIGHT AND SPREAD: 15 to 20 ft. × 15 to 25 ft.

GROWS WELL IN: Reflected heat; stems tolerate cold to 25°F

The twining stems of orchid vine, lush with smooth, narrow, evergreen leaves, will quickly scramble up a trellis or fence. Clusters of orchid-like yellow flowers produce soft, chartreuse-colored, winged fruits that ripen to papery brown by October. Slow to start, water new plants weekly for a few summers to encourage them to cover, then soak once or twice a month in summer to keep plants vigorous. After unusual cold events, plants may die back to the ground, recovering from the roots and delaying blooming until summer. Pruning out frost damage in spring rejuvenates plants. The related *Mascagnia lilacina* has purple flowers but is otherwise very similar.

Bougainvillea (*Bougainvillea glabra*). RIGHT Yellow orchid vine (*Calleaum macropterum*).

Trumpet vine

BLOOM PERIOD: **May to September**

HEIGHT AND SPREAD: **40 ft. × 15 ft.**

GROWS WELL IN: **Extreme reflected heat with weekly water in summer; cold hardy to -30°F**

My love for its clusters of large, deep red-orange flowers—an outrageous show against lush, dark green compound leaves—is tempered by trumpet vine's aggressive root-sprouting and unruly winter appearance. Hummingbirds are drawn to the flowers and arid conditions help check its wanderlust, but it takes deep watering at least twice a month during the growing season to be attractive. There are several hybrids with an Asian species that are less cold hardy and less rampant growers, including soft red 'Madame Galen' and butter yellow *Campsis radicans* f. *flava*.

Trumpet vine (*Campsis radicans*).

Scarlet clematis

BLOOM PERIOD: **March to August**

HEIGHT AND SPREAD: **6 to 8 ft. × 4 to 6 ft.**

GROWS WELL IN: **Heat in partial shade; cold hardy to -15°F, possibly colder when dormant**

Scarlet clematis is not your grandmother's vine—unless she lives on the Edwards Plateau in Texas. Delicate in appearance but tolerant of extremes of heat and cold in rocky soils, this resilient native has long, slender leaflets, and thin, twining stems. Clusters of urn-shaped, red flowers with leathery sepals substituting for petals surround the frilly stamens. There are several hybrids with star-shaped, red flowers available from specialty growers; these are best grown in afternoon shade. Flowers are produced on new growth, so plants can be trimmed back to the first buds above ground in spring.

Scarlet clematis (*Clematis texensis*).

Silver lace vine

BLOOM PERIOD: June through September
HEIGHT AND SPREAD: 20 ft. × 15 ft.
GROWS WELL IN: Moderate heat; cold hardy
to -25°F

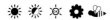

Silver lace vine is the most xeric large vine for shading pergolas in cold desert gardens. Dry soil limits the spread of rhizomes, and it rarely self-sows, so it is less likely to escape cultivation than in more temperate areas. Its small oval leaves are light green and cover the thin stems profusely. Lightly scented panicles of small white flowers cover the plant in a cool froth and provide nectar for butterflies all summer. Plant it where monsoon rains can flood it, or water deeply twice a month in summer to keep it blooming.

Creeping fig

HEIGHT AND SPREAD: 10 to 15 ft. × 10 to 15 ft.
GROWS WELL IN: Extreme heat in shade; cold
hardy to 20°F

Its small evergreen leaves, fine stems that cling to walls, and preference for shade in arid climates make creeping fig a great choice for shaded entry alcoves and the perennially dark north sides of tall buildings, especially when there is limited surface area for rooting. It can also be used as a ground cover in fully shaded spaces. Once well-established, creeping fig is fast growing but easy to manage and can be watered well twice monthly to maintain dense coverage.

Silver lace vine (*Fallopia baldschuanica*).

Creeping fig (*Ficus pumila* 'Minima').

Lilac vine

BLOOM PERIOD: November through May in frost-free areas

HEIGHT AND SPREAD: 15 ft. × 10 ft.

GROWS WELL IN: Well-drained soil in extreme heat; foliage damage at 25°F, root hardy to 20°F

This vigorous Australian twining plant can be grown on a fence or trellis, or allowed to sprawl without support as a shrubby ground cover. Fast growing with dark evergreen leaves, it is valued for the winter color of its purple flower clusters. Once established, lilac vine requires monthly soaking, producing surprisingly little litter for a plant that blooms so profusely. 'Happy Wanderer' is a robust cultivar with larger flowers.

Hop vine

BLOOM PERIOD: May to September

HEIGHT AND SPREAD: 15 to 20 ft. × 10 to 15 ft.

GROWS WELL IN: Moderate heat; cold hardy to -40°F

The lush-lobed leaves of this vigorous climber are bright green, deeply veined, and hairy, rough to the touch. The flowers are inconspicuous, but the papery brown clusters of hop heads that droop from the stems of female plants are ornamental and a key ingredient in brewing beer. European varieties are favored for beer crafting because the flavor is more consistent, but the adaptability of native hops is important when growing it as an ornamental in our extreme climate. Deep watering twice a month in summer keeps it robust. Cool night temperatures in fall blush the leaves purple before they drop.

Hop vine (*Humulus lupulus* var. *neomexicanus*). LEFT Lilac vine (*Hardenbergia violacea*).

Coral honeysuckle

BLOOM PERIOD: April to September

HEIGHT AND SPREAD: 8 to 15 ft. × 4 to 6 ft.

GROWS WELL IN: Extreme heat with shade; cold hardy to -30°F when dormant

Coral honeysuckle has a very large native range, mostly east and north of the arid Southwest, but its large clusters of orange flowers and the hummingbirds they attract have made it a garden favorite. Several cultivars seem especially well-adapted, with crisp, oval to oblong leaves less likely to mildew when grown in the shade here. 'Blanche Sandman' is a rosy coral color, 'Magnifica' is clear tangerine-orange, 'Major Wheeler' is deep red-orange, and hybrid *Lonicera ×brownii* 'Dropmore Scarlet' is the only fragrant one. They tend to be nearly evergreen, leafless only during freezing winter months.

Coral honeysuckle (*Lonicera sempervirens*). RIGHT Catclaw vine (*Macfadyena unguis-cati*).

Catclaw vine

BLOOM PERIOD: March to May

HEIGHT AND SPREAD: 25 ft. × 25 ft.

GROWS WELL IN: Extreme heat; cold hardy to 15°F

One of the best options for shading south- and west-facing walls in hot desert gardens, this fast-growing vine will adhere to any surface, quickly covering it with dark evergreen foliage. Clusters of large yellow flower trumpets are profuse in spring, followed by foot-long, slender seedpods. Established plants have a network of tuberous roots that help this subtropical native endure drought. In wet east Texas it is considered invasive, but is less likely to naturalize in arid places.

Yellow morning glory, yuca vine

BLOOM PERIOD: June to October

HEIGHT AND SPREAD: 10 ft. × 10 ft.

GROWS WELL IN: Extreme heat; foliage burns at 32°F, stems are cold hardy to 25°F, roots to 15°F

☀ ☼

This Baja native is stunning for seasonal color in spaces too extreme for less heat-loving vines. Its large yellow flower trumpets open along the twining stems, strung out like spotlights amid star-like, segmented, dark green leaves. Connoisseurs of seedpods will like the papery brown capsules that contain the large seeds. In frost-free spots it will remain evergreen, but consistent cold to 25°F will kill the stems to the ground, allowing winter sun to warm spaces shaded in summer. It will regrow quickly from the starchy roots in spring without compromising a strong color show, since it is a summer-flowering plant.

Woodbine

HEIGHT AND SPREAD: 10 to 25 ft. × 10 to 25 ft.

GROWS WELL IN: Extreme heat with shade; cold hardy to 0°F

☀ ☁ ☼ ⦿

Woodbine is a vigorous Western relative of moisture-loving Virginia creeper, with lush, dark green palmate leaves that turn brilliant red before they fall in autumn. 'Hacienda Creeper' is a slower-growing, more compact form, smaller in leaf as well as in overall size. In the hottest desert areas, it is best grown in the shade in rainwater basins with supplemental watering, but in high desert it does just as well in full sun with deep watering once or twice monthly.

Yellow morning glory (*Merremia aurea*).

Woodbine (*Parthenocissus vitacea*).

Blue passion flower

BLOOM PERIOD: June to September

HEIGHT AND SPREAD: 10 to 20 ft. × 5 to 10 ft.

GROWS WELL IN: Extreme heat; root hardy to 5°F

☀ ☀ ☀ ✿ 🐝▸

Fragrant passion flowers are nothing short of fantastic. Ivory petals enclose a ring of dark blue, fringed by a crown of pale blue filaments that resemble a sea creature more than a flower. Butterflies intent on sipping nectar add to the display. Native to Brazil and Argentina, in mild winter areas the slender stems and leaves are evergreen. Where winters are persistently freezing, plants rapidly regrow from root-sprouts in spring, flowering on new growth. It climbs by tendrils and its deep green leaves are glossy and variable, averaging five lobes. *Passiflora incarnata*, a smaller plant with equally bizarre flowers that produce edible fruit called maypops, is root hardy to -15°F.

Blue passion flower (*Passiflora caerulea*). RIGHT Silk vine (*Periploca graeca*).

Silk vine

BLOOM PERIOD: May and June

HEIGHT AND SPREAD: 15 to 20 ft. × 15 to 20 ft.

GROWS WELL IN: Moderate heat; cold hardy to -15°F

☀ ☀ ☀ 🐝▸

Silk vine has glossy, dark green, lance-shaped leaves creating a deep shade canopy when used to cover an arbor. Velvety, dark maroon, star-shaped flowers hang in inconspicuous clusters against the dark foliage, a nice surprise at close range. The leaves drop after hard freezes, revealing the elegant, smooth, twining stems. Short, thick seedpods are rarely produced but are similar to those of milkweed, a related butterfly host, and contain papery seeds attached to silken parachutes to help dispersal.

Banksia rose

BLOOM PERIOD: March to April

HEIGHT AND SPREAD: 20 ft. × 15 ft.

GROWS WELL IN: Extreme heat; cold hardy to 0°F, old wood and roots hardy to -10°F when dormant

Banksia rose, unusual in being fast-growing, evergreen, and long-lived, was brought to the Southwest more than a century ago and at least one of those plants is still thriving, a tourist attraction in Tombstone, Arizona. Its long, arching, nearly thorn-free stems easily cover a large trellis or arbor, and since it flowers on old wood, the most impressive display of blossoms in spring is from plants that are thinned occasionally rather than pruned back like a conventional rose. Sprays of small, pale yellow or white flowers have a light violet scent and last only a few weeks.

Banksia rose (*Rosa banksiae*).

Canyon grape

BLOOM PERIOD: May to June

HEIGHT AND SPREAD: 10 to 15 ft. × 5 to 10 ft.

GROWS WELL IN: Extreme heat when shaded; cold hardy to -15°F

☀ ⛅ ☼ 📍

Compared with grape vines grown for food and drink, canyon grape is smaller in plant size and in the size of its lightly lobed, deciduous leaves. The flowers are inconspicuous but the clusters of small fruits are enjoyed by songbirds. It is a good choice for summer shade in the intermediate and high desert, and its three-lobed leaves add texture to a wall surface. Arizona grape ivy (*Cissus trifoliata*) is a better option for green walls and ground cover for hot desert gardens. Evergreen to 30°F, roots survive cold to 20°F.

Wisteria

BLOOM PERIOD: May to June

HEIGHT AND SPREAD: 15 to 25 ft. × 15 to 25 ft.

GROWS WELL IN: Moderate heat; cold hardy to -30°F

☀ ☼ ⚙ 🐝

Not as well-known as the Asian species, American wisteria is more compact and blooms while younger, a better choice for smaller gardens. Its tolerance of alkaline soil and the fact that it blooms slightly later in spring (often repeating through summer) reduces the problems of chlorosis and frost-killed flower buds that are common with *Wisteria sinensis* and *W. floribunda*. Wisteria needs deep watering twice a month through the growing season. 'Aunt Dee' and 'Blue Moon' are two widely available cultivars.

Canyon grape (*Vitis arizonica*). RIGHT Wisteria (*Wisteria macrostachya*).

Acacia berlandieri
syn. *Senegalia berlandieri*

Guajillo

BLOOM PERIOD: March intermittently to November

HEIGHT AND SPREAD: 8 to 12 ft. × 10 to 15 ft.

GROWS WELL IN: Rocky soils in extreme heat; tolerates cold to 20°F, probably briefly to 15°F

Native from south central Texas down into Mexico, guajillo is multi-stemmed and sparsely armed with small spines, lush with delicate-looking, light green leaflets, and fragrant, creamy white puffball flowers. It thrives in areas receiving 6 to 20 inches of rainfall and seems to produce most of its growth after summer heat abates in fall and early winter. Prune sparingly to remove any frost damage and to enhance its sculptural form in late spring. Evergreen when winter is mild, guajillo works well in patios and around pools, and is just opaque enough to provide light screening without blocking cooling summer breezes. Recently renamed *Senegalia berlandieri*, but the transition to a new name will take some time.

Guajillo (*Acacia berlandieri*, syn. *Senegalia berlandieri*).

Leather leaf acacia

BLOOM PERIOD: Intermittently April through September

HEIGHT AND SPREAD: 15 ft. × 15 ft.

GROWS WELL IN: Rocky alkaline soils in extreme heat; tolerates cold to mid-teens °F

Resilient leather leaf acacia is native to western Australia and is well adapted to our hottest desert areas. Evergreen, with a slow to moderate growth rate when watered every few weeks in summer, it can be maintained with deep watering every month or two once established. Small yellow flowers with frilly stamens are paired at the branch tips and produce heavily veined, bronze seedpods that make attractive mulch when they drop. Leather leaf acacia suffers no pest problems and is attractive with little maintenance, an effective screen or backdrop for plants with more dramatic forms or colorful flowers.

Catclaw acacia

BLOOM PERIOD: May through August

HEIGHT AND SPREAD: 10 to 15 ft. × 15 ft.

GROWS WELL IN: Extreme heat; survives -10°F briefly

Unlike the acacias described as trees, catclaw has low, sprawling, thorny branches that make pruning to tree form painful. Use it as a barrier, planting where its frilly, pale yellow, wonderfully fragrant flowers hum with bees. Conspicuous, flat, cocoa-brown seedpods are decorative and add habitat value, as does its thicket of prickly branches that are refuge for nesting songbirds. Occasional soaking in summer spurs flowering and maintains a dense cover of tiny compound leaves. A recent name change to *Senegalia greggii* means there will be a transitional period when both names may be found and used.

Leather leaf acacia (*Acacia craspedocarpa*).

Catclaw acacia (*Acacia greggii*, syn. *Senegalia greggii*).

Aloysia wrightii

Oreganillo

BLOOM PERIOD: May through September

HEIGHT AND SPREAD: 5 ft. × 4 ft.

GROWS WELL IN: Extreme heat, cold hardy to -10°F

The small, pale green, crinkled leaves of oreganillo are a subtle complement to the sprays of tiny white flowers it produces on its wiry white stems. The whole plant is wonderfully aromatic and abuzz with bees while blooming. Its compact size and soft color and texture make it an excellent foil for more brilliantly colored and boldly spiky evergreen plants, providing the counterpoint that keeps our prickly plant palette from feeling overtly hostile.

Amorpha canescens

Leadplant

BLOOM PERIOD: May to August

HEIGHT AND SPREAD: 2 to 3 ft. × 3 to 4 ft.

GROWS WELL IN: Moderate heat; root hardy to -30°F, probably colder

Leadplant is an important nitrogen-fixing component of prairie and oak savannah grasslands. Tough and resilient, it behaves like a large, herbaceous perennial, browsed by wildlife and resprouting after wildfire. In gardens, it is refined and quite elegant, with its compound silver leaflets and racemes of blue-purple flowers on slender, upright stems, filling in among wildflowers, culinary herbs, xeric shrubs and succulents.

Oreganillo (*Aloysia wrightii*).

Leadplant (*Amorpha canescens*).

Amorpha fruticosa

False indigo

BLOOM PERIOD: May to June

HEIGHT AND SPREAD: 4 to 12 ft. × 4 to 10 ft.

GROWS WELL IN: Moderate heat; cold hardy to -30°F

☀ ☁ 💧 📍 🐝

False indigo has elegant, slender branches that together form a mounded canopy of compound, dark green, deciduous leaves. Its spikes of navy blue flowers with orange-gold stamens are striking close up, but go unnoticed at a distance. Small seedpods are inconspicuous compared with other legumes such as mesquite and acacia, but wildlife readily finds and consumes them. False indigo stabilizes soil along perennial streams, reclaims abandoned farm fields where the groundwater is shallow, enriches heavy clay soils in rainwater catchments in mid-elevation gardens, and is an excellent thornless substitute for mesquite in areas too cold for such heat-requiring plants.

False indigo (*Amorpha fruticosa*).

Anisacanthus quadrifidus var. wrightii

Flame anisacanthus

BLOOM PERIOD: June to September

HEIGHT AND SPREAD: 3 to 5 ft. × 3 to 4 ft.

GROWS WELL IN: Reflected heat; cold hardy to -5°F

☀ ☀ ☀ 📍 🐝

The slender stems of flame anisacanthus are strongly vertical, pale gray, and only partly obscured by its small, dark green leaves. Ablaze with orange tubular flowers during the hottest time of the year, it is a magnet for hummingbirds all summer. Slow to leaf out in spring, it is rarely bothered by the late winter deep freezes that undermine plants already actively growing when the temperature plummets. Flame anisacanthus provides lots of summer color on a small water budget.

Flame anisacanthus (*Anisacanthus quadrifidus* var. *wrightii*).

'Chieftain' manzanita

BLOOM PERIOD: April

HEIGHT AND SPREAD: 2 to 3 ft. × 3 to 6 ft.

GROWS WELL IN: Well-drained soil in moderate heat; cold hardy to -20°F in well-drained soil

'Chieftain' is a robust selection of *Arctostaphylos* ×*coloradensis*, a compact evergreen plant with contrasting, smooth, cinnamon-colored bark, small, urn-shaped, white flowers and pea-sized russet fruits. It requires a bit of patience while it slowly establishes itself. Resist the urge to speed growth by adding water and fertilizer, as that will have the opposite effect. The reward for benign neglect is a handsome companion to brilliant flowering plants—and it never has an off season.

Threadleaf sage, sand sage

BLOOM PERIOD: July to September

HEIGHT AND SPREAD: 3 to 4 ft. × 3 to 4 ft.

GROWS WELL IN: Heat; cold hardy to -20°F

Threadleaf sage looks windswept, as it anchors dune sand and dominates miles of mid-elevation desert. Evergreen except in times of extreme drought, it is filmy in texture with thready silver-blue leaves and tiny sprays of silver flowers. It adds a sense of motion in gardens like ornamental grasses do, and its moderate size makes it a versatile background for colorful flowering plants. Pruning the oldest stems down to the ground in spring keeps plants young and vigorous.

'Chieftain' manzanita (*Arctostaphylos* × *coloradensis* 'Chieftain').

Threadleaf sage (*Artemisia filifolia*).

Artemisia frigida

Fringed sage

BLOOM PERIOD: May to August

HEIGHT AND SPREAD: 1 ft. × 2 ft.

GROWS WELL IN: Heat; cold hardy to -30°F

Since the woody part of this subshrub is within a few inches of the ground, gardeners treat it as an herbaceous perennial, trimming off the fringe of tiny yellow and silver flower stems to encourage a flush of soft new growth. The fine leaves and stems are covered with minute silver hairs that protect the plant from intense sunlight and drying wind. An excellent soft filler between wildflowers in beds and borders, it is a subtle color and textural contrast with grasses in prairie ground covers.

Fringed sage (*Artemisia frigida*).

Artemisia tridentata

Big leaf sage

BLOOM PERIOD: July to September

HEIGHT AND SPREAD: 3 to 6 ft. × 3 to 5 ft.

GROWS WELL IN: Moderate heat; extreme cold to -30°F

A dryland evergreen shrub with tiny flowers in a fine fringe above the silky, silver, aromatic foliage and gnarled, charcoal gray stems, this sage has big leaves only when compared to other Western artemisias with even finer foliage. Sage offsets colorful flowering plants, adding texture and depth to the garden. Big leaf sage is best above 7000 ft. in deep, arable soil. Bigelow's sage (*Artemisia bigelovii*) grows 1 to 2 ft. tall and wide and is the most heat loving of the large-leaved artemisias, best at lower elevations in rocky or sandy soils.

Big leaf sage (*Artemisia tridentata*).

Desert milkweed

BLOOM PERIOD: May to September

HEIGHT AND SPREAD: 4 ft. × 3 ft.

GROWS WELL IN: Extreme reflected heat; hardy for short episodes of cold to 20°F

☀ ☼ ◉ 🐝▸

Slender, silver-green stems stand stiffly upright in clumps tipped with clusters of pale yellow flowers and pairs of elongated, pendant seedpods. Pods split open to release the papery seeds, attached to parachutes of silken hairs. This is the most heat and drought adapted of the milkweeds; beautiful for its elegant, spare lines. All milkweeds are essential larval food and nectar plants for many butterfly species, including monarchs. Their milky sap contains cardiac glycosides which are toxic to butterfly predators but harmless to the butterflies and their larva.

Desert milkweed (*Ascelpias subulata*).

Fourwing saltbush

BLOOM PERIOD: May to July

HEIGHT AND SPREAD: 3 to 5 ft. × 4 to 8 ft.

GROWS WELL IN: Saline, alkaline soils in extreme heat; cold hardy to -30°F

☀ ☼ ◉ 🐝▸

Fourwing saltbush is not a garden plant, though its mounded shape, clusters of papery tan seedpods, and small, pale, evergreen leaves are quite attractive. It is an excellent habitat and reclamation plant, as it will thrive on sites too harsh for most other desert plants. Because wildlife devours the seeds, priming them to germinate, and since the plant grows easily with no encouragement, it quickly becomes a weed in cultivated settings. The pollen is also a potent aero-allergen, so use the seed-producing females at the edges of large habitat gardens, and quail will thank you.

Fourwing saltbush (*Atriplex canescens*).

Mat saltbush

BLOOM PERIOD: April to June

HEIGHT AND SPREAD: 1 to 2 ft. × 2 to 3 ft.

GROWS WELL IN: Extreme heat; cold hardy to -25°F

☀ ☼ 📍

Mat saltbush is a compact, mounded plant with thumbnail-sized, silver evergreen leaves that turn pale opalescent shades of pink and blue after hard freezes. Native in mid-elevation deserts receiving 4 to 8 in. annual rainfall and adapts to many soils, including saline clay. It is best used with other drought lovers, such as agave and yucca, and is a soft color contrast for dark green creosote bush and turpentine bush. Shadscale (*Atriplex confertifolia*) and Gardner's saltbush (*A. gardneri*) are similar species with great potential as ground covers on harsh sites with low water budgets.

Mat saltbush (*Atriplex corrugata*).

Dwarf butterfly bush

BLOOM PERIOD: May to October

HEIGHT AND SPREAD: 5 to 7 ft. × 4 to 6 ft.

GROWS WELL IN: Moderate heat; cold hardy to -25°F

☀ ☼ ☼ ⚙ 🐝

The slender silver foliage and thin arching stems give this buddleja a feeling of airiness. Lightly fragrant, 6-in.-long, tapered spikes of small blue or purple flowers keep coming for months, making it worth its weight in gold to the steady stream of both hummingbirds and butterflies that find it a reliable source of nectar. Breeders have been successful in producing even more compact plants in a wider range of colors. Peter Podaras's 'Flutterby' Series includes a yellow-orange hybrid called 'Peach Cobbler'.

Dwarf butterfly bush (*Buddleja davidii* var. *nanhoensis*).

Woolly butterfly bush

BLOOM PERIOD: March or April through August
HEIGHT AND SPREAD: 3 to 5 ft. × 3 to 5 ft.
GROWS WELL IN: Extreme heat; cold hardy to 0°F
briefly and infrequently

☀ ☼ ◉ 🐝

This native buddleja has many garden-worthy traits. Its oval, blue-green leaves are densely covered in white hairs nicely contrasted by its quarter-sized globes of bright orange flowers. The woolly leaves, warm-toned blossoms, and the compact form of the plant all give the impression of softness in a landscape where prickly and spiky are more typical. Leaves are evergreen in all but the coldest areas. Once it is well-rooted, a plant will survive unirrigated, but will flower all summer with deep monthly soaks when rain fails to provide the needed encouragement.

Yellow bird of paradise

BLOOM PERIOD: May through September
HEIGHT AND SPREAD: 4 to 6 ft. × 5 to 8 ft.
GROWS WELL IN: Extreme heat; root hardy to -20°F, stems hardy to 0°F, possibly colder when dry

☀ ☼ 🐝

This Argentine émigré has been at home in the Southwest for at least a century. The tiny leaflets of its compound foliage scarcely hide its metallic, light green stems—hardly a plant to draw much attention. Soon clusters of yellow, pea-shaped flowers feathered with exotic red stamens appear in profusion, much to the delight of nectar-sipping humming-birds. This is when bird of paradise earns its spot in the garden. Sandpapery seedpods follow the flower display, and as they dry, they open with an audible "pop," to the surprise of anyone close enough to be pelted with the shiny brown seeds. Recently the name was changed to *Erythrostemon gilliesii*, but the new label will take time to find its way into nurseries and common usage.

Woolly butterfly bush (*Buddleja marrubiifolia*). RIGHT Yellow bird of paradise (*Caesalpinia gilliesii*, syn. *Erythrostemon gilliesii*).

Red bird of paradise

BLOOM PERIOD: June to October

HEIGHT AND SPREAD: 4 to 6 ft. × 4 to 6 ft.

GROWS WELL IN: Extreme reflected heat; sustains tip damage at 30°F, roots are hardy to 20°F

The fine foliage and rich color of red bird of paradise provide a brilliant show that lasts for months during the hottest time of year. It's well worth the extra water needed to sustain this Caribbean native. It dies back substantially when winter temperatures drop much below freezing, but grows quickly, and since flowers are produced on new growth, the frost and cleanup pruning afterward keeps plants young and colorful. Use it paired with palo verde or mesquite to give a courtyard the lush feel of an oasis, or in rainwater catchment basins where it will benefit from the extra moisture.

Red bird of paradise (*Caesalpinia pulcherrima*).

Baja fairy duster

BLOOM PERIOD: April to September, lightly almost year-round where frosts are rare

HEIGHT AND SPREAD: 4 ft. × 4 ft.

GROWS WELL IN: Extreme, reflected heat; at 25°F branch tips freeze, stems die back near 18°F

The ample but tiny compound leaflets lend an airy lushness to this shrub, but its bright red, frilly blossoms and bundles of brilliantly colored stamens are the reason this Baja California native finds its way into gardens north of the border. The gamble is in the sudden cold snaps inland desert gardens experience. If plants are watered deeply every few weeks year-round, they respond by blooming all year as well, but when tender growth freezes back, plants require more restorative pruning and flowering is halted for months at a time. Better to stop watering in early autumn and wait until the spring to spur new growth.

Baja fairy duster (*Calliandra californica*).

Fairy duster

BLOOM PERIOD: February to May, and flushes in response to summer rains

HEIGHT AND SPREAD: 2 to 3 ft. × 3 to 4 ft.

GROWS WELL IN: Extreme, reflected heat; cold hardy to 10°F, possibly lower

A paradox of desert shrubs is how innocuous, even dainty, some of them appear—when in fact they are some of the most tenacious plants on the planet. The small leaf and plant size make fairy duster easy to miss until it is clouded in a haze of pink powder-puff flowers in spring. Since it is so inconspicuous and so heat and drought hardy, it is best to plant fairy duster in masses, where on a small water budget it lends a soft glow among contrasting boulders and spiky succulents.

Fairy duster (*Calliandra eriophylla*).

Hairy mountain mahogany

BLOOM PERIOD: Inconspicuous flowers in May; feathery silver seed plumes in October

HEIGHT AND SPREAD: 6 to 15 ft. × 4 to 12 ft.

GROWS WELL IN: Rocky soils with heat intermittently above 100°F; cold hardy to at least -20°F

Hairy mountain mahogany is drought adapted by default, as it grows on steep, exposed slopes where rain often runs off before soaking into the soil. Its small, dark evergreen leaves are covered with fine hairs that shade it from intense sunlight. Branches are upright, eventually fanning out to form a strong vase shape as the plant matures. It is a reliable evergreen for screening and a companion for buddlejas, salvias, and eriogonums, as well as hesperaloes, agaves, and other colorful or striking specimen plants. *Cercocarpus montanus* is a deciduous species suited to higher elevations, a good companion to pines and oaks that rarely grow more than 5 ft. tall and 4 ft. wide.

Hairy mountain mahogany (*Cercocarpus breviflorus*).

Littleleaf mountain mahogany

BLOOM PERIOD: Inconspicuous flowers in May and June; feathery silver seed plumes in October

HEIGHT AND SPREAD: 6 to 8 ft. × 4 to 6 ft.

GROWS WELL IN: Heat intermittently above 100°F; cold hardy to at least -25°F

Young plants resemble upright forms of rosemary, with small, dark evergreen leaves, except the aroma of this native rose is a sweet, spicy one when leaves are bruised. Littleleaf mountain mahogany is slow-growing initially and compact at maturity, so it fits well in smaller spaces where a long-lived subdued evergreen is needed. It has a naturally vertical shape, rarely if ever needs pruning, and is the most heat and drought tolerant of all the mountain mahoganies.

Littleleaf mountain mahogany (*Cercocarpus ledifolius* var. *intricatus*).

Curl-leaf mountain mahogany

BLOOM PERIOD: Inconspicuous flowers in May; feathery silver seed plumes in October
HEIGHT AND SPREAD: 8 to 25 ft. × 6 to 15 ft.
GROWS WELL IN: Heat; cold hardy to -30°F

Curl-leaf mountain mahogany is a reliable evergreen that thrives in exposed, sunbaked places where most conifers struggle to survive. It has the same long-lived, stoic character as the other mountain mahoganies, a handsome plant requiring little pruning and only monthly deep watering once it is well rooted. Too much water too often seems to inhibit growth. With benign neglect, curl-leaf mountain mahogany eventually grows quite large, and given the region-wide pine die-off from bark beetles, it makes a suitable substitute for pinyon where conditions have become too dry for the pines.

Fernbush

BLOOM PERIOD: May through September
HEIGHT AND SPREAD: 4 to 8 ft. × 4 to 10 ft.
GROWS WELL IN: Heat intermittently above 100°F; cold hardy to at least -30°F

There are many native roses that look and act nothing like garden roses, yet are wonderful additions to arid gardens. Fernbush is so called for its soft, sage-green, finely divided leaves that resemble tufts of small fern fronds. When established plants are watered deeply once or twice a month during the growing season, they produce conical spikes of small white blossoms throughout the summer. Seed heads are rusty brown and contrast with the leaf color nicely. Mostly deciduous by late autumn, the few remaining frost-gray leaves and russet stems have winter presence, and fernbush is one of the first shrubs to announce the arrival of spring.

Fernbush (*Chamaebatiaria millefolium*). LEFT Curl-leaf mountain mahogany (*Cercocarpus ledifolius*).

Damianita

BLOOM PERIOD: March to June, September to November

HEIGHT AND SPREAD: 1 to 2 ft. × 1 to 2 ft.

GROWS WELL IN: Well-drained soil in extreme, reflected heat; cold hardy to 0°F in dry soil

Damianita grows a perfect mound of soft, fine, dark evergreen leaves densely covering woody stems, which are smothered in impossible-to-ignore chromium yellow daisies for months at a time. Its compact size makes damianita perfect for courtyard gardens and clustering near pathways, where the scent of its foliage can be appreciated. Butterflies and bees work the nectar-rich flowers that are only suppressed by truly extreme heat and cold. Excess watering while plants are resting is the best way to kill them; monthly water while in bloom is all that is needed.

Littleleaf cordia

BLOOM PERIOD: February to November

HEIGHT AND SPREAD: 4 to 6 ft. × 5 to 7 ft.

GROWS WELL IN: Extreme heat; cold hardy to 18°F

Evergreen shrubs of these proportions are useful for informal borders, screening, and creating enclosed spaces inexpensively. The bonus of littleleaf cordia is the explosion of trumpet-shaped, clustered white blossoms it produces in response to soaking rains or pulses of irrigation that mimic rainfall. Deep gray-green leaves an inch long and half as wide make the pure white of the flowers more pronounced. Keeping plants dry when there is the probability of deep freezes can reduce the need for spring cleanup and allows plants to grow larger.

Damianita (*Chrysactinia mexicana*). RIGHT Littleleaf cordia (*Cordia parvifolia*).

Dalea capitata

Golden or lemon dalea

BLOOM PERIOD: April to May, September to October

HEIGHT AND SPREAD: 1 ft. × 3 to 4 ft.

GROWS WELL IN: Extreme reflected heat; tolerates cold to 0°F when dormant

A soft mounding ground cover with tiny green leaves on thread-thin stems, this is a fine plant to cover hot spots between showier wildflowers, specimen succulents, and flowering shrubs. Its pale lemon-yellow flowers are unusual for the genus, a characteristic shared with woolly dalea (*Dalea lanata*), a smaller, silver-leaved species that occurs at the northern edge of the Chihuahuan Desert and is even more cold tolerant, but rarely offered in nurseries. Although considered subshrubs because they have a woody crown and deep, long-lived root system, these daleas are best treated as herbaceous perennials and pruned back hard in the spring.

Dalea frutescens

Black dalea

BLOOM PERIOD: September

HEIGHT AND SPREAD: 3 to 4 ft. × 3 to 5 ft.

GROWS WELL IN: Extreme reflected heat; cold hardy briefly to -15°F

This is a shrub to celebrate the end of blistering summer heat, with its abundant show of brilliant wine-colored flowers. It has small, dark green leaves that hide the stems until hard freezes, when the leaves drop, exposing what looks to me like a mound of crumpled, charcoal-gray wire. Inelegant as this may sound, the effect is actually quite striking when paired with blue or silver evergreens such as blue ephedra, Havard agave, or blue forms of Rocky Mountain juniper. Watered deeply once or twice a month, less in winter, it needs little pruning. *Dalea pulchra* is a similar species, more evergreen and spring blooming, but only cold hardy to 15°F.

Golden or lemon dalea (*Dalea capitata*).

Black dalea (*Dalea frutescens*).

Dalea greggii

Trailing dalea

BLOOM PERIOD: March to June

HEIGHT AND SPREAD: 1 to ft. × 3 to 5 ft.

GROWS WELL IN: Well-drained soil in extreme reflected heat; tolerates cold briefly to near 0°F when dormant

☀ ☀ ☀ ♀ 🐝▸

The tiny, silver-gray leaves on thread-like stems create an undulating carpet across sunbaked soil. Clusters of small, rose-pink flowers add a soft blush to the ground cover for a few months in spring. Given thorough soakings once or twice a month during warm weather and every six weeks to two months in late fall and winter, it fills in quickly, creating a soft counterpoint when planted among boulders, between large yucca, agave, or beargrass, or at the edge of the canopy of mesquite or palo verde.

Trailing dalea (*Dalea greggii*).

Encelia farinosa

Brittlebush

BLOOM PERIOD: March to May and after soaking summer rain

HEIGHT AND SPREAD: 2 to 3 ft. × 3 to 4 ft.

GROWS WELL IN: Rocky, well-drained soil in extreme reflected heat; cold to 25°F burns leaves, dies out below 20°F

☀ ☀ ♀ 🐝▸

Light intensity and dryness determine whether its hairy foliage appears silver-white or green; the sunnier and drier, the whiter the leaves. Plants defoliate under extremely dry and cold conditions. Once the plant is established, a deep soak every few months is enough to cause a flush of blooms, a shining yellow halo of daisies. Under prime conditions, soaking rain or irrigation several times a year, brittlebush has a decade-long lifespan and self-sows readily, so there are always young plants ready to replace those in decline.

Brittlebush (*Encelia farinosa*).

Bluestem joint fir, *ma huang*

BLOOM PERIOD: **April to June**

HEIGHT AND SPREAD: **4 to 5 ft. × 6 to 10 ft.**

GROWS WELL IN: **Heat; cold hardy to -20°F**

Bluestem joint fir is noteworthy for its year-round decorative features in climates where extremes of heat and cold and aridity limit evergreens to a miserly number. It is also known for its medicinal value in Asian pharmacopeias, where it is known as *ma huang*. Springtime brings a show of frilly yellow flowers, followed by berry-like red fruits. The slender, steel-blue stems form great mounds that will pile up against a wall or sprawl across the ground. Extreme cold will cause the stems to turn pewter gray, then back to blue when temperatures moderate. Deep soaking monthly during the growing season maintains vigorous growth once well rooted.

Green ephedra

BLOOM PERIOD: **April to June**

HEIGHT AND SPREAD: **4 to 6 ft. × 5 to 9 ft.**

GROWS WELL IN: **Extreme heat; cold hardy to -20°F**

Though it rarely dominates, green ephedra is always vibrant green and its slender vertical stems add texture and depth to any garden composition. Its frilly yellow flowers look like lace draped across the plant and the papery brown seed cones are interesting when viewed up close. Large enough to use as evergreen screening in very dry spaces, it is a great companion for larger bunchgrasses like deer muhly and big bluestem. Fast growing in response to deep watering a few times a month while young; established plants need water monthly or less to remain in top form.

Bluestem joint fir (*Ephedra equisetina*).

Green ephedra (*Ephedra viridis*).

Eremophila glabra ssp. carnosa

Emu bush

BLOOM PERIOD: Intermittently February to November

HEIGHT AND SPREAD: 3 to 4 ft. × 4 to 5 ft.

GROWS WELL IN: Reflected extreme heat; cold hardy to 20°F

A gift from western Australia, this compact evergreen's common name means desert loving. It has a long bloom season, nearly year-round with occasional deep watering and cutting back to encourage new growth. Ideal for small spaces that would roast lesser xerics, 'Winter Blaze' is a cultivar with tubular, coral-red flowers for cool season color. Hummingbirds will appreciate having this plant on the menu. Keep winter watering to a minimum and in the event of heavy frost don't assume you've lost it. It may resprout from old wood and look better than ever.

Eremophila hygrophana

Blue bells

BLOOM PERIOD: Intermittently January through December

HEIGHT AND SPREAD: 2 to 3 ft. × 3 ft.

GROWS WELL IN: Extreme reflected heat; tip damage at 17°F, dieback at 15°F

Another of the desert-loving Aussie émigrés that are great additions to low desert gardens, blue bells has small, silver evergreen leaves on silver stems that are blanketed in blue-purple tubular flowers in flushes throughout the year. It seems like the Australian counterpart to our native Texas ranger, but smaller and even less thirsty, it needs only occasional deep watering and a bit of touch-up pruning. Please don't shear this naturally well-shaped plant.

Blue bells (*Eremophila hygrophana*). LEFT Emu bush (*Eremophila glabra* ssp. *carnosa*).

Eremophila maculata 'Valentine'

Spotted emu bush

BLOOM PERIOD: January through March
HEIGHT AND SPREAD: 3 to 4 ft. × 4 to 5 ft.
GROWS WELL IN: Extreme reflected heat; established plants are cold hardy to 15°F

Yet another emu bush for low desert gardens, 'Valentine' is a widely grown cultivar, especially showy in winter. Its red buds open to tubular, deep rose-colored flowers heavily visited by hummingbirds. In response to cooler temperatures, the deep green leaves blush red. Since it blooms on younger growth it should be trimmed back after flowering to encourage new growth. This is not an invitation to make a naturally shapely plant into a gumball.

Spotted emu bush (*Eremophila maculata* 'Valentine').

Ericameria laricifolia

Turpentine bush

BLOOM PERIOD: August to November
HEIGHT AND SPREAD: 2 to 3 ft. × 3 to 4 ft.
GROWS WELL IN: Extreme reflected heat; cold hardy to -15°F briefly when dormant

This is an easy shrub to find a place for in the dry garden. It's compact in size, deep green year-round, grows in a dense, mounding shape without pruning, and is smothered in chromium yellow flowers come autumn—so what's not to love about turpentine bush, except maybe its name? There are two widely available selections: 'Aguirre' is the gold standard, a more cold-tolerant cultivar also vigorous in extreme heat and seasonally covered in dime-sized daisies; 'Desert Mountain', a cultivar of hot desert origin, has less attractive flowers and is mostly used for reclamation projects where its natural ranginess is less noticeable.

Turpentine bush (*Ericameria laricifolia*).

Flattop buckwheat

BLOOM PERIOD: March to November

HEIGHT AND SPREAD: 1 to 1½ ft. × 2 ft.

GROWS WELL IN: Extreme heat; northern seed sources may be cold hardy to 10°F

Buckwheat is an important nectar plant for butterflies; luckily for gardeners it is beautiful all year. Unlike many desert plants that seem to change little over the seasons, flattop buckwheat transforms from a clump of green and silver leaves into slender silver stems and tight clusters of tiny white or pink flowers, and then into rusty red seed heads as the months progress. Established plants are very long-lived unless watered excessively in heavy soil. Prune off the previous year's flower stems in early spring to start the cycle anew.

Flattop buckwheat (*Eriogonum fasciculatum*).

Wright's buckwheat

BLOOM PERIOD: June to November

HEIGHT AND SPREAD: 1 to 1½ ft. × 2 ft.

GROWS WELL IN: Extreme heat; cold hardy briefly to -10°F

Wright's buckwheat is quite similar to flattop buckwheat, with a few important distinctions. It is much more cold tolerant than flattop and the flowers are borne along the stems, so the impression is that of a cloud of blossoms rather than clusters of buttons. The butterflies show no concern for these differences, working whichever species is at hand. It self-sows easily, and the only maintenance needed is thinning volunteer seedlings and cutting back in the spring.

Wright's buckwheat (*Eriogonum wrightii*).

Apache plume

BLOOM PERIOD: March to May; August to October

HEIGHT AND SPREAD: 4 to 10 ft. × 5 to 12 ft.

GROWS WELL IN: Extreme heat with extra water; cold hardy to -20°F

☀ ☼ ◉ 🐝▸

Apache plume was one of the first southwestern shrubs grown for landscape use, thanks to its adaptability, its display of apple blossom–like white flowers, and the silky pink seed plumes that glow when backlit by the sun. Its small leaves are partly evergreen even in the coldest areas, and the hint of red dormant foliage is a nice contrast to the silver stems. It will thrive with a soaking monthly once established, but also tolerates weekly watering, responding by growing larger and flowering more—so, drought or deluge, it performs masterfully.

Desert lavender

BLOOM PERIOD: January to May

HEIGHT AND SPREAD: 6 to 10 ft. × 4 to 6 ft.

GROWS WELL IN: Extreme heat; 20°F cold causes significant leaf drop, roots are hardy to 15°F

☀ ☼ ◉ ✿ 🐝▸

Some plants are valued for their brassy color or bold form, but desert lavender is all about soft in a climate that is anything but mellow. Softly hairy silver leaves are a perfect complement to its pale purple flower spikes, icy cool when temperatures sizzle. After rain, the leaves exude a lavender scent in areas too hot for true lavenders to thrive. Cold is a limitation and there can be substantial stem dieback after a severe cold snap in the low desert, but established plants rebound rapidly in spring. 'Silver Lining' is a cold-hardy, higher-elevation selection.

Apache plume (*Fallugia paradoxa*). RIGHT Desert lavender (*Hyptis emoryi*).

Chuparosa

BLOOM PERIOD: **Intermittently all year but most abundant March to May**

HEIGHT AND SPREAD: **3 to 4 ft. × 4 to 6 ft.**

GROWS WELL IN: **Well-drained soil in extreme reflected heat; cold hardy to 25°F**

Attractive though they are, the small, fleshy, deep green leaves and slender silver-gray stems take a backseat to the brilliant red, tubular, 1-in. flowers that attract hummingbirds all year. Native in arroyos, chuparosa responds best to occasional pulses of water rather than frequent shallow irrigation. Withhold water in autumn to avoid encouraging soft, cold-tender growth.

Chuparosa (*Justicia californica*).

Mexican honeysuckle

BLOOM PERIOD: February to November

HEIGHT AND SPREAD: 2 to 3 ft. × 2 to 3 ft.

GROWS WELL IN: Extreme reflected heat; cold hardy to 20°F

Mexican honeysuckle has slender orange flowers favored by hummingbirds. This justicia may tolerate a bit more cold, but judicious watering is the best strategy. Where temperatures frequently drop to 20°F at night in winter, more protected microclimates in courtyards or close to buildings, boulders, or other warm niches helps to protect plants.

Mexican honeysuckle (*Justicia spicigera*).

Creosote bush

BLOOM PERIOD: March to November in response to water

HEIGHT AND SPREAD: 2 to 8 ft. × 2 to 6 ft.

GROWS WELL IN: Extreme reflected heat; clones vary but some selections are root hardy to -15°F

Because creosote bush covers so much ground in harsh open desert throughout the Southwest, it is sometimes passed up for garden use, but there are several reasons to reconsider. Its small, resinous, dark evergreen leaves are vibrant and prolific after rain or a deep watering (sparser when drought is persistent), and its open-layered growth habit is quite attractive. Yellow flowers are likely to appear anytime the temperature is above freezing and a bit of water is available. The fragrance of creosote bush is from the leaves rather than the flowers—fresh and clean like a rain-washed breeze, the signature scent of the desert.

Creosote bush (*Larrea tridentata*).

Lavandula angustifolia

Lavender

BLOOM PERIOD: June to August
HEIGHT AND SPREAD: 1 to 2 ft. × 2 to 2½ ft.
GROWS WELL IN: Lean, well-drained alkaline soils in moderate heat; most selections tolerate cold to -15°F when dry

Loved worldwide for its purple flower spikes and aromatic silver foliage, lavender has been cultivated for at least a millennium. There are hundreds of cultivars, each just slightly different in its shade of purple, scent, and cold tolerance. Lavender adapts to temperatures spiking above 100°F in summer and cold dropping to 0°F and lower in winter—what causes failure is the occasional 70°F day that suddenly plummets to -5°F overnight, especially when the soil is kept too wet.

Lavandula ×intermedia

Lavandin

BLOOM PERIOD: May to September
HEIGHT AND SPREAD: 2 to 3 ft. × 4 to 4 ft.
GROWS WELL IN: Well-drained soil in moderate heat; most cultivars tolerate cold to 0°F

'Grosso' and 'Provence' are two of the most widely available lavandins, hybrids of true lavender (*Lavandula angustifolia*) and spike lavender (*L. latifolia*). Originally these hybrids occurred naturally where the range of the two species overlapped, but their robust growth, vigor, and disease resistance have earned them a place in gardens. There are many new cultivars available with slightly different variations in size, leaf hue, and flower spike color (blues, purples, and whites). A higher concentration of camphor in their essential oil may account for their resilience.

Lavender (*Lavandula angustifolia*).

Lavandin (*Lavandula × intermedia*).

Leucophyllum candidum

Violet silverleaf

BLOOM PERIOD: Late May to October

HEIGHT AND SPREAD: 3 to 4 ft. × 3 to 4 ft.

GROWS WELL IN: Well-drained soil in extreme reflected heat; cold tolerant to 5°F

☀ ☀ ☼ ◉ 🐝▸

Violet silverleaf describes two of the characteristics that distinguish this easy-to-grow, compact shrub from other *Leucophyllum* species. The cultivar 'Thunder Cloud' has a particularly vivid contrast between the small silver leaves and deep purple blooms. Its dense evergreen leaf cover and stiff stems are attractive without pruning. Too much water in heavy soil and hungry rabbits finding new transplants account for most plant losses.

Leucophyllum frutescens

Texas ranger, rain sage

BLOOM PERIOD: Late May through October, especially after summer rain

HEIGHT AND SPREAD: 4 to 8 ft. × 4 to 8 ft.

GROWS WELL IN: Reflected heat; the species is cold hardy to 5°F and cultivars survive 0°F or colder when dormant

☀ ☀ ☼ ◉ 🐝▸

There is quite a range of leaf and flower color and mature size among the cultivars of this species. 'Compacta' is a tidy 4 ft. × 4 ft. plant with silver leaves and bright pink flowers sought after by hummingbirds. 'Green Cloud' has leaves that are green above and silver on the undersides, with deep rose-purple flowers. Both of these cultivars are among the most cold tolerant, but plants may defoliate in extreme cold, especially in wind-exposed locations.

Violet silverleaf (*Leucophyllum candidum*).

Texas ranger (*Leucophyllum frutescens*).

Leucophyllum langmaniae
'Lynn's Legacy'

'Lynn's Legacy' Texas sage

BLOOM PERIOD: May to November or until hard frost

HEIGHT AND SPREAD: 4 ft. × 4 ft.

GROWS WELL IN: Reflected heat; cold hardy to -5°F, root hardy to -10°F when dormant

This resilient desert shrub is deceptively cultivated looking, compact in growth habit, lush with leaves, and bursting into opulent bloom with very little watering. 'Lynn's Legacy' has soft, rounded, pale green leaves and tubular, light purple flowers that appear in flushes throughout the growing season. Clustered to define spaces, as a backdrop for bold-leaved succulents, or as a seductive nectar source for hummingbirds, it fills many garden roles. 'Lynn's Legacy' and similar 'Rio Bravo' are two of the cold hardiest of the *Leucophyllum* genus, having survived -5°F with little damage. When winters are milder, plants remain evergreen.

'Lynn's Legacy' Texas sage (*Leucophyllum langmaniae* 'Lynn's Legacy').

Fragrant rain sage

BLOOM PERIOD: June into November

HEIGHT AND SPREAD: 6 to 8 ft. × 6 to 8 ft.

GROWS WELL IN: Extreme reflected heat; cold hardy to 10°F

This *Leucophyllum* is the most fragrant of all the species, likened to grape bubblegum or soda with small, curled, silver-white leaves and dark purple flowers. It grows rapidly with occasional deep soaking while blooming, but like all its xeric cousins, too much water can cause an unhappy ending due to root rot. Since it blooms on new growth, prune out the oldest woody stems in spring to maintain the plant's natural shape and stimulate new flowering shoots. 'Sierra Bouquet' is an especially fragrant cultivar.

Blue ranger

BLOOM PERIOD: June into November

HEIGHT AND SPREAD: 3 to 4 ft. × 4 to 6 ft.

GROWS WELL IN: Extreme reflected heat; cold hardy to 10°F when dormant

One of the smaller species, with blue-purple flowers nicely contrasted by dense, cupped, gray-green leaves. 'Cimarron' is a selection that is particularly compact and blooms in cool waves through summer heat. While it grows best in lean, well-drained soil, it is reportedly more tolerant of heavy clay than most *Leucophyllum*. The flower and leaf colors blend well with just about any equally xeric companion, be it the deep magenta of canyon penstemon or giant four o'clock, the cheery yellow of desert zinnia or turpentine bush, or the screaming scarlet of Mexican red sage or red bird of paradise. Blue ranger is also an excellent nectar plant for hummingbirds.

Fragrant rain sage (*Leucophyllum pruinosum*).

Blue ranger (*Leucophyllum zygophyllum*).

Fremont's mahonia

BLOOM PERIOD: Late March to June

HEIGHT AND SPREAD: 4 ft. × 5 ft.

GROWS WELL IN: Entire region

The abundant, holly-like, evergreen leaves of Fremont's mahonia are pale blue, an inch long, and half as wide—an elegant backdrop for the honey-scented yellow flowers in spring and ¾-in., round red fruits that form in summer. Songbirds love the fruit and the cover of its prickly leaves. This Colorado Plateau native is the most compact of three similar mahonias in our region. Redberry mahonia (*Mahonia haematocarpa*), the most widespread of the trio, grows 6 ft. tall and wide with narrow, gray-green leaves and abundant, pea-sized red fruits. Algerita, (*M. trifoliata*), native across southern Texas, New Mexico, and Arizona, is similar in overall size, leaf form, and fruit, but its leaves are steel gray. All three make excellent security barriers and beautiful companions for deciduous shrubs and flowers.

Fremont's mahonia (*Mahonia fremontii*).

Creeping mahonia

BLOOM PERIOD: March to June

HEIGHT AND SPREAD: 1 ft. × 2 ft.

GROWS WELL IN: Gardens above 5000 ft. elevation

This mahonia's deep green, holly-like leaves turn shades of purple and red in winter, and are still the color of merlot when the fragrant yellow flowers appear in spring. Creeping mahonia prefers a cool, shady spot in the garden and although it spreads by rhizomes to create a dense ground cover, it's easy to contain by limiting the moisture available. Since aspen needs a cool, moist niche to thrive, creeping mahonia makes a perfect soil-shading companion in gardens above 7000 ft. Compact mahonia (*Mahonia aquifolium* 'Compacta') grows 2 ft. tall and twice as wide; it's more heat tolerant and so a better choice for intermediate desert gardens.

Creeping mahonia (*Mahonia repens*).

Malvaviscus drummondii

Turk's cap mallow

BLOOM PERIOD: March to September

HEIGHT AND SPREAD: 3 to 5 ft. × 2 to 5 ft.

GROWS WELL IN: Reflected heat with shade;
freezes back at 15°F, recovers quickly in spring

☀ ☼ 📍 🐝▸

Although you'll find Turk's cap growing in washes and on boulder-strewn hillsides, its soft green, tropical-looking leaves and brilliant red-orange blossoms are welcome in oasis courtyards where the enclosure helps to limit frost damage from occasional deep cold events. Deep watering twice a month in summer keeps it lush and blooming. Plant it in the dappled shade of palo verde or mesquite, or at the base of palms.

Parthenium incanum

Mariola

BLOOM PERIOD: July to September

HEIGHT AND SPREAD: 2 to 4 ft. × 2 to 3 ft.

GROWS WELL IN: Well-drained soil in extreme
reflected heat; cold hardy to -20°F

☀ ☼ 📍 ⚙ 🐝▸

From its small-lobed, silver-green leaves to its ivory-colored, clustered flower heads and compact mounded form, mariola bears all the hallmarks of a heat and drought lover, requiring only occasional deep soaking once established. Its muted coloration is a soft contrast for dark green creosote bush or turpentine bush, and a subtle echo of the larger fern-bush. It mediates clashes between spiky and prickly plants, keeping a cactus garden looking hospitable.

Turk's cap mallow (*Malvaviscus drummondii*).

Mariola (*Parthenium incanum*).

Poliomintha incana

Frosted mint, rosemary-mint

BLOOM PERIOD: April to May and September to October

HEIGHT AND SPREAD: 2 to 3 ft. × 3 to 4 ft.

GROWS WELL IN: Well-drained soil in extreme, reflected heat; cold hardy to -20°F

Comparing this small shrub to rosemary is apt, as it bears spikes of similar pale lavender flowers and a sweet herb scent appreciated by native people who have used it as savory flavoring for as long as anyone remembers. Like rosemary, it is also an attractive garden plant, but in color and growth habit, frosted mint is quite different. Its silver-white leaves are less rigid and its lax, sprawling stems arch and mound, rooting into loose sand when buried by wind or storm runoff (or gardeners who want more of it in their gardens).

Poliomintha maderensis

Mexican oregano

BLOOM PERIOD: May, repeating through summer with monsoon rain or occasional watering

HEIGHT AND SPREAD: 1 to 3 ft. × 1 to 3 ft.

GROWS WELL IN: Well-drained soil in heat; cold hardy to 10°F when dormant and in dry soil

Its leaves, form, and brittle stems resemble another more widely planted shrub mint, *Salvia greggii*, but Mexican oregano's pale lavender flowers deepen in color as they mature, so plants have flowers of many shades of purple at the same time, and its leaves have a distinctly oregano scent. Where winters are mild, it is evergreen and shrubby, needing only light pruning, but where it freezes hard, the plant is treated as an herbaceous perennial and cut back to 6 in. from the ground when new buds appear in spring.

Frosted mint (*Poliomintha incana*).

Mexican oregano (*Poliomintha maderensis*).

Western sand cherry

BLOOM PERIOD: April to June

HEIGHT AND SPREAD: 4 to 5 ft. × 5 to 6 ft.

GROWS WELL IN: Well-drained soil in intermediate and high deserts, where it tolerates heat; cold hardy to -20°F

Sand cherry marks the seasons. Its sprays of fragrant white flowers signal that spring is underway and are soon replaced by glossy green leaves that conceal the cherries forming along the stems. As the fruits ripen, they turn blue-black; birds make short work of the feast. In autumn, leaves turn beautiful shades of red before they fall, leaving a skeleton of slender reddish stems in winter. 'Pawnee Buttes' is a low-spreading form of sand cherry. It grows only 2 ft. high and 5 to 6 ft. wide, and is an easy-care ground cover on slopes and along paths.

Western sand cherry (*Prunus besseyi*). BELOW Western sand cherry fruits ripening.

Western chokecherry

BLOOM PERIOD: April to May

HEIGHT AND SPREAD: 6 to 10 ft. × 6 to 12 ft.

GROWS WELL IN: Foothills arroyos where it tolerates heat; cold hardy to -30°F

Sprays of pure white flowers in spring ripen to clusters of pea-sized, juicy red-purple fruits. Jams, syrups, and wine are made from the fruit—if you can beat the birds to the harvest. Western chokecherry is smaller and more xeric than those native in cooler, wetter parts of the country. It is amenable to receiving pulses of rainwater or irrigation every few weeks in summer, monthly or less the rest of the year. It root-sprouts to form groves. With its purple-gray stems and lush green foliage, it is a beautiful plant for controlling erosion in storm water swales and basins.

Purple sage, broom dalea

BLOOM PERIOD: Late May and August

HEIGHT AND SPREAD: 2 to 3 ft. × 3 to 4 ft.

GROWS WELL IN: Well-drained soil in extreme heat, cold hardy to -25°F in dry soil

This is the purple sage of deep, windblown sands, native in a few isolated areas across the Southwest where it perfumes the sunbaked hillsides with clusters of intensely blue or purple flowers, and, to the joy of beekeepers, increases honey crops prodigiously. Purple sage is one of the few desert plants that resents too much water even immediately after planting, and thrives on benign neglect in hot, dry places. It rarely has leaves, photosynthesizing in its slender blue-gray stems, which have a sweet, soapy scent.

Purple sage (*Psorothamnus scoparius*). LEFT Western chokecherry (*Prunus virginiana* var. *demissa*).

Rhus aromatica 'Gro-low'

'Gro-low' sumac

BLOOM PERIOD: **March to April**

HEIGHT AND SPREAD: **2 to 3 ft. × 5 to 7 ft.**

GROWS WELL IN: **Moderate heat; cold hardy to -30°F**

☀ ☀ ☀ ⚲ ⚙ 🐝

'Gro-low' sumac has slender, purple-gray stems that sprawl along the ground, quickly covering slopes or low-lying areas with its lush, glossy, lobed leaves. The clusters of yellow flowers are only conspicuous because they bloom before the leaves emerge, and the plants hum with bees eager to turn the nectar into honey. The foliage turns bright scarlet in autumn and is a beautiful contrast for conifers in foothills gardens. 'Gro-low' is an easy-care, fast-growing ground cover for large spaces when drip irrigated twice a month.

'Gro-low' sumac (*Rhus aromatica* 'Gro-low').

Rhus lanceolata

Prairie flameleaf sumac

BLOOM PERIOD: **July to August**

HEIGHT AND SPREAD: **12 to 25 ft. × 15 to 25 ft.**

GROWS WELL IN: **Extreme heat; cold hardy to 0°F, probably colder when dormant**

☀ ☀ ☀ ⚲ 🐝

The rich green compound leaves and strong branch pattern of this sumac lend a tropical feel to the garden. It doesn't root-sprout as aggressively as similar species, especially if the root zone is left undisturbed, so it can be used in smaller, more controlled settings for screening and light shade. In autumn, flameleaf sumac is as advertised, ablaze with shades of orange and red foliage, accented by panicles of coriander-sized red fruits at the ends of branches.

Prairie flameleaf sumac (*Rhus lanceolata*).

Rhus microphylla

Littleleaf sumac

BLOOM PERIOD: **April to May**

HEIGHT AND SPREAD: **4 to 8 ft. × 6 to 10 ft.**

GROWS WELL IN: **Extreme heat; cold hardy to -30°F**

☀ ☀ ☀ ◉ 🐝▸

Perhaps the most heat and drought loving of all sumacs, due to its finely divided deep green leaves. Littleleaf sumac's tiny clusters of white flowers are inconspicuous, but the golf ball–sized clusters of red-orange fruits they produce are showy in August and September, until voracious birds make a meal of them. The plant grows large with only periodic deep soaking, developing a mass of crisscrossing gray twigs, which provides nesting space for desert songbirds. Fall color is a subdued burgundy-red. Mix it with Arizona rosewood, curl-leaf mountain mahogany, or other evergreens as a wind buffer or screen.

Rhus trilobata

Threeleaf sumac

BLOOM PERIOD: **March to April**

HEIGHT AND SPREAD: **4 to 8 ft. × 5 to 10 ft.**

GROWS WELL IN: **Extreme heat; cold hardy to -30°F**

☀ ☀ ☀ ◉ ⚙ 🐝▸

Threeleaf sumac is a versatile and resilient shrub with many landscape uses. Its clusters of honey-scented, pale yellow flowers appear in spring just before its oak-like, lobed, dark green leaves unfold. Clusters of sticky red seeds are welcomed by songbirds. Foliage is dense and lush-looking on a very limited water budget all summer, turning shades of yellow and orange before dropping in fall. *Rhus trilobata* 'Autumn Amber' is a low-growing selection, 2 to 3 ft. tall and spreading 6 to 10 ft. wide, a beautiful, easy-care ground cover in harsh conditions. Once established, monthly deep watering is all they require.

Littleleaf sumac (*Rhus microphylla*).

Threeleaf sumac (*Rhus trilobata*).

Rhus virens var. *choriophylla*

Evergreen sumac

BLOOM PERIOD: May to August

HEIGHT AND SPREAD: 6 to 9 ft. tall × 8 to 12 ft. wide

GROWS WELL IN: Well-drained soil in heat at 2000 to 5000 ft. elevation; cold hardy to 0°F when dormant

☀ ☼ ☼ 📍 🐝▸

In desert gardens where many of the arid-adapted plants are feathery, prickly, or silver, evergreen sumac's dense cover of glossy, vividly green leaves lends mass and contrast to the composition . Clusters of tiny white flowers provide nectar for butterflies and bees. Similarly evergreen sugarbush (*Rhus ovata*) rarely grows larger than 6 ft. tall and 8 ft. wide, has larger leaves, and tolerates more shade but less cold to 10°F. Both prefer occasional deep watering. Young plants will fill out faster when watered every few weeks to monthly in summer, but constantly wet soil in winter can be fatal.

Evergreen sumac (*Rhus virens* var. *choriophylla*).

Rosmarinus officinalis

Rosemary

BLOOM PERIOD: January to February and October to November

HEIGHT AND SPREAD: 4 to 6 ft. × 4 to 6 ft.

GROWS WELL IN: Extreme heat; cold tolerance varies with cultivar. 'Arp' survives -10°F when dormant

☀ ☼ ✿ 🐝▸

Whether or not you light a grill or bake bread, the aroma of rosemary is an asset in the garden. Cultivated for a few thousand years, there are lots of selections to choose from. The scent can be slightly piney; the needle-like evergreen leaves may be bright, dark, or dusky gray-green; the flowers pale to deep, clear blue; and the form prostrate to columnar, compact to rangy. Mediterranean natives respond to moisture with growth, so plants weather cold better when they are hardened off in fall and not urged out of dormancy with water too early in spring.

Rosemary (*Rosmarinus officinalis*).

Desert ruellia

BLOOM PERIOD: Most prolific March to May, lightly all year in frost-free areas

HEIGHT AND SPREAD: 3 to 4 ft. × 4 to 6 ft.

GROWS WELL IN: Extreme, reflected heat; significant tip damage at 25°F, root hardy to 20°F, possibly colder

Purple tubular flowers dot the oval, resinous green leaves, densely covering the white stems of this heat lover. Desert ruellia tolerates a wide range of watering, but to thrive only needs a deep soak once or twice a month in summer, and less than monthly in cooler weather. Its role in the garden is more complementary companion than drama queen. Planting it in the shelter of a patio or against a south- or west-facing wall can limit freeze burning, and hard pruning to repair frost damage keeps it compact and fresh with a stronger color show.

Desert ruellia (*Ruellia peninsularis*).

Firecracker plant

BLOOM PERIOD: February through November

HEIGHT AND SPREAD: 3 to 5 ft. × 3 to 5 ft.

GROWS WELL IN: Extreme, reflected heat; frost damage at 25°F, root hardy to 22°F

Insouciant is the best word to describe this plant. Its growth is almost grasslike; thin green stems are mostly leafless, contributing to this tropical native's surprising adaptability to dry climates. The stems arch and sprawl in no particular pattern, yet appear refined rather than unruly. Best planted in good garden soil, it may need watering weekly during the hottest summer months. This will maintain the show of brilliant red, tubular flowers scattered at branch tips throughout the thready growth, but once the heat abates, monthly watering suffices.

Firecracker plant (*Russelia equisetiformis*).

Mexican blue sage

BLOOM PERIOD: **April through October**

HEIGHT AND SPREAD: **1 to 2 ft. × 2 to 3 ft.**

GROWS WELL IN: **Extreme heat; cold hardy to -15°F when dormant**

☀ ☼ ✿ 🐝

A neat little shrub with slender silver stems covered with small, rounded silver leaves, Mexican blue sage's clustered flowers are deep China blue. In intense sunlight, the flower stems are strongly vertical and the display of color is strongest, a flush of blooms in spring, repeating sporadically all summer where temperatures are not persistently above 100°F, and returning with a strong display in fall. The plant does well in heavy clay soils with watering every two weeks (at most) in summer, monthly when it's cooler, and without water at all when night temperatures are persistently freezing. It is longer-lived in high desert gardens.

Chaparral sage

BLOOM PERIOD: **March to June**

HEIGHT AND SPREAD: **3 to 4 ft. × 3 to 4 ft.**

GROWS WELL IN: **Extreme heat, cold hardy to 10°F**

☀ ☼ ✿ 📍 ✿ 🐝

This chaparral salvia's rounded, pale gray leaves are strongly aromatic and used in tea and seasoning. Despite being fairly short-lived, its outstanding display of tufted blue-violet flowers stacked an inch apart on stiff stems, and the butterflies and hummingbirds those blooms attract, are the reasons it finds its way into Southwest gardens. Adapted to winter moisture and summer rest, it grows best with monthly watering during cooler weather, and just enough summer moisture to keep it from defoliating and to avoid root rot. Prune it back and resume watering when temperatures cool a bit, to spur growth of the next season's flower stems.

Mexican blue sage (*Salvia chamaedryoides*). RIGHT Chaparral sage (*Salvia clevelandii*).

Sage

BLOOM PERIOD: Varies with hybrid

HEIGHT AND SPREAD: 2 to 3 ft. × 1 to 4 ft. (varies with hybrid)

GROWS WELL IN: Extreme heat, given cooler night temperatures; cold hardy to -5°F unless noted

The wealth of salvia species, the relative ease in hybridizing them, and the opportunities to create something different all combine to constantly yield new variations on the autumn sage theme. Crosses of _Salvia greggii_ × _S. microphylla_ typically grow 2½ ft. tall × 3 ft. wide, tolerate cold to at least -5°F and include 'Wild Thing', a deep fuchsia pink; 'Raspberry Delight', with rose-purple flowers and a pleasant fruity aroma; and 'Marachino', with bright scarlet flowers. _S._ 'Ultra Violet' grows 1½ ft. tall and wide, blooms from July until frost, and is root hardy to -15°F.

Sage (_Salvia greggii_ hybrid).

Mexican bush sage

BLOOM PERIOD: July to November

HEIGHT AND SPREAD: 3 to 4 ft. × 3 to 4 ft.

GROWS WELL IN: Extreme heat; top freezes to the ground at 20°F

A handsome plant, this salvia has long, narrow olive-green leaves on stiff, arching white stems that end in 6- to 8-in. spikes of violet-purple flowers. Although its common name is bush sage, it could be listed among herbaceous perennials, since in much of the Southwest it will freeze and need to be pruned back to the woody crown each spring. In frost-free areas, this tropical native benefits from hard pruning as well, since the result is more flower stems per plant. It is an important plant for bee and hummingbird nectar.

Mexican bush sage (_Salvia leucantha_).

Culinary sage

BLOOM PERIOD: **March to May**

HEIGHT AND SPREAD: **1 to 2 ft. × 3 to 4 ft.**

GROWS WELL IN: **Moderate heat; cold hardy to -15°F when dormant**

Cultivated for at least a thousand years, this is the sage of poultry stuffing, casseroles, soups, and stews. Its steel-gray, semi-evergreen leaves, pungent aroma, and blue-purple flower spikes earn it a space in ornamental gardens. Given the human urge to tinker, it's not surprising that there is a form with wider, paler leaves called 'Berggarten' and a mini-sage called 'Nana' or 'Compacta'. There are also variegated forms—including one called 'Tricolor', with white leaf margins and pink-flushed new growth that would be stunning if it didn't burn badly even in partial shade.

Culinary sage (*Salvia officinalis*).

Mojave sage

BLOOM PERIOD: **May to July**

HEIGHT AND SPREAD: **2 ft. × 3 ft.**

GROWS WELL IN: **Well-drained soil in moderate heat; cold hardy to -25°F when dormant**

This compact evergreen salvia is mounded in shape, with round silver leaves crowned by spikes of bicolored flowers. The calyces are purple and remain on the stems long after the tubular blue flowers have served the last of their nectar to bees and hummingbirds. It absolutely requires careful irrigation, as this gem seems to have a chronic dislike of consistently damp soil. Purple sage (*Salvia dorrii*) is a Great Basin desert native similar to Mojave sage in plant size and love of aridity and well-drained soil. Its leaves and flower spikes are smaller but important to all pollinators.

Mojave sage (*Salvia pachyphylla*).

'Trident' sage

BLOOM PERIOD: March to May; October

HEIGHT AND SPREAD: 3 ft. × 3 ft.

GROWS WELL IN: Well-drained soil in extreme heat; cold hardy to -10°F when dormant

This cultivar is a three-way cross between *Salvia mojavensis*, *S. clevelandii*, and *S. dorrii*, resulting in a compact form with spikes of tufted flowers like chaparral sage. It has aromatic foliage similar to desert sage, and a deeper violet-blue flower color than any of the parents. It tolerates heat in the hottest low desert areas much better than any other salvia, but still prefers well-drained soil and occasional deep watering, especially while plants are in bloom.

'Trident' sage (*Salvia* 'Trident').

Silverleaf cassia

BLOOM PERIOD: December to March

HEIGHT AND SPREAD: 5 to 6 ft. × 5 to 6 ft.

GROWS WELL IN: Extreme heat; cold hardy to 20°F

Australian *Senna*, formerly classified as *Cassia*, is grown for its light texture and show of brilliant yellow flowers. Silverleaf cassia has sickle-shaped phyllodes instead of leaves, and begins flowering in December, continuing through spring. Feathery cassia (*Senna artemisiodes*) has an open branch pattern and silver needle-like leaves that give it a wispy appearance, except when smothered in flowers. Desert cassia (*S. nemophila*) is similar, except its leaves are green. Feathery cassia stays a bit smaller, 4 to 5 ft. tall and wide. Mature plants of all species get large and woody if they are watered too much.

Silverleaf cassia (*Senna phyllodinea*).

Simmondsia chinensis

Jojoba, goat nut

BLOOM PERIOD: December to July

HEIGHT AND SPREAD: 6 to 8 ft. × 6 to 8 ft.

GROWS WELL IN: Extreme heat; cold hardy to 15°F

Jojoba is a slow-growing evergreen shrub with narrow, stiff blue-green leaves paired along arching stems—lush and cool looking despite its ability to thrive with little water in hot, rocky spaces. Its flowers are inconspicuous, but its acorn-like seeds are the source of fine oil with many commercial uses. In the garden, it is valued for its consistency, a soothing companion for spiny, spiky succulents and intense flower displays. 'Vista' is a compact, cutting-grown selection, consistently 4 ft. tall and wide with denser leaf cover.

Syringa meyeri

Dwarf Korean lilac

BLOOM PERIOD: May to June

HEIGHT AND SPREAD: 4 to 5 ft. × 4 to 6 ft.

GROWS WELL IN: Cooler areas above 6000 elevation; cold hardy to -30°F

Old-fashioned lilacs had been easy to establish and grow in higher-elevation, cooler gardens in the Southwest, but given the increasing summertime heat and warmer winter temperatures, the best option for maintaining the wonderful fragrance is dwarf Korean lilac. More compact, with smaller leaves and flower clusters, it blooms a bit later in spring. Although it seems to be the most heat tolerant of the lilacs, it still requires consistent watering during the growing season to keep it healthy.

Jojoba (*Simmondsia chinensis*).

Dwarf Korean lilac (*Syringa meyeri*).

Orange bells 'Orange Jubilee'

BLOOM PERIOD: **March to December**
HEIGHT AND SPREAD: **5 to 10 ft. × 4 to 8 ft.**
GROWS WELL IN: **Extreme heat; foliar damage at 25°F, but roots survive to 10°F**

☀ ☼ 🐝▸

A hybrid between the South American *Tecoma alata* and the native desert yellow bells (*Tecoma stans* var. *angustata*), 'Orange Jubilee' has rich green foliage contrasting with soft orange trumpet flowers that attract hummingbirds. The not-quite-rigid upright stems look best against a wall or fence. In hot desert areas, frosts will blacken leaves; in intermediate desert areas, orange bells will freeze to the ground and regrow quickly in spring. Limiting water in fall and winter improves cold tolerance. Growing 3 to 6 ft. tall, orange bells are valued pollinator plants. Watering deeply every two weeks helps keep it blooming in summer heat.

Orange bells 'Orange Jubilee' (*Tecoma alata* 'Orange Jubilee').

Teucrium fruticans

Shrubby germander

BLOOM PERIOD: June to October

HEIGHT AND SPREAD: 2 to 3 ft. × 3 to 4 ft.

GROWS WELL IN: Extreme heat; cold hardy to 5°F in dry soil

The sky-blue flowers of shrubby germander look more like tiny orchids than mint, the family to which this plant belongs. It small, slender leaves are silver-blue above and white on the underside. Together with white stems, these hues give the whole plant a hazy cool look that is soothing when summer temperatures bake. Thorough watering once a month keeps plants healthy, watering a bit more often in summer helps keep it blooming. It is evergreen where winters are mild, and freezes to the ground where winters dip to those temperatures persistently, but recovers quickly when the soil warms in spring.

Shrubby germander (*Teucrium fruticans*).

Vauquelinia californica

Arizona rosewood

BLOOM PERIOD: May to July

HEIGHT AND SPREAD: 10 to 12 ft. × 8 to 10 ft.

GROWS WELL IN: Extreme heat; cold hardy to -15°F when dormant

The adjective used most often to describe this large evergreen is "handsome." Its strongly vertical stems, densely covered with narrow dark green leaves, are crowned with lacy white flower clusters. The blooms ripen to deep rust-brown seed heads that persist for months before breaking off in the wind. Clustered or lined out as a green wall, Arizona rosewood makes an excellent wind and noise buffer or screen. Plants in extremely exposed locations survived a sudden deep freeze to -20°F, but died back to half their height, recovering to their former glory in two years, after deadwood was pruned out.

Arizona rosewood (*Vauquelinia californica*).

Vauquelinia corymbosa ssp. angustifolia

Chisos rosewood

BLOOM PERIOD: June to August

HEIGHT AND SPREAD: 10 to 15 ft. × 10 ft.

GROWS WELL IN: Heat, wind, and cold to -20°F

Slender, glossy, bright evergreen leaves and umbels of fragrant white flowers on dark rusty branches give this large shrub great garden appeal. Try it clustered as a wind buffer, or as a tall backdrop for succulents and contrasting shrubs such as Texas sages and woolly butterfly bush. Frost doesn't dull its foliage color, so it remains vibrant all through winter. Unusual for broad-leaved evergreens, rosewoods seem to prefer windy exposures and are leafier and more vigorous for the buffeting.

Chisos rosewood (*Vauquelinia corymbosa* ssp. *angustifolia*).

Viguiera deltoidea parrishi

Golden eye, desert sunflower

BLOOM PERIOD: March intermittently to October

HEIGHT AND SPREAD: 3 ft. × 3 ft.

GROWS WELL IN: Extreme reflected heat; cold hardy to 25°F when established

Sandpapery, triangular leaves cover the mound of stems. Small, 1-in. yellow daisies bloom spring through summer if plants are watered deeply once or twice a month. Thin out any deadwood in late winter to freshen it for the surge of spring blooms. Occasional deep watering makes the plant leafier, but too much too often produces lanky, sprawling growth and fewer flowers. It's a good companion for blue and purple flowers, making them stand out more in contrast. Also try mixing with red- and orange-flowering plants to accent the blazing color. Skeleton-leaf goldeneye (*Viguiera stenoloba*) has similar large yellow flowers; bright green, thread-like leaves on wiry white stems; and is cold hardy to 10°F.

Golden eye (*Viguiera deltoidea parrishi*).

SUCCULENTS

Desert rose

BLOOM PERIOD: February through August
HEIGHT AND SPREAD: 3 to 5 ft. × 2 to 10 ft.
GROWS WELL IN: Well-drained soil, extreme heat; tolerates no frost

Desert rose has smooth, gray, succulent stems that taper to a bulbous base, creating a striking silhouette against a hot wall whether in leaf, in bloom, or bare branched due to drought. Its large tubular flowers are deep rose-pink; the hybrid *Adenium obesum × A. swazicum* has larger deep red blooms. Heat loving but not at all cold tolerant, desert rose needs scant watering, and the hottest spot in low desert gardens if planted in the ground. It also thrives in a pot, which allows its use on patios throughout all desert areas; move indoors when frost threatens.

Desert rose (*Adenium obesum*). RIGHT Smooth agave (*Agave desmettiana*).

Smooth agave

BLOOM PERIOD: May to July once before dying
HEIGHT AND SPREAD: 3 ft. × 3 ft.
GROWS WELL IN: Well-drained soil in low desert only; severe cold damage at 25°F

Smooth agave is an elegant plant with wide, deep green leaves that curve outward and downward. Usually spineless on the margins, the brittle leaves have a sharp barb at their tips. It is a Florida native but is quite xeric, requiring only monthly watering once well-established when grown in the shade. Young plants will grow faster when watered more frequently, if drainage is sharp. *Agave desmettiana* 'Variegata' is streaked with bands of yellow: Lady Gaga to the all-green, classy Kate Middleton species.

Agave geminiflora

Twin-flowered agave

BLOOM PERIOD: September to October once before dying

HEIGHT AND SPREAD: 2 to 3 ft. × 2 to 3 ft.

GROWS WELL IN: Well-drained soil, filtered sun in the low desert; cold hardy to 25°F

Its thick crown averaging more than a hundred very narrow, smooth-margined leaves bordered with curling white fibers, twin-flowered agave is easily mistaken for soapweed yucca—until the slender, 10-ft.-tall flower spike shoots skyward, sheathed in yellow flowers tinged with purple. The party is then over for this solitary agave, which must be grown from seed. Unlike most agaves, though, this one is slow to die out, losing color gradually, sometimes taking a few years to fade completely. The process from planting to removal can take decades.

Twin-flowered agave (*Agave geminiflora*).

Agave havardiana

Havard agave

BLOOM PERIOD: May to August once before dying

HEIGHT AND SPREAD: 3 to 4 ft. × 4 to 5 ft.

GROWS WELL IN: Well-drained soil, reflected heat; tolerates cold briefly to -15°F

Havard agave has broad blue-green leaves tipped with black spines, arranged densely in a spiral, forming a magnificent rosette. Like most agave, once it produces its towering spike of yellow flowers, it dies—but it can take many decades for a plant to flower, growing increasingly impressive in the process. So there's no reason not to plant it, unless the soil is poorly drained or stays too wet, which is the other cause of plant loss. Leave a few feet around the perimeter of this agave to allow access to nearby plants. Water sparingly in summer.

Havard agave (*Agave havardiana*).

Agave lophantha

Agave

BLOOM PERIOD: June once before dying

HEIGHT AND SPREAD: 2 to 3 ft. × 2 to 3 ft.

GROWS WELL IN: Well-drained soil, extreme heat; tolerates cold to 5°F occasionally

Although armed with gray spines along the margins and at the leaf tips, this is one of the rare agaves with deep green leaves. The most common form has a faint, pale stripe down the middle of most leaves and there are several variegated selections with bright yellow striping. It grows best in alkaline soil, as it is native to limestone slopes in the desert foothills of south Texas into Mexico. Plants grown from northern seed sources are likely to be cold hardier; the variegated forms and those from deep into Mexico may not tolerate temperatures lower than 10°F.

Agave multifilifera

Chahuiqui

BLOOM PERIOD: May to June once before dying

HEIGHT AND SPREAD: 3 ft. × 4 ft.

GROWS WELL IN: Well-drained soil in extreme heat; cold hardy to 20°F and possibly 15°F, if grown dry in fall and winter

A rare agave that slowly develops a trunk, raising the crown of leaves a few feet above the ground. Its many dark green leaves are flat on the inner surface and curved on the underside, with coarse white fibers on the margins rather than spines. The flower stem towers 15 ft. above the ground, its hundreds of pale green flowers tinged with pink, and open from the base to the tip. It could be mistaken for a young soaptree yucca, except for the rigidity of the leaves and the striking, once-in-a-lifetime floral display.

Agave (*Agave lophantha*).

Chahuiqui (*Agave multifilifera*).

Hohokam agave

BLOOM PERIOD: Once in a lifetime March to April, sometimes earlier when winter is mild

HEIGHT AND SPREAD: 3 ft. × 3 ft.

GROWS WELL IN: Well-drained soil, extreme heat with light shade; cold hardy to 10°F when dry

There is evidence that this agave has been cultivated in Arizona as a staple food and fiber source for at least 500 years, and that "wild" plants are descendants of ancient crop fields. The plants are medium sized, have stiff leaves that range in color from dusky green to blue-gray with short spikes at the tip, and small hooked spines along the margins. A striped yellow cultivar is available as well.

Whale tongue agave

BLOOM PERIOD: June or July once before dying

HEIGHT AND SPREAD: 2 to 5 ft. × 3 to 6 ft.

GROWS WELL IN: Well-drained soil, extreme heat; tolerates brief periods of cold to 0°F in dry soil

Whale tongue has distinctive, wide, powder-blue leaves with small hooked spines on the margins and short barbs at the leaf tips. It is not unlike other agaves, though whale tongue leaves are sculpted, with a gutter down the center which is ideal for collecting and funneling rain to the roots. Producing no plantlets around its perimeter, it grows as a symmetrical rosette, needs little supplemental watering, benefits from filtered shade in low-desert infernos, and tolerates greater cold when grown dry. The flowers are pale yellow-green, borne on a towering stalk at the end of its long, beautiful life.

Hohokam agave (*Agave murpheyi*). RIGHT Whale tongue agave (*Agave ovatifolia*).

Parry's agave

BLOOM PERIOD: April to July once before dying

HEIGHT AND SPREAD: 1½ to 2 ft. × 2 ft. (plus offsets)

GROWS WELL IN: Well-drained soil, extreme heat with light shade; most varieties tolerate cold to -20°F

This is one of the most widely distributed and variable of the beautiful artichoke-form agaves, featuring blue-gray leaves with black spines on the margins and at the tips. One of the cold hardiest (as long as it is watered sparingly and only during warm weather), it usually produces many offsets, plantlets clustered around its base. *Agave parryi* var. *truncata* is stunning with wider, bluer leaves that curve inward toward the center of the rosette. *A. parryi* var. *parryi* 'Estrella' is a solitary clone produced by tissue culture. All have flower stems to 15 ft. tall with yellow flowers tinged red; plants die after blooming.

Parry's agave (*Agave parryi*).

Hairy agave

BLOOM PERIOD: May to July once before dying

HEIGHT AND SPREAD: 2 ft. × 3 ft.

GROWS WELL IN: Well-drained soil, extreme heat; tolerates cold to 15°F when grown dry

One of the smaller agave, this plant produces offsets very rarely and so maintains a compact, symmetrical shape. Its leaves are dark green, curved inward. Instead of marginal spines, it produces fine, curling white or tan filaments which help filter intense sunlight on its smooth leaf surfaces. The flower stem when it does finally appear is distinctive, a tall spike with greenish-yellow flowers tinged purple, opening from the bottom of the spike upward, reminiscent of foxtail lily on steroids. This modest plant ends life with a grand flourish, and deserves space in any garden warm enough to shelter it in winter.

Hairy agave (*Agave schidigera*).

Queen Victoria agave

BLOOM PERIOD: June or July once before dying
HEIGHT AND SPREAD: 1 to 1½ ft. × 1 to 2 ft.
GROWS WELL IN: Well-drained soil, extreme heat in filtered shade; tolerates cold to -10°F when grown dry

☀ ☼ ◉ ☼ 🐝▸

This royal name-dropper is one of the smallest and most distinctive agaves, with deep green leaves that are narrow but thick, wedge-shaped, and unarmed except at the tips. The leaves are marked with white at the edges of the plane surfaces, arranged in a tight rosette, giving the plant mighty presence in a small space. It needs good drainage and very little water; no water in winter except in low desert. Its spear-like flower stem, sheathed in reddish-purple, blooms on a tower 10 ft. or more above the plant. Some forms offset prolifically even when young, others grow as solitary rosettes.

Queen Victoria agave (*Agave victoriae-reginae*). RIGHT Weber's agave (*Agave weberi*).

Weber's agave

BLOOM PERIOD: May to June once before dying
HEIGHT AND SPREAD: 4 to 5 ft. × 7 to 10 ft.
GROWS WELL IN: Well-drained soil in extreme heat; survives cold briefly to 10°F when dormant

☀ ☼ ◉ ◉ 🐝▸

Easy to distinguish from other agave by its size and its 6-in.-wide, smooth-margined, flexible green leaves, this is a plant that makes a statement. Its bold form extends to its branched flower stem, a heady 20 feet of yellow blooms. Bulbils (small plantlets) form after flowering, and can be rooted to grow a replacement for the dying diva. There are variegated forms streaked pale yellow, for those who find the natural form a bit subtle. If agave turns yellow in low desert heat, move it under the shade of a mesquite or palo verde, or give it a good soaking if the soil is very dry.

Aloe vera

BLOOM PERIOD: **February to July**

HEIGHT AND SPREAD: **1½ ft. × 2 ft.**

GROWS WELL IN: **Well-drained soil in extreme heat; tolerates cold to 25°F**

☀ ☀ ☼ 🐝▸

Widely cultivated in containers for its burn-soothing sap, aloe vera is a fine garden plant as well. More tolerant of the intense sun and heat in low desert areas than most aloes, it develops tight clusters of strongly upright, fleshy pale green leaves when watered every few weeks in summer, and only occasionally in cooler weather. Tubular yellow flowers rise on branched stems up to 3 ft. tall, and are stunning when massed with desert verbenas. Having been cultivated for millennia, there are many forms and hybrids that may tolerate a bit more cold.

Aloe vera (*Aloe barbadensis*).

'Blue Elf' aloe

BLOOM PERIOD: January to April and intermittently the rest of the year

HEIGHT AND SPREAD: 1½ ft. × 2 ft.

GROWS WELL IN: Well-drained soil, extreme heat; tolerates cold to 18°F

'Blue Elf' is widely grown commercially, available in large numbers, and mass planted for winter color. The thick, upright, pale blue leaves surround stems of coral-orange tubular flowers enjoyed by hummingbirds. It needs good drainage and light watering in summer only. Since it blooms when frost is most likely, it is more vulnerable to cold than plants that are dormant. Plants may need thinning every few years; removing old flower stalks keeps plantings neat. It can be grown in pots in colder areas and brought indoors before deep frost to offer winter color near a sunny window.

'Blue Elf' aloe (*Aloe* 'Blue Elf').

Coral aloe

BLOOM PERIOD: February to May

HEIGHT AND SPREAD: 2 ft. × 2½ ft.

GROWS WELL IN: Well-drained soil, extreme heat; tolerates cold to 22°F

The wide, smooth, pale blue leaves form an open rosette that sometimes offsets to a multi-headed cluster. While the form and foliage are reason enough to grow this aloe, tubular coral flowers droop from several branched stems in spring, creating a lavish buffet for hummingbirds. Like all early-blooming aloes, it can suffer frost damage, especially if kept too wet. Planting under the canopy of palo verde or mesquite is ideal for light frost protection, as well as for preventing sunburn in summer. It thrives in pots small enough to move indoors for winter.

Coral aloe (*Aloe striata*).

Saguaro cactus

BLOOM PERIOD: **May and June**
HEIGHT AND SPREAD: **2 to 50 ft. × 1 to 15 ft.**
GROWS WELL IN: **Well-drained soil, extreme heat once several feet tall; cold hardy to 10°F when mature**

Saguaros are magnificent focal points in gardens; the elder statesmen of the Sonoran Desert. They prefer alkaline, rocky soil, especially on south-facing slopes. Waxy white flowers, edible fruits, and nest holes for savvy flickers are a bonus. It is slow growing and long-lived, but native stands are shrinking due to development disturbance, wild collecting, and climate change. Grow in native soil with minimal watering, as the plants themselves are elegantly ribbed water storage tanks, towering above their leafy neighbors. Saguaro is undermined by bacterial disease when wounded, and wind thrown when poorly rooted, so benign neglect is the best strategy.

TOP Saguaro in bloom. LEFT Saguaro cactus (*Carnegiea gigantea*).

Silver cholla

BLOOM PERIOD: March to April

HEIGHT AND SPREAD: 2 to 3 ft. × 3 to 4 ft.

GROWS WELL IN: Well-drained soil, extreme heat; cold hardy to -20°F

Cholla differ from prickly pear in that they have cylindrical, cane-like stems rather than flattened pads. Silver cholla is a compact, bushy plant covered with papery white spines that glow when backlit by the sun. The spines shade the stems, allowing it to thrive in the most intense light and heat. Yellow flowers blushed with red appear in spring, followed by dry, prickly fruit best left as dinner for wildlife. This is another great option for barrier planting viewed from a distance, where the gleaming spines add an unexpected flourish to the landscape.

Pencil cholla

BLOOM PERIOD: April to June

HEIGHT AND SPREAD: 3 to 4 ft. × 3 to 5 ft.

GROWS WELL IN: Well-drained soil, extreme heat and cold to -20°F; seems to prefer dry clay soils

The stems of this cholla are dark green and truly pencil thin, well-armed with 1-in. spines and glochid tufts. Selected plants have beautiful golden spines that glow when backlit, worth looking for at local nurseries. Flowers are small and pale yellow, less conspicuous than the glistening spines, but abundant, grape-sized, bright red fruits are showy and persist through fall and winter unless eaten by wildlife. The winter fruit gives the plant another common name, Christmas cholla. *Cylindropuntia kleiniae* is another species with slender stems that grows twice as large, with dusky coral-pink blossoms and less-conspicuous fruits.

Silver cholla (*Cylindropuntia echinocarpa*).

Pencil cholla (*Cylindropuntia leptocaulis*).

Dasylirion quadrangulatum

Mexican grass tree

BLOOM PERIOD: May and June

HEIGHT AND SPREAD: 3 to 10 ft. × 2 to 8 ft.

GROWS WELL IN: Well-drained soil, reflected heat; cold hardy to 15°F

Young plants resemble large clumps of graceful evergreen grass, but in time a stout trunk develops, gradually raising the grassy crown well above the ground. The blue-green leaves shimmer in the breeze. Mexican grass tree plays well with others as a neutral backdrop for brightly colored flowers, or as a striking accent specimen silhouetted against a wall in dry gardens. Older plants produce tall spikes of frothy white flowers. Established plants may need water every month or two; in areas receiving 10 in. of annual rainfall, no supplemental watering is necessary.

Dasylirion wheeleri

Desert spoon

BLOOM PERIOD: May to July

HEIGHT AND SPREAD: 3 to 5 ft. × 3 to 5 ft.

GROWS WELL IN: Well-drained soil, extreme reflected heat; tolerates cold briefly to -15°F when dry

Desert spoon is an elegant evergreen plant with narrow, limber leaves in dense clumps, eventually growing a stem to 3 ft. tall. Its blue-green leaves have prickly toothed margins. The flower stem of mature plants can reach 15 ft. tall, the top fourth covered with a froth of tiny white florets. It grows best in permeable volcanic or limestone soil with minimal watering. Texas sotol (*Dasylirion texanum*) differs in having pale green leaves and being native only in Texas, although it does well in all areas below 7000 ft., where winter is relatively mild and deep cold is infrequent.

Desert spoon (*Dasylirion wheeleri*). LEFT Mexican grass tree (*Dasylirion quadrangulatum*).

Golden barrel cactus

BLOOM PERIOD: June or July

HEIGHT AND SPREAD: 1 to 2 ft. × 1 to 2 ft.

GROWS WELL IN: Well-drained soil, extreme heat; tolerates cold to 15°F

Golden barrel exactly describes this cactus, with its low, squat profile and rows of bright yellow spines. The spines entirely hide the body of young plants—protecting them from hungry wildlife and intense sunlight. Its yellow flowers are beautiful, but pale in comparison to the sensational spines. A single plant is an eye-catching accent; a group of plants is show-stopping. Monthly watering in summer will grow plants to size faster. Planting near a south-facing wall or on the south side of large boulders helps protect plants on sites otherwise just a bit too cold.

Claret cup cactus

BLOOM PERIOD: April or May

HEIGHT AND SPREAD: 1 ft. × 1½ ft.

GROWS WELL IN: Well-drained soil, extreme heat; cold hardy to -15°F

Claret cup in bloom is a sign that spring is here to stay in the high desert. Seedlings are a single, short green column, ribbed with protective black or tan spines. In time, they cluster into dense mounds of multiple stems. Even young plants produce large, crimson, cup-like flowers, but a mature mounded plant covered with intense red flowers is impossible to ignore. Individual stems grow 4 in. in diameter and 1½ ft. tall, bearing similar red flowers in spring. All claret cups grow well in containers. 'White Sands' is a selection that is particularly robust.

Golden barrel cactus (*Echinocactus grusonii*).

Claret cup cactus (*Echinocereus triglochidiatus*).

Candelilla

BLOOM PERIOD: March to October

HEIGHT AND SPREAD: 1 ft. × 3 ft.

GROWS WELL IN: Well-drained soil, extreme reflected heat; cold hardy to 5°F occasionally

Candelilla's waxy, blue-green, pencil-thin evergreen stems grow strongly upright in dense mounds. Tiny pink and white flowers speckle the stems on and off throughout the growing season, but the beauty of candelilla is its vertical growth habit and subtle coloration. At home between boulders on hillsides, and in gardens mixed with other succulents and desert wildflowers, it also succeeds in pots as long as they're moved indoors where winters are too harsh. Deep monthly watering in summer is all that is needed to keep plants healthy.

Fishhook barrel cactus

BLOOM PERIOD: July through September

HEIGHT AND SPREAD: 1 to 3 ft. × 1 to ½ ft.

GROWS WELL IN: Well-drained soil, extreme heat; cold hardy occasionally to 5°F

Very slow growing, a young fishhook barrel is a squat pancake prodigiously armed with beautiful reddish, curved spines. Its form changes to globular and finally to a stout ribbed column that expands accordion-like with extra moisture and contracts in drought and cold. Fishhook barrels are crowned with large orange flowers July through September, followed by plump lemon-yellow fruits. Creosote bush, flame anisacanthus and perky Sue play well with this sturdy cactus.

Candelilla (*Euphorbia antisyphilitica*). RIGHT Fishhook barrel cactus (*Ferocactus wislizenii*).

Ocotillo

BLOOM PERIOD: April through September, in response to rain

HEIGHT AND SPREAD: 5 to 15 ft. × 10 ft.

GROWS WELL IN: Well-drained soil, extreme heat; tolerates occasional cold briefly to -20°F

☀ ◉ ☼ 🐝▸

A plant of many surprises, ocotillo begins as a bundle of thorny gray sticks, but given a good location with reflected heat and occasional water in summer, it grows to be a striking specimen. Once it is well rooted, even light rains will cover the stems with small green leaves that remain as long as the moisture supports. Ocotillo photosynthesizes in its stems, so the ephemeral leaves are a source of extra energy. Given a surge of moisture, the stem tips seem to flame with dense clusters of scarlet flowers, to the delight of hummingbirds and bats in the neighborhood.

Ocotillo (*Fouquieria splendens*).

Hesperaloe parviflora

Red yucca

BLOOM PERIOD: April to September

HEIGHT AND SPREAD: 2 ft. (leaves) 4 ft. (flower stems) × 4 ft.

GROWS WELL IN: Well-drained soil, heat and cold tolerant to -20°F

The foliage of red yucca resembles a large clump of coarse evergreen grass, but that illusion is dispelled with the appearance of graceful, arching stems of waxy, tubular, coral-colored flowers. Mature plants will have dozens of stems. It is a favorite of gardeners—and hummingbirds—for its long blooming season. The color and form blend well with lavender-blooming plants in cooler areas: 'Ultra Violet' salvia at mid-elevations, and violet silverleaf (*Leucophyllum*) in hot desert gardens. 'Brakelights' and 'Perpa' are smaller cultivars, 2 ft. tall and wide, with intensely red flowers.

Red yucca (*Hesperaloe parviflora*).

Hesperaloe funifera

Giant hesperaloe

BLOOM PERIOD: May through August

HEIGHT AND SPREAD: 4 ft. (leaves) 8 to 10 ft. (flower stems) × 3 ft.

GROWS WELL IN: Well-drained soil, extreme heat; occasional cold to -10°F

Giant hesperaloe is, as advertised, a robust plant. The evergreen leaves are strongly vertical, 1 in. wide at the base tapering to a point, with thin curling fibers along the leaf margins. The flower stems are tall-branched candelabras dotted with small, waxy white flowers. The flowers are much less conspicuous than the coral and red species. It is their clumps of light green, vertical leaves that make interesting patterns in the landscape. Highlighted against a wall, both the bold leaves and contrasting, delicate flowers have maximum impact.

Giant hesperaloe (*Hesperaloe funifera*).

Spice lily

BLOOM PERIOD: May through August

HEIGHT AND SPREAD: 8 to 12 in. (leaves), 18 to 36 in. (flower stems) × 12 in.

GROWS WELL IN: Well-drained soil, low desert heat; cold hardy to -20°F in dry soil

Spice lily deserves more attention on multiple counts. Its brittle, concave leaves resemble a spotted aloe during the growing season, but the leaves are deciduous, so the plant disappears like an herbaceous perennial in cold winter areas, reappearing in spring. The flower stems persist through most of the summer with fragrant, tubular blossoms that open white and turn gradually deeper rose-pink while new buds open, so there are flowers of deepening color together on a single stem. Rhizomatous, it eventually forms a small colony, blending nicely with ornamental grasses, or in a bed of desert zinnia and purple verbena or similarly xeric wildflowers.

Ribbon grass

BLOOM PERIOD: May to July

HEIGHT AND SPREAD: 2 ft. × 3 ft.

GROWS WELL IN: Well-drained soil, reflected heat; cold hardy to -20°F in dry soil

The leaves of ribbon grass are dark green and narrow, curving outward and spiraling from the center of the evergreen mound, making this plant the most refined of the cultivated nolinas. Its flower stem grows 4 ft. tall with clusters of tiny white florets displayed well above the foliage. Because of its compact size and tolerance of a bit more moisture and light shade, it is easy to find places to tuck it into the garden. It pairs well with any number of wildflowers and subshrubs, including giant four o'clock, salvias, Mexican gold poppy, and trailing dalea.

Spice lily (*Manfreda maculosa*). RIGHT Ribbon grass (*Nolina lindheimeriana*).

Nolina microcarpa

Beargrass

BLOOM PERIOD: June to August

HEIGHT AND SPREAD: 3 to 5 ft. × 5 to 6 ft.

GROWS WELL IN: Well-drained soil, reflected heat; cold hardy to -10°F

☀ ◉ ☼ 🐝▸

The slender olive-green leaves of beargrass look like huge evergreen clumps of grass, until summer, when flower stalks arch to 6 ft., bearing clusters of tiny yellow-green flowers. Massive enough to be used singly, in small groups as accent, or as a backdrop for more colorful flowering plants, it thrives on benign neglect. Leaf tips end in curling fibers, but the leaf margins are finely serrated and sharp. A similar species, *Nolina texana*, grows 2 ft. tall and 4 ft. wide, with frothy white blooms nestled among the leaves. It is cold hardy to -20°F.

Beargrass (*Nolina microcarpa*).

Nolina nelsoni

Blue nolina

BLOOM PERIOD: May to July

HEIGHT AND SPREAD: 3 to 12 ft. × 4 ft.

GROWS WELL IN: Well-drained soil, reflected heat; cold hardy to 5°F in dry soil

☀ ◉ ☼ 🐝▸

The stiff blue leaves and slowly developing stem distinguish blue nolina from its closest relatives. It's easily confused with yuccas until it blooms and reveals the froth of tiny flowers characteristic of nolinas. It endures cold at the upper reaches of its native range in Mexico, and it's probable that plants grown from seed collected above 8000 ft. elevations will be significantly hardier than those from lowland collections. It is less prone to stabbing you in the back while its leaves remain limber and within reach, but the leaf margins could be used for filleting steaks so handle them with care.

Blue nolina (*Nolina nelsoni*).

Opuntia basilaris

Beavertail prickly pear

BLOOM PERIOD: April to May

HEIGHT AND SPREAD: 2 to 3 ft. × 4 to 6 ft.

GROWS WELL IN: Well-drained soil, extreme heat; cold hardy to near 0°F

☀ ◉ ☼ 🐝

Beavertail is noteworthy for its pale blue pads that appear thornless from a distance, but are well armed with irritating glochids if touched. The satiny flowers are deep magenta and line the edges of the pads. It is slow growing for a prickly pear and so is easily contained when planted among other plants. It needs plenty of sun, and very little water to thrive. In colder areas, keep plants away from rainwater basins and stop watering in midsummer, so plants go into freezing weather dry and can avoid winter damage.

Beavertail prickly pear (*Opuntia basilaris*).

Opuntia canacapa 'Ellisiana'

Spineless prickly pear

BLOOM PERIOD: June to August

HEIGHT AND SPREAD: 4 ft. × 6 ft.

GROWS WELL IN: Well-drained soil, extreme heat; cold hardy to 0°F

☀ ☼ ☼ ◉ 🐝

The smooth, pale green pads of this prickly pear answer the prayers of gardeners who love the sculptural form of prickly pear, but have been impaled by spines or endlessly annoyed by glochids. 'Ellisiana' has neither, but it does have large, lemon-yellow flowers and edible red fruits. If that doesn't satisfy your checklist of opuntia options, its ability to thrive in low desert summers and survive high desert winters should push it to the top of your I-need-this-plant list.

Spineless prickly pear (*Opuntia canacapa* 'Ellisiana').

Engelmann's prickly pear

BLOOM PERIOD: April to May

HEIGHT AND SPREAD: 2 to 4 ft. × 8 to 12 ft.

GROWS WELL IN: Well-drained soil, reflected heat; cold hardy to -15°F when dry; best between 3500 and 7500 ft. elevation

The largest of the cold-hardy prickly pears, its dinner platter–sized pads are held perpendicular to the sun's rays, shielding the smooth green skin. Abundant large, satiny yellow or vermillion blooms make a grand spring show. Clusters of stiff tan spines and minute but extremely irritating glochids protect the pads from predation and make harvesting the large juicy purple "pears" a challenge. Long-handled barbeque tongs are a handy tool for the job, and fruits must be peeled carefully to remove small spines. As cold weather approaches, the pads shrink, allowing space for sap to freeze and thaw.

Indian fig

BLOOM PERIOD: May to July

HEIGHT AND SPREAD: 5 to 12 ft. × 4 to 8 ft.

GROWS WELL IN: Well-drained soil, reflected heat; not tolerant of hard frost

Indian fig has been cultivated for so long that its native origins are obscure. Some of the farmed varieties are nearly spineless and produce bumper crops of large red-purple tunas, the traditional name for the melon-berry-flavored fruits. The tender new pads are harvested, thinly sliced, and eaten raw or cooked as a xeric substitute for green beans. As an ornamental, it is a statuesque evergreen specimen plant; grow it as a low-water green wall in places where temperatures rarely drop more than a few degrees below freezing.

Engelmann's prickly pear (*Opuntia engelmannii*). RIGHT Indian fig (*Opuntia ficus-indica*).

'Old Mexico' prickly pear

BLOOM PERIOD: May to June

HEIGHT AND SPREAD: 4 to 5 ft. × 6 to 8 ft.

GROWS WELL IN: Well-drained soil, extreme heat; cold hardy to 10°F

'Old Mexico' is a spineless prickly pear cultivar with satiny, pale yellow flowers in late spring and red tunas in late summer and fall. Its pads are pale green and broadly oval, with wavy margins that give it a distinctive texture. 'Old Mexico' will thrive in more shade than most cacti.

'Old Mexico' prickly pear (*Opuntia gomei* 'Old Mexico').

Polka dot prickly pear

BLOOM PERIOD: June to August

HEIGHT AND SPREAD: 2 to 3 ft. × 3 to 5 ft.

GROWS WELL IN: Well-drained soil, extreme heat; cold hardy to 12°F, possibly colder when dry

Polka dot is an apt descriptor for this small-padded, compact prickly pear. It has no large spines, but gets its common name from the dense tufts of glochids that dot the stems. There are three varieties, one with pale cream-colored glochids, another with golden-yellow bristles, and one with rust-brown tufts. All have pale yellow flowers and small red fruits. The pads appear in pairs above the old growth and spawned the other common name: bunny ears cactus.

Polka dot prickly pear (*Opuntia microdasys*).

Santa Rita prickly pear

BLOOM PERIOD: April to May

HEIGHT AND SPREAD: 2 to 5 ft. × 2 to 5 ft.

GROWS WELL IN: Well-drained soil, extreme reflected heat; tolerates cold to 0°F when dry

☀ ◉ ☼ 🐝

The purple flush of color on the rounded pads makes even those who think they aren't fans of cactus look twice. Santa Rita prickly pear has few large spines but plenty of pesky glochids, so while it appears more benign, it should still be planted away from places where people and pets are likely to pass. The color is most intense when plants are drought or cold stressed, and contrasts beautifully with lemon-yellow flowers that appear when the winter-induced blush is still vivid. Extreme cold kills this plant but *Opuntia macrocentra* is a similar but spinier species that is hardy to -20°F.

Santa Rita prickly pear (*Opuntia santa-rita*).

Slipper plant

BLOOM PERIOD: February to May and August to October

HEIGHT AND SPREAD: 2 to 3 ft. × 2 ft.

GROWS WELL IN: Well-drained soil, reflected heat; old growth survives to 22°F

☀ ◉ ☼ 🐝

The slender, light green stems are leafless most of the time, and their strongly vertical lines contrast and complement the mounded forms of many desert shrubs. Its oddly shaped coral-red flowers are a great patio party conversation starter. Limited to the warmest parts of the region as a landscape plant, it can be used to echo Mexican grass tree in form but contrast that same tree in stature. Use it as a silhouette against a wall or boulder, or against deep green foliage such as turpentine bush or rosemary. In cold areas, it can be grown in a pot and wintered indoors.

Slipper plant (*Pedilanthus macrocarpus*).

Hens and chicks

BLOOM PERIOD: June to August

HEIGHT AND SPREAD: 6 in. × 12 in.

GROWS WELL IN: A cool climate; hardy to -30°F

In temperate climates, hens and chicks grow on green roofs and rockeries, in pots, and along pathways, but in the desert Southwest, they do best in cooler, shaded places. Above 7500 ft. in elevation, sempervivum can tolerate more direct sunlight, but even there (except for the self-shading woolly white varieties) sunburn can be a problem if plants aren't buffered part of the day. They are exquisitely symmetrical and user-friendly, like unarmed dwarf agave with cupped flowers on short, thick stems. Like agave, the hen that flowers dies, but there are so many chicks that the gaps fill quickly.

Hens and chicks (*Sempervivum tectorum*).

Banana yucca

BLOOM PERIOD: May to July

HEIGHT AND SPREAD: 2 to 3 ft. × 3 to 5 ft.

GROWS WELL IN: Well-drained soil, reflected heat; cold hardy to -30°F when dry

Banana yucca is so called for the pendulous, starchy fruits that droop from the flower stem; these were a dietary staple of Southwestern native people. In contemporary gardens it is a dependably spiky accent plant, with waxy cream-colored blossoms. Relatively slow growing, it takes many years to develop a short trunk which elevates the rosette of thick, guttered blue-green leaves above ground; by then, the oldest rosettes are usually wreathed in smaller offsets. A mature plant may produce a dozen or more flower stems each year. Curling white fibers along the leaf margins add texture.

Banana yucca (*Yucca baccata*).

Joshua tree (*Yucca brevifolia*).

Joshua tree

BLOOM PERIOD: **May to June**
HEIGHT AND SPREAD: **15 to 30 ft. × 15 to 30 ft.**
GROWS WELL IN: **Well-drained soil, extreme heat; cold hardy to -15°F**

A single Joshua tree is an impressive sight; a forest of them is truly amazing. This yucca is the most tree-like of all, with a trunk that begins to branch several feet above ground and continues to divide and grow new heads—rosettes of stiff, narrow, pale green leaves developing into a wide-crowned, spreading canopy. Even more magnificent is the annual display of white lily blooms atop spikes growing from the leafy rosettes. Slow growing and undermined by excess water or fertilizer, Joshua tree takes many decades to mature, but even a young plant makes a fine accent specimen.

Soap tree

BLOOM PERIOD: **May to June**

HEIGHT AND SPREAD: **6 to 20 ft. tall × 4 to 6 ft. wide**

GROWS WELL IN: **Well-drained soil, extreme heat; cold hardy to -30°F**

Soap tree grows in large colonies on rocky slopes and open desert. An elegant white-flowered candelabra towers 6 to 10 ft. above the leafy heads; when the woody seed capsules dry, split, and release the flat black seeds, those seeds pepper the ground with every strong gust of wind. Plants grow 10 ft. in 15 years with 10 or 12 in. of summer rain, and begin to flower after 5 or 6 years. *Yucca rostrata* is a narrow-leaved species growing 6 to 12 ft. tall, easy to distinguish from soap tree by its yellow leaf margins and shorter flower stem.

Soap tree (*Yucca elata*). LEFT Flowering soap tree spire.

Yucca faxoniana

Faxon yucca

BLOOM PERIOD: May to June

HEIGHT AND SPREAD: 15 ft. × 8 ft.

GROWS WELL IN: Well-drained soil, extreme heat; cold hardy to -20°F

☀ ◉ ◔ 🐝▸

This broad-leaved yucca has a fairly shallow mat of pencil-thin roots, and stores so much food that it is one of the few yuccas that transplant well as mature specimens. Young plants resemble banana yucca for a few years but begin to develop a thick trunk relatively quickly. The dead leaves that sheathe the trunk (absorbing moisture and protecting the live tissue) are sometimes removed; in areas with little winter cold, this grooming seems to cause no ill effect. The creamy, 2-ft.-tall flower spike, shielded within the bright green leaves, is quite showy.

Yucca glauca

Soapweed

BLOOM PERIOD: April to June

HEIGHT AND SPREAD: 1 to 3 ft. × 2 to 4 ft.

GROWS WELL IN: Well-drained soil, extreme heat; cold hardy to -40°F

☀ ◉ ◔ 🐝▸ 🌡

Perhaps the most common lily of desert grasslands and the adjacent prairie, soapweed provided one-stop shopping in prehistoric times: a source of food, personal hygiene, and fiber. Its starchy root is still a traditional shampoo, as well as a foaming agent in root beer. Stiff, narrow, light green leaves crown a short stem, from which 3-ft.-high flower stems branch, graced with pendulous white flowers that are sometimes tinged pink. Woody seed capsules containing stacks of flat black seeds have habitat value. There are several similar but smaller yuccas, including *Yucca harrimaniae* and the petite *Y. nana*, that can be massed as small, ornamental evergreen grass.

Faxon yucca (*Yucca faxoniana*). RIGHT Soapweed (*Yucca glauca*).

Pale yucca

BLOOM PERIOD: May to June

HEIGHT AND SPREAD: 2 ft. × 2½ ft.

GROWS WELL IN: Clay soils, extreme heat; tolerates cold to 0°F

☀ ☁ ☼ 📍 🐝▸

This small plant's rosette of wide, frosted blue leaves makes it a fine evergreen placeholder in perennial beds, or for textural contrast in a mass of ground cover such as prairie sage. It is equally at home as a companion to dark-leaved shrubs such as rosemary or turpentine bush. Flower stems may be 4 to 6 ft. tall depending on age of the plant, and available light and moisture. Plants will grow in fairly deep shade, but won't bloom reliably, and the sight of its silken white flower bells is worth finding pale yucca a place in the sun.

Pale yucca (*Yucca pallida*).

Blue yucca

BLOOM PERIOD: May to July

HEIGHT AND SPREAD: 10 to 15 ft. × 5 to 6 ft.

GROWS WELL IN: Well-drained soil, extreme heat; cold hardy briefly to 5°F in dry soil

☀ ☼ 🐝▸

Blue yucca grows to tree size, usually with only one or two heads per trunk. The leaves are stiff, an inch wide and a foot long, ending in a brown spine and clustered in a fan above the mat of dead leaves covering the stem. The 2-ft.-tall flower stems are partly hidden in the leaves, and are congested with creamy white buds. The frosty leaf color, stature, and flower display make blue yucca an obvious choice as an accent in dry gardens.

Blue yucca (*Yucca rigida*).

Twistleaf yucca

BLOOM PERIOD: April to June

HEIGHT AND SPREAD: 1 to 2 ft. × 2½ ft.

GROWS WELL IN: Well-drained soil, extreme heat;
cold hardy to 0°F

☀ ☁ ☼ ◉ 🐝

Twistleaf yucca's native range overlaps that of pale
yucca, and the plants hybridize, so there are plants
with intermediate characteristics, but the species are
quite distinct. Twistleaf has deep green leaves with
red- or yellow-toothed margins; as the leaves age
they have a natural torque that gives the plant its
common name and an undulating sense of motion.
Flower stems are strongly vertical with the waxy,
cream-colored blossoms dangling from short side
shoots. Plants benefit from occasional deep watering in summer, especially in full-sun, low desert areas.

Mountain yucca

BLOOM PERIOD: June to July

HEIGHT AND SPREAD: 6 to 10 ft. × 3 to 6 ft.

GROWS WELL IN: Well-drained soil, extreme heat;
cold hardy to -20°F

☀ ❄ ☼ 🌡 ◉ 🐝

This is one of the most cold tolerant of the tall yuccas, forming a dense crown of stiff, wide, blue-green
leaves with contrasting brown margins and tips.
Plants often sprout new heads at the base of mature
trunks. Native to the rocky Arizona foothills, it is an
excellent companion for live oak and Gambel oak, as
well as for hot desert flowering shrubs such as bird
of paradise and woolly butterfly bush.

Mountain yucca (*Yucca schottii*). LEFT Twistleaf yucca (*Yucca rupicola*).

Thompson's yucca

BLOOM PERIOD: June to July

HEIGHT AND SPREAD: 5 to 8 ft. × 6 to 8 ft.

GROWS WELL IN: Well-drained soil, extreme heat; cold hardy to -10°F when dormant

☀ ☼ ◉ 🐝▸

Thompson's yucca is small compared with other tree-forming yuccas, ideal for spaces too confined for the big ones. Stems burst from multiple branches, and heads are nearly spherical with short, narrow, light green leaves and pale yellow margins. Each head can produce several 3-ft. flower stems, candelabra lit with waxy, bell-shaped, cream-white blossoms.

Thompson's yucca (*Yucca thompsoniana*).

Achillea millefolium

Common yarrow

BLOOM PERIOD: May to September

HEIGHT AND SPREAD: 1 to 3 ft. × 1 to 2 ft.

GROWS WELL IN: Rich organic soil; moderate heat; cold hardy to -30°F when dormant

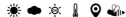

This is such a widely cultivated plant and has been grown in temperate climates for so long that there are many cultivars available. Look for a wide range of shades in yellow, pink, coral, red, wine, and scarlet. All grow a mat of soft, fern-like leaves and tiny flowers clustered together in flat-topped umbels on stiff stems. The western native is the toughest, has white flowers, and is most commonly found growing in woodland clearings above 6000 ft. in the mountains of the Southwest. The colorful cultivars are somewhat less heat and drought tolerant—best grown in part shade in good garden soil, as nectar sources for butterflies and bees.

Common yarrow (*Achillea millefolium*).

Hollyhock

BLOOM PERIOD: **May to August**

HEIGHT AND SPREAD: **4 to 6 ft. × 1 to 2 ft.**

GROWS WELL IN: **Heat; cold hardy to -40°F**

From clumps of large scalloped leaves, stout vertical stems emerge: columns of 3-in. flower trumpets in shades from white to deep burgundy, pale pink, and buttery yellow. The show goes on for a month or longer when plants are given a good soaking every two weeks. Cultivated since the sixteenth century, to say this is an old garden favorite may be a bit of an understatement. From Tucson to Taos, it is a common sight in the Southwest, growing along walls and fences. Our dry winters make it a long-lived perennial that self-sows quite prolifically if given any encouragement.

Arizona bluestar

BLOOM PERIOD: **March to May**

HEIGHT AND SPREAD: **1 ft. × 1 ft.**

GROWS WELL IN: **Moderate heat; cold hardy to -20°F**

Arizona bluestar and the closely related Colorado native *Amsonia jonesii* (Jones bluestar) have clusters of flowers that are white with a blue cast. All species of *Amsonia* develop deep, shrub-like roots, giving plants an edge in our dry climate. Their fine, deep green foliage and mounded shape look well-groomed with little care other than cutting back to the crown in spring. Arkansas bluestar (*A. hubrichtii*) was selected perennial plant of the year in 2011 for its overall garden presence; brief display of clusters of pale, tubular flowers; willowy foliage; and spectacular gold fall foliage. Shrub-like in size, 2 to 3 ft. tall × 3 ft. wide, and cold hardy to -30°F, it does well in higher-elevation gardens in the Southwest.

Arizona bluestar (*Amsonia grandiflora*). LEFT Hollyhock (*Alcea rosea*).

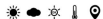

Antennaria rosea

Pussytoes

BLOOM PERIOD: **March to April**

HEIGHT AND SPREAD: **6 in. × 12 in.**

GROWS WELL IN: **Moderate heat; cold hardy to -30°F**

☀ ☁ ☼ 🌡 📍

Found carpeting crevices between boulders on mountaintops across the West, pussytoes is remarkably heat adapted when grown in afternoon shade at lower elevations. It evades heat and drought stress by blooming early in the year. Although it grows a dense mat of foliage, the leaves are small, reflective silver, and evergreen. Nestled between paving stones or boulders that condense moisture, which trickles down to keep its deep roots hydrated, this very efficient plant expends little energy. Its common name refers to the small clusters of hairy flower buds on short stems that appear early in spring, looking very much like tiny white or pink cat paws.

Aquilegia chrysantha

Golden columbine

BLOOM PERIOD: **March to June**

HEIGHT AND SPREAD: **1 to 2½ ft. × 2 ft.**

GROWS WELL IN: **Moderate heat; cold hardy to -30°F**

☀ ☁ ☼ 🌡 📍 🐝

The intricately fluted flowers of columbine have been a garden favorite since Victorian times. Golden columbine is the most heat and drought enduring of the many species and cultivars. Even in low desert gardens, it will produce a strong spring show in the shade if watered once a week while in bloom. Its pale green, scalloped leaves are beautiful, and seem resistant to the leaf miners that plague other columbines. The butter yellow flowers continue their nectar buffet for hummingbirds until 100-degree heat brings the feast to an end for the year, but the lacy leaves continue to offer textural contrast.

Pussytoes (*Antennaria rosea*). RIGHT Golden columbine (*Aquilegia chrysantha*).

'Sea Foam' artemisia

HEIGHT AND SPREAD: **6 to 12 in. × 24 in.**

GROWS WELL IN: **Heat tolerant; cold hardy to -30°F**

This hybrid is all about texture, its small leaves are a silky, pale silver-green, densely growing along short stems that branch and twist, creating a tight carpet resembling the froth along the edge of the sea as it breaks on the beach. It prefers our low humidity and lean soils, and is an excellent ground cover for small spaces or filler between other perennials or grasses.

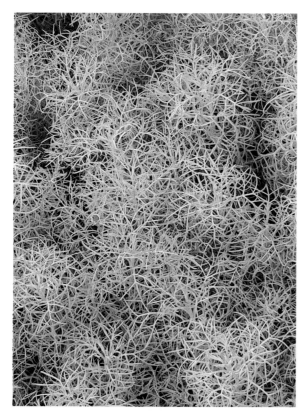

'Sea Foam' artemisia (*Artemisia versicolor* 'Sea Foam').
RIGHT Milkweed (*Asclepias* species).

Milkweed

BLOOM PERIOD: **June to September**

HEIGHT AND SPREAD: **1 to 2½ ft. × 1 to 2 ft.**

GROWS WELL IN: **Moderate to extreme heat; cold hardy to -30°F**

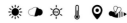

Essential to the life cycle of many butterflies, there are milkweeds adapted to nearly every Southwestern ecosystem. All have attractive flower clusters, interesting foliage, and large seedpods that split open to release papery seeds adrift on silken fibers. Whorled milkweed (*Asclepias subverticillata*) has willowy stems and leaves and 1-in. balls of tiny fragrant flowers. Showy milkweed (*A. speciosa*) occurs at higher elevations and has pairs of wide, glossy leaves on stiff vertical stems, topped with clusters of pink flowers. Butterfly weed (*A. tuberosa*), native in our shady canyons, is well suited to rainwater swales in desert gardens. Select plants and seeds from local clones, as the seeds and plants offered for sale are often from cooler, wetter regions, not as well adapted as they need to be to survive desert conditions.

221

Bahia absinthifolia

Bahia

BLOOM PERIOD: **April to October**

HEIGHT AND SPREAD: **6 to 10 in. × 24 in.**

GROWS WELL IN: **Extreme and reflected heat; cold hardy to -22°F when dry**

☀ ☼ ◉ 🐝

Although there are plenty of yellow daisies for Southwest gardens, if you have a sunbaked spot in sandy or rocky soil that's too harsh for other plants, bahia is a gem worth considering. Its dense, silver-blue foliage forms a thick mat topped by 1-in., clear yellow flowers that bloom on short stems in flushes in response to water. A thorough soaking every few weeks in summer will keep it blooming almost continuously. Monthly soakings will produce stronger surges of color and show off the attractive leaf carpet to advantage.

Berlandiera lyrata

Chocolate flower

BLOOM PERIOD: **April through October**

HEIGHT AND SPREAD: **1 to 1½ ft. × 2 ft.**

GROWS WELL IN: **Extreme reflected heat; cold hardy to -30°F in dry soil**

☀ ☼ ◉ ⚙ 🌡 🐝

The rich, chocolaty aroma of this yellow daisy with a dark maroon-red eye is unmistakable, especially early in the morning when the flowers are fresh. By midday the heads droop, avoiding the hot sun and looking a bit forlorn. Late in the day they perk up again. The crisp, gray-green leaves are coarsely dissected, lyre-like in shape. Easy to grow from seeds or transplants, chocolate flower establishes quickly and self-sows prolifically in well-drained soil with deep watering once or twice a month.

Bahia (*Bahia absinthifolia*).

Chocolate flower (*Berlandiera lyrata*).

Poppy mallow, winecups

BLOOM PERIOD: April to October

HEIGHT AND SPREAD: 1 ft. × 2 to 3 ft.

GROWS WELL IN: Moderate heat; cold hardy to -25°F in dry soil

The sprawling, cord-like stems of poppy mallow will scramble between boulders, weave their way through grasses and other wildflowers, and cascade over low walls, seeking sunlight for the round, scalloped-edged leaves and satiny, cupped, deep burgundy flowers. While plants will survive extreme heat, they do so by going dormant, shrinking to a cluster of a few leaves above the starchy roots, and waiting until temperatures cool before they resume their garden rambling. Plants need protection from hungry rabbits, who seem to consider this plant candy and will even eat the roots if reachable.

Poppy mallow (*Callirhoe involucrata*).

Sundrops

BLOOM PERIOD: March to September

HEIGHT AND SPREAD: 1 to 2 ft. × 2 to 3 ft.

GROWS WELL IN: Extreme heat; cold hardy to -20°F

Sundrops' narrow, medium green leaves and spreading mound shape are a simple backdrop for the waves of square yellow flowers with translucent petals that fade from clear yellow to salmon orange in a single day. Pollinated by sphinx moths that add their own movement and color, the display is most intense in spring and fall, when temperatures are cooler. Even with thorough watering every few weeks, flower size and numbers will decrease during the summer. Sundrops are related to evening primrose, the favorite lunch of flea beetles, which can skeletonize plants stressed by heat, but rarely do permanent damage to otherwise healthy specimens.

Sundrops (*Calylophus hartwegii* subsp. *fendleri*).

Indian paintbrush

BLOOM PERIOD: March to May

HEIGHT AND SPREAD: 1 ft. × 1 ft.

GROWS WELL IN: Moderate heat; cold hardy to
-30°F

This extraordinary wildflower boasts red-orange
blooms held erect like a brush of plump bristles
on a stiff, upright stem. Though not truly parasitic,
Indian paintbrush has the distinction of requiring
a compatible host plant to share resources. My
favorite sympathetic pairings are with fringed sage
for a scarlet-silver contrast, and with paperflower
for a hot scarlet and yellow mix. Plants are sometimes sold growing in a pot with blue grama, as both
can be started from seeds together. Paintbrush
blooms brilliantly through spring, and then its slender, pale green leaves recede innocuously into the
background.

Red valerian, Jupiter's beard

BLOOM PERIOD: March to September

HEIGHT AND SPREAD: 1 ft. × 2 ft.

GROWS WELL IN: Dry heat; cold hardy to -30°F

This is a deeper-hued variety of the old garden
favorite that migrated from the Mediterranean
to the Southwest long ago. You'll find it in flower
beds both well tended and neglected. Its rounded
clusters of tiny star flowers are rich coral-pink, but
there are white and pale pink selections as well. It
self-sows abundantly in good garden soil, less so in
unamended native soils with limited water. Hummingbirds and butterflies probe its nectar-rich
blooms, which continue as long as water is available
every week or two during the growing season. I like
to pair it with blue and purple flowers like catmint
and sandpaper verbena.

Indian paintbrush (*Castilleja integra*).

Red valerian (*Centranthus ruber* var. *coccineus*).

Dwarf plumbago, leadwort

BLOOM PERIOD: June to September

HEIGHT AND SPREAD: **8 to 10 in. × 18 to 24 in.**

GROWS WELL IN: **Moderate heat; cold hardy to -25°F**

In middle elevation gardens, this is the go-to ground cover under shade trees. It is slow to wake up in spring so I pair it with grape hyacinth, to provide spring color. The plant's new growth hides the fading hyacinth bulb foliage by mid-May. Five-petaled, China blue flowers cover its small rounded leaves all summer and early autumn, and then the foliage turns red with the first frosts. It spreads to form a thick, weed-resistant cover in shade with deep watering every few weeks. In full sun it takes twice the water and is compact to the point of looking stressed unless rains are ample.

Dwarf plumbago (*Ceratostigma plumbaginoides*). LEFT Cool nights bring red foliage to dwarf plumbago.

Conoclinium dissectum

Mist flower

BLOOM PERIOD: March to July; September to November

HEIGHT AND SPREAD: 1 to 2 ft. × 2 to 3 ft.

GROWS WELL IN: Extreme heat; cold hardy to -20°F in dry soil

Sometimes likened to the bedding ageratums, mist flower is a taller, more robust plant, with finely dissected, soft green leaves and flat clusters of thready lavender-purple flowers that attract a dozen or more species of butterfly to their nectar feast. The color blends easily with other plants and the soft texture is a nice contrast for succulents. Watering every week or two keeps the plant blooming in full sun; water is needed less often in part shade. Be miserly with water in winter and wait until early spring before pruning back old growth.

Mist flower (*Conoclinium dissectum*).

Dalea purpurea

Purple prairie clover

BLOOM PERIOD: June to July

HEIGHT AND SPREAD: 1 to 2 ft. × 2 to 2½ ft.

GROWS WELL IN: Moderate heat; cold hardy to -30°F

A valuable member of the high-plains shortgrass prairie community, prairie clover transitions to garden use quite easily. Its fine-textured foliage and fans of stiff, wiry stems are topped with tight heads of tiny rose-purple flowers. Easily grown from seed, it is most effective massed between ornamental grasses or shrubs where its deep, nitrogen-fixing roots help feed its companions. Inconspicuous until it begins to bloom, when a soft, rosy haze offers a wash of color and nectar for pollinators. Songbirds find the seeds appealing once the flower show ends.

Purple prairie clover (*Dalea purpurea*).

Cheddar pinks

BLOOM PERIOD: April through June

HEIGHT AND SPREAD: 10 in. × 24 in.

GROWS WELL IN: Well-drained soil; moderate heat; cold hardy to -35°F

☀ ☼ ☼ 🌡 ⚙

It's easy to see the kinship between cheddar pinks and carnations, and *Dianthus gratianopolitanis* has probably been cultivated just as long as carnations. In high and intermediate desert gardens it is a winner on several counts. Its evergreen foliage is a dense mat of blue-green, grass-like leaves. Depending on the variety, the flowers stand on limber stems—8 to 10 in. for the pale pink species; 6 in. in the case of dark pink 'Firewitch' or the clustered heads of 'Tiny Rubies'. All are wonderfully fragrant and easily grown in gritty native soil with weekly watering while in bloom, less often to maintain the lush cushions of foliage.

Cheddar pinks (*Dianthus gratianopolitanis*).

Sulfur buckwheat

BLOOM PERIOD: May to July

HEIGHT AND SPREAD: 1 to 2 ft. × 1½ to 2½ ft.

GROWS WELL IN: Dry heat; cold hardy to -30°F

☀ ☼ 🌡 📍 🐝

A robust selection of a widespread wildflower, 'Kannah Creek' is beautiful year-round. Its rosettes of oval leaves are dark green on the upper surface, silver below, and turn reddish in cold weather. In spring, slender flower stalks emerge, topped with open clusters of small, winged yellow flowers, replaced by dark rust seed heads that persist for months after the last flowers fade. Deep soaks every few weeks during the growing season and monthly or less in winter keep plants vigorous. Antelope sage (*Eriogonum jamesii*) is similar, with pale yellow flowers, and there are at least a dozen related species that vary mostly in blooming white or pink and having burgundy-red seed heads.

Sulfur buckwheat (*Eriogonum umbellatum* var. *aureum*).

Euphorbia rigida

Gopher spurge

BLOOM PERIOD: January to May

HEIGHT AND SPREAD: 1 to 3 ft. × 2 to 4 ft.

GROWS WELL IN: Well-drained soil; extreme heat; cold hardy to -20°F in dry soil

The triangular silver-blue leaves spiral up dozens of thick but flexible stems, looking like something a designer might invent rather than the resilient arid Mediterranean émigré that it is. Even more striking are the clusters of fluted chartreuse flower bracts at the tips of the stems. Once they bloom, the stem dies and should be pruned back to the crown of the plant (where next year's stems are emerging). The latex sap causes contact dermatitis in many people, so wearing gloves is highly recommended. Easily grown, it may self-sow in loose, gritty soil with only occasional irrigation.

Gaura lindheimeri

Gaura

BLOOM PERIOD: March to October

HEIGHT AND SPREAD: 2 to 3 ft. × 1½ to 2 ft.

GROWS WELL IN: Extreme heat; cold hardy to -15°F in dry soil

One of the cultivars is called 'Whirling Butterflies' and it's easy to imaging a flight of pink-tinged white butterflies when looking at gaura, especially when the plant is backlit by a rising or setting sun. The tall, slender stems, often infused with red pigment, fan out from the crown and nearly half the stem holds flowers that gracefully shimmer in the breeze. Plants tend to be short-lived, especially when kept constantly moist in heavy soil. In low desert areas, flowering stops June through August. Flea beetles can cut flowering short in the heat at higher elevations, but the blooms resume with shorter days and cooler temperatures in autumn.

Gopher spurge (*Euphorbia rigida*). RIGHT Gaura (*Gaura lindheimeri*).

Trailing gold gazania

BLOOM PERIOD: March to July

HEIGHT AND SPREAD: 10 in. × 24 in.

GROWS WELL IN: Well-drained soil; extreme, reflected heat; cold hardy to at least 15°F in dry soil

☀ ☀

The mat of narrow leaves is densely covered in fine silver hairs, offsetting large yellow daisies that cover the plants when they first come into bloom. Stems trail along the ground, tapping any moisture available with rootlets that form where stems touch the soil. Terracotta gazania (*Gazania krebsiana*) is close kin from arid South Africa, with deep rust-orange flowers. Both will self-sow in the loose, gravelly soil they prefer.

Trailing gold gazania (*Gazania rigens*).

Rock verbena

BLOOM PERIOD: March to June; September to November

HEIGHT AND SPREAD: 1 ft. × 3 ft.

GROWS WELL IN: Well-drained soil; extreme heat; cold hardy to 15°F

☀ ☀ 🐝

This South American transplant lights up low desert gardens with its umbels of purple blossoms in spring and fall, drifts of color that mix well with the yellow daisies common in the Southwest (including perky Sue and desert mule's ears). Considered a potential invasive in Texas, there are several native species you could grow instead, including pale lavender *Glandularia gooddingii,* that tends to burn out in summer heat but self-sows to form a roving colony of new plants each spring. It is cold hardy to 0°F and may be longer-lived where summers are cooler. Prairie verbena (*G. bipinnatifida*) tolerates cold to -30°F, blooming deep lavender spring through fall, whenever enough moisture is available.

Rock verbena (*Glandularia pulchella*).

Maximilian sunflower

BLOOM PERIOD: **September to October**
HEIGHT AND SPREAD: **5 to 7 ft. × 3 to 5 ft.**
GROWS WELL IN: **Heat; cold hardy to -30°F**

☀ ☼ 🌡 📍 🐝

Early in spring, dark green shoots emerge, and as the growing season progresses the dozens of stems grow taller and their leaves grow longer, until fat flower buds begin to develop. Rhizomatous roots are held in check by the water available. As the days grow shorter, large, bright yellow flowers open, until dozens of blooms line the stems—columns of gold along rainwater swales, making fences and walls things of splendor. A spectacular sign of autumn, this long-lived sunflower ends the year hosting songbirds with a feast of seeds, before it's time to cut down the weathered stalks.

Candytuft

BLOOM PERIOD: **March to May**
HEIGHT AND SPREAD: **6 to 10 in. × 18 in.**
GROWS WELL IN: **Heat in full shade; cold hardy to -30°F**

☀ ☁ ☼ 🌡

Candytuft develops a low cushion of small, shiny evergreen leaves obscured by fragrant clusters of snow white flowers in spring. It is a popular perennial in more temperate gardens and is so resilient, adapted to lean, alkaline soils, that it works well in all but the hottest desert areas. In cold desert regions it can be grown in full sun, but the hotter the spot, the more shade is needed to limit water use and keep plants evergreen. In small gardens and courtyards, along paths, spilling over retaining walls, and weaving through boulders, candytuft can be grown with deep watering a few times a month once well established.

Candytuft (*Iberis sempervirens*). LEFT Maximilian sunflower (*Helianthus maximiliani*).

'New Gold' lantana

BLOOM PERIOD: **March through September**

HEIGHT AND SPREAD: **1 to 2 ft. × 2 to 3 ft.**

GROWS WELL IN: **Extreme heat; evergreen to 25°F, roots survive to 10°F**

Because of its long and brilliant blooming season, attractive (though abrasive) foliage, and ability to thrive under harsh growing conditions, there are many hybrids and cultivars of lantana. 'New Gold', a nearly sterile hybrid with butter-yellow flowers, continues to bloom despite extreme desert heat and produces few seeds, limiting its potential for invasiveness. It remains evergreen, needing only light pruning to remove frosted tips where winters are mild, freezes to the roots in colder areas, and in extreme winter areas is planted as an annual. Butterflies and hummingbirds find the nectar irresistible.

'New Gold' lantana (*Lantana* 'New Gold').

Gayfeather

BLOOM PERIOD: **September**

HEIGHT AND SPREAD: **1½ to 2 ft. × 2 to 3 ft.**

GROWS WELL IN: **Lean, well-drained soil; intermittent spikes above 100°F; cold hardy to -30°F in dry soil**

In early spring, gayfeather's tuft of leaves emerges from carrot-like, succulent deep roots, looking like a clump of dark green, wide-bladed grass. It conserves resources and photosynthesizes through much of the growing season in this innocuous manner. As the days begin to shorten, the leafy flower stems quickly lengthen, ending in 6- to 12-in. spikes of thready purple flowers. A seedling may produce only one or two stems, while a well-established 5-year-old plant in lean, well-drained soil may have dozens of flower spikes. Infrequent deep watering produces the best display.

Gayfeather (*Liatris punctata*).

Blackfoot daisy

BLOOM PERIOD: **April to October**

HEIGHT AND SPREAD: **1 ft. × 1½ to 2 ft.**

GROWS WELL IN: **Well-drained soil; extreme heat; cold hardy to -20°F**

Across the Southwest, especially after a wet winter, the deserts and adjacent foothills will be strewn with tidy bouquets of yellow-centered white daisies. Blackfoot daisy is one of several wildflowers that look well tended with absolutely no care from the gardener. It takes weeks of triple digit temperatures to end its flower show, and with occasional deep watering or good summer monsoons breaking the heat, it will start blooming afresh. Too much water too often will produce floppy growth and shorten its lifespan. Benign neglect suits blackfoot daisy just fine.

Blackfoot daisy (*Melampodium leucanthum*).

Wild four o'clock

BLOOM PERIOD: **April to October**

HEIGHT AND SPREAD: **1 ft. × 2 to 4 ft.**

GROWS WELL IN: **Well-drained soil; dry heat; cold hardy to -30°F in dry soil**

 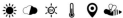

An easy-care ground cover with lush, heart-shaped leaves on thick, sprawling stems. Prolific dark pink, tubular flowers open every afternoon, attracting sphinx moths and hummingbirds. Plants bloom for months with deep watering every few weeks at most. At the end of the season, after frost, stems dry and detach from the succulent roots, making cleanup simple and fast. Wet soil in winter is the undoing of wild four o'clock.

Wild four o'clock (*Mirabilis multiflora*).

White tufted evening primrose

BLOOM PERIOD: February through October

HEIGHT AND SPREAD: 1 ft. × 2 ft.

GROWS WELL IN: Extreme heat; cold hardy to -20°F

The 3-in. flowers, with silken, cupped white petals, nestle in rosettes of velvet-soft, long, narrow pale green leaves with lightly notched margins. Flowers fade to pink, finished after a day's heat, but new flowers open every evening to lure the sphinx moths that pollinate them. The flowers glow in moonlight, making them ideal for planting near pathways and around patios. Yellow evening primrose (*Oenothera macrocarpa*) is similar, except the leaves are glossy green and the spring-blooming flowers are clear yellow, fading to salmon-orange, with roots hardy to -30°F.

White tufted evening primrose (*Oenothera caespitosa*).

Sand penstemon, bush penstemon

BLOOM PERIOD: April to June, August to October

HEIGHT AND SPREAD: 1 to 2 ft. × 2 to 3 ft.

GROWS WELL IN: Well-drained soil; extreme heat; cold hardy to -30°F in dry soil

If you have walked up an arroyo or down a city street, and seen a billowing mound of thousands of pale pink, orchid-like flowers with deeper rose reverse, you've seen sand penstemon in its glory. You may have walked past it a thousand times when not in bloom, as its wiry stems and tiny leaves are quite inconspicuous. This is by far the longest-lived species of *Penstemon*; 50 years or more is possible for plants growing in fast-draining soil and intense sun and heat, and receiving soaking surges of water once a month or less while in bloom.

Sand penstemon (*Penstemon ambiguus*).

Rock penstemon

BLOOM PERIOD: April to June

HEIGHT AND SPREAD: 2 to 3 ft. × 3 to 4 ft.

GROWS WELL IN: Well-drained soil; extreme heat; cold hardy to -15°F

There are more than a dozen red-flowering penstemon, all of them worth trying. They bloom at slightly different times, have different foliage and different shades of tubular red flowers, but they all guarantee hummingbird activity. A sampling includes rock penstemon, shrubby with small leaves and scarlet flowers on wand-like stems; pineleaf penstemon (*Penstemon pinifolius*), a low cushion of needle-like leaves and flowers ranging from deep red to yellow, depending on variety; Eaton's penstemon (*P. eatoni*), with glossy, spoon-shaped leaves and scarlet flowers on 2-ft. stems; and cardinal penstemon (*P. cardinalis*), with deep garnet-red flowers on 2½-ft. stems above a rosette of crisp, oval leaves.

Rock penstemon (*Penstemon baccharifolius*). RIGHT Rocky Mountain penstemon (*Penstemon strictus*).

Colorado narrowleafed penstemon

BLOOM PERIOD: April to August

HEIGHT AND SPREAD: 8 to 10 in. × 12 to 18 in.

GROWS WELL IN: Well-drained soil; heat in part shade; cold hardy to -25°F

There are nearly as many blue-purple penstemons as there are red species, all adapted to a range of elevations. Some of the best-adapted selections for both heat and cold are Colorado narrowleafed penstemon, with short spikes of tubular, pale lavender-blue flowers emerging from a mat of fine, needle-like, silver leaves. In mild winters the leaves are evergreen, and when summer rain cools the air, plants will bloom through summer. 'Silverton' is an excellent selection. The other blue treasure is Rocky Mountain penstemon (*Penstemon strictus*), with a mat of glossy, dark green leaves and 18-in. spikes of violet-purple flowers in May and June.

Palmer penstemon

BLOOM PERIOD: **April to May**

HEIGHT AND SPREAD: **2 to 4 ft. × 1 to 2 ft.**

GROWS WELL IN: **Well-drained soil; extreme heat; cold hardy to -30°F**

☀ ☀ ☀ 🌡 ◉ ✿ 🐝▸

Of the many penstemons with pink flowers, one of the easiest to grow from seeds is Palmer penstemon, the tallest and only fragrant choice in this large genus. Its crisp, angular leaves are pale blue and the flowers are large and inflated, pale pink on rigid upright stems. Longer-lived when watered sparingly and not allowed to go to seed. Both conditions also apply to canyon penstemon (*Penstemon pseudospectabilis*), whose flowers are deep rose-pink on stems that are 2½ ft. tall; its leaves are dark blue-green blushed pink in full sun.

Parry's penstemon

BLOOM PERIOD: **February to April**

HEIGHT AND SPREAD: **2 to 4 ft. tall × 1 to 2 ft. wide**

GROWS WELL IN: **Well-drained soil; extreme heat; cold hardy to -10°F for brief periods**

☀ ☀ ☀ ◉ 🐝▸

You know it's spring in low desert gardens when you see masses of sunrise-pink wildflowers swaying in the breeze. Parry's penstemon has slender, lance-shaped pale green leaves and strong vertical stems supporting tubular flowers in a range of pink shades. The nectar-rich blooms are abuzz with hummingbirds as long as the flower show continues. While removing most of the seed stalks may prolong the lifespan of individual plants, allowing some plants to go to seed can build up a reserve in the soil and create spectacular displays—especially after wet winters.

Palmer penstemon (*Penstemon palmeri*).

Parry's penstemon (*Penstemon parryi*).

Fameflower

BLOOM PERIOD: June to September

HEIGHT AND SPREAD: 10 in. × 6 in.

GROWS WELL IN: Well-drained soil; extreme heat with afternoon shade; cold hardy to -30°F

☀ ☼ 🌡 📍

This little gem is distinctive for several reasons. Its leaves look like small tufts of succulent grass that sprout wiry gold flower stems topped with 1-in., translucent rose-pink flowers. New flowers open every afternoon through the summer, and seem to float above ground. In the fall, when days become shorter but well before frost, the plant shrivels and the show is over. Take care when cleaning up, as fameflower's succulent stem, not the root system, is what overwinters. It self-sows abundantly, so if you do mistakenly remove old plants, there will likely be lots of seedlings to replace them in spring.

Fameflower (*Phemeranthus calycinus*).

Santa Fe phlox

BLOOM PERIOD: June to September

HEIGHT AND SPREAD: 1 ft. × 1 to 1½ ft.

GROWS WELL IN: Moderate heat; cold hardy to -30°F

☀ ☼ 🌡 📍 🐝▸

There are many wonderful species and cultivars of phlox, but they need frequent watering and protection from intense sunlight and wind in the arid Southwest. Although it grows sporadically from West Texas through Arizona, the New Mexico city of Santa Fe claims title to *Phlox nana*, for its resilience in a harsh climate. The small, narrow leaves densely cover wiry stems that form a flat mound—almost hidden by deep pink, star-shaped flowers much of the summer. It is perfect along pathways, in rockeries, and in open areas between shrubs in gardens above 5000 ft. in elevation, with deep watering monthly.

Santa Fe phlox (*Phlox nana*).

Paperflower

BLOOM PERIOD: February to September

HEIGHT AND SPREAD: 1 to 2 ft. × 1 to 2 ft.

GROWS WELL IN: Well-drained soil; extreme heat; cold hardy to -20°F

Clusters of small, bright yellow daisies cover the silver-green leaves and stems on compact mounded plants, gradually fading to papery tan. Although individual plants are short-lived, in gritty native soils, plants self-sow abundantly, creating brilliant washes of color—especially eye-catching contrasting trailing dalea or lavender in spring, or black dalea in autumn. Cut plants back to the basal leaves once their seeds disperse, as part of a seasonal cleanup.

Paperflower (*Psilostrophe tagetina*).

Mexican petunia

BLOOM PERIOD: April to October

HEIGHT AND SPREAD: 1 to 2 ft. × 1 to 2 ft.

GROWS WELL IN: Extreme heat in part shade; root hardy to 15°F

Striking a perfect balance between deep violet-purple flowers and long, narrow, dark green leaves is this elegant plant, suited to shaded garden spots where the soil stays moist. Given good soil and weekly watering during 100°F weather, this plant blooms prolifically all summer. 'Katie', 'Rosa', and 'Blanca' are blue, pink, and white cultivars (respectively) of a dwarf selection that stays a foot tall. This is an ideal choice for a lush oasis spot in a courtyard surrounding a small water feature. It can be used as an annual in colder areas.

Mexican petunia (*Ruellia brittoniana*).

Mexican red sage

BLOOM PERIOD: July to October

HEIGHT AND SPREAD: 2½ to 3 ft. tall × 1½ to 2 ft. wide

GROWS WELL IN: Lean, well-drained soil; extreme heat; cold hardy to -10°F in dry soil

Of the many red salvias, Mexican red sage is my favorite. From its clumps of heart-shaped, scalloped-edge, pale green leaves, to its strong, arching stems, to its scarlet-lipped flowers that seem to glow from within, there is much to admire about this plant. Hummingbirds have their own opinions and judging from the constant stream of nectar-sipping birds, I'd say we agree. 'Vermilion Bluffs' is a selection thought to be more cold tolerant than the species. Water it twice monthly while actively growing, weekly while in bloom, and remove the old flower stems down to the ground in spring.

Meadow sage

BLOOM PERIOD: April to June

HEIGHT AND SPREAD: 1 to 2 ft. × 1 to 2 ft.

GROWS WELL IN: Moderate heat; roots are cold hardy to -30°F

There are several blue salvias that work well in southwestern gardens. From a basal clump of narrow, crinkled gray-green leaves, slender stems emerge, lined with pairs of smaller leaves. By midspring, deep blue flower spikes lure butterflies and bumble bees to their nectar. Deep watering monthly until flower stems emerge, then twice a week to maintain blooming in lean native soil, nets more color on shorter, sturdier plants. Blue sage or pitcher sage (*Salvia azurea* var. *grandiflora*) blooms in late summer, with resplendent spikes of sky-blue flowers on stems 3 ft. and taller. Other smaller options that bloom spring into summer with weekly watering include meadow sage cultivars 'East Friesland' (sky blue) and 'Caradonna' (violet) as well as *S.* ×*sylvestris* 'Blue Queen' (rich blue) and 'Rose Queen' (wine).

Mexican red sage (*Salvia darcyi*). RIGHT Meadow sage (*Salvia nemorosa* 'May Night').

'Fireworks' goldenrod

BLOOM PERIOD: **August to October**

HEIGHT AND SPREAD: **2½ to 3 ft. × 3 to 4 ft.**

GROWS WELL IN: **Moderate heat in shade; cold hardy to -30°F**

There are several cultivars and hybrids of soligado that are spectacular in bloom and particularly useful in partly shaded rainwater basins, in intermediate and high desert gardens. Pollinated by bees and butterflies, goldenrods don't deserve their reputation as allergy triggers. 'Fireworks' has tall, leafy stems topped with sprays of tiny yellow flowers—an explosion of color when combined with ornamental grasses. More compact and drought tolerant *Soligado* 'Little Lemon' has leafy stems 14 in. tall, with plants spreading 18 in. wide. Its flowers are tapered pale yellow spikes, blooming in summer and again in autumn if stems are cut back to basal leaves after the initial flush of color wanes.

'Fireworks' goldenrod (*Soligado rugosa* 'Fireworks').

Desert globemallow

BLOOM PERIOD: February to November

HEIGHT AND SPREAD: 1½ to 2 ft. × 2 to 3 ft.

GROWS WELL IN: Well-drained soil; extreme heat; cold hardy to -20°F in dry soil

One of the first wildflowers to light up the desert in spring, with its abundant, creamy orange flowers; contrasting woolly, pale green stems; and 3-lobed, scalloped leaves. Of the many globemallows, this is the most prolific in bloom, and easiest to establish. Grown from seed, the color ranges from clear pink to salmon and coppery orange, and a beauty with grenadine-coral flowers called 'Louis Hamilton' is available. Watering deeply but infrequently and cutting plants back periodically keeps them from becoming rangy. Since the tiny hairs that help shade the leaves and stems can be an irritant, wear gloves when pruning.

Desert globemallow (*Sphaeralcea ambigua*).

Mt. Lemmon marigold, Mexican marigold

BLOOM PERIOD: October to November; February to March

HEIGHT AND SPREAD: 2 to 4 ft. × 3 to 5 ft.

GROWS WELL IN: Extreme heat with light shade; root hardy to 5°F

When most other perennials are dormant, this plant's lush, finely divided, dark evergreen leaves on sprawling stems are nearly obscured by orange-centered, golden yellow daisies. It's at its best in intermediate deserts, where summers are hot but less intense than Phoenix, and winters are cool but less extreme than Albuquerque. Nicely aromatic, the oils that keep wildlife at bay can cause contact dermatitis in gardeners. Use care (and gloves) when cutting it back to induce branching new growth and more intense flowering.

Mt. Lemmon marigold (*Tagetes lemmonii*).

Angelita daisy

BLOOM PERIOD: February to June; August to November

HEIGHT AND SPREAD: 1 ft. × 1 ft.

GROWS WELL IN: Extreme heat; leaves die back at 15°F, root hardy to -20°F

This hard-working little plant blooms almost constantly in the warm-winter low desert, and April to October in cold desert gardens. It is a graceful plant, with tufts of grassy dark green leaves and showy yellow daisies on slender, leafless stems that come in waves, as long as extreme heat and hard freezes allow. Plants self-sow easily and small colonies tend to develop, adding to the colorful display. Perky Sue (*Tetraneuris scaposa*) is similar, distinct in having silver foliage. Removing the spent stems when blooming slows can spur another round of fresh buds.

Angelita daisy (*Tetraneuris acaulis*).

Wall germander

BLOOM PERIOD: May through August

HEIGHT AND SPREAD: 1 ft. × 2 to 3 ft.

GROWS WELL IN: Extreme heat in part shade; cold hardy to -15°F

Wall germander has small evergreen leaves that are dark gray-green, spade-shaped, and densely cover its short stems. It root-sprouts close to the crown, making a compact mound that roots along as it grows wider. Short spikes of rose-pink mint flowers crown the plants in summer. Creeping germander (*Teucrium chamaedrys* var. *prostratum*) is a low, spreading form with shiny green leaves and similar rose-pink flower spikes. Greek germander (*T. capitatum* ssp. *Majoricum*—sometimes sold as *T. aroanium* or *T. cossonii*) has flat clusters of tiny pink flowers smothering a mat of sweet-scented evergray leaves in spring and summer.

Creeping germander (*Teucrium chamaedrys* var. *prostratum*).

Dogweed, wild marigold

BLOOM PERIOD: April through October

HEIGHT AND SPREAD: 6 to 8 in. × 10 to 12 in.

GROWS WELL IN: Well-drained soil; extreme heat; cold hardy to -25°F in dry soil

☀ ☼ ◉ 🐝▸

This pretty little yellow daisy suffers from a bad reputation. I know it from years of handling it, leading tours through stands of it, and planting it in many gardens. I've read descriptions calling it malodorous and prickly. It is neither. It has a faint resinous scent and tiny leaves clustered like soft bristles along its stems, in a compact dark green cushion. It thrives in sandy and rocky native soil, with 6 in. of rain or several thorough waterings a year when in bloom.

Dogweed (*Thymophylla acerosa*).

Sandpaper verbena

BLOOM PERIOD: April to October

HEIGHT AND SPREAD: 1 ft. × 2 to 3 ft.

GROWS WELL IN: Extreme heat; cold hardy to 5°F in dry soil

☀ ☼ 🐝▸

The thistle-like leaves of this fast-spreading heat-lover are scratchy to touch; the flat clusters of tiny purple flowers, like velvet. There are two main color variations: unnamed deep royal purple and pale lavender 'Polaris'. Both are easy to find, but for our intense sunlight I love to mix the deep purple with prairie zinnia or angelita daisy, the yellow-purple combination is a traffic stopper. Sandpaper verbena has a tendency to roam. It spreads by rhizomes; the original plant dies, replaced by half a dozen or more offshoots a few feet from the original.

Sandpaper verbena (*Verbena rigida*).

Desert mule's ears

BLOOM PERIOD: May to July

HEIGHT AND SPREAD: 1 to 2 ft. × 2 to 3 ft.

GROWS WELL IN: Well-drained soil; extreme heat; cold hardy to -25°F in dry soil

☀ ☼ ♀ ⚙ 🐝

I first saw the winter skeleton of mule's ears: a sprawling clump of wiry white stems, each tipped with a domed, chocolate-brown seedpod. I collected seeds and grew it the following spring; to my surprise, it turned out to be a long-lived perennial sunflower, with 3-in. yellow flowers that smelled deliciously like vanilla. Needless to say, I've been in love ever since and recommend it to anyone with a dry patch of ground in blazing sun, especially anyone who likes to feed butterflies and songbirds, as the nectar and seeds attract both. Deep monthly watering will keep plants healthy.

Desert mule's ears (*Wyethia scabra*).

Prairie zinnia

BLOOM PERIOD: May through October

HEIGHT AND SPREAD: 4 to 10 in. × 8 to 18 in.

GROWS WELL IN: Well-drained soil; extreme heat; cold hardy to -30°F

☀ ☼ 🌡 ♀ 🐝

This is a wonderful ground cover for lean native soils, spreading by rhizomes to create colonies sometimes 6 to 10 ft. across. The fine grassy leaves are pale green, turning straw-colored in winter, and are hidden by 1-in. yellow flowers with yellow or orange centers most of the growing season. Thoroughly soaking plants once a month while in bloom is best. Too much water, especially in heavy clay, will slow growth and can be deadly. Use it to fill seams in flagstone paving, border paths and patios, and to soften the strong personalities of succulents.

Prairie zinnia (*Zinnia grandiflora*).

BULBS AND EPHEMERALS

Allium species

Chives

BLOOM PERIOD: June through July

HEIGHT AND SPREAD: 12 in. × 6 to 12 in.

GROWS WELL IN: Moderate heat; root hardy to at least -30°F

☀ ◑ ⬤ ⚙ 🌡 🐝

Chives (*Allium schoenoprasum*) have grassy leaves and slender stems 12 in. tall, with tight oval clusters of purple flowers in June and July. Garlic chives (*A. tuberosum*) self-sow readily in the shade, forming a lush, grassy ground cover with flat umbels of white flowers in summer. Smell oniony and can be used as chives. *A. schubertii* is one of the most heat-tolerant species, with wide, strap-like basal leaves and strong stems 12 to 24 in. tall, bearing a cluster of tiny rose-pink flowers on flower stems of varied lengths. Each main stem resembles a rose-pink sparkler—an appropriate descriptor, as it blooms in July.

Chives (*Allium schoenoprasum*). RIGHT Rain lily (*Cooperia pedunculata*).

Cooperia pedunculata

Rain lily

BLOOM PERIOD: March to August

HEIGHT AND SPREAD: 8 to 12 in. × 4 to 6 in.

GROWS WELL IN: Extreme heat; cold hardy to -5°F

☀ ☀ ◉ ☀ 🐝

Rain lily has grassy blue-green leaves that sprout after a soaking rain, closely followed by fragrant white flowers, 3 petals held by 3 sepals that are funnel-like early in the evening but flared wide open by the following midday. Pink *Zephyranthes grandiflora*, white *Z. candida*, and yellow *Z. citrina* are Central and South American rain lilies that survive the freezing air temperatures, as long as the bulbs are insulated with mulch. Occasional soaking with a hose or drip irrigation will simulate rain and wake up sleeping bulbs, but consistently moist soil can result in rot, especially when the soil is cold.

Crinum

BLOOM PERIOD: May to June

HEIGHT AND SPREAD: 2 to 3 ft. × 1 to 2 ft.

GROWS WELL IN: Moist heat; cold hardy to -5°F

Clumps of wide, strappy leaves give rise to stout stems holding several trumpet-shaped, fragrant flowers with succulent white or pink petals, striped with deeper rose. There are many cultivars of this South African wetland native. In the desert, it is a showy accent plant for the rare spot where the soil is rich in organic matter and can be kept moist during the late spring bloom time. Avoid disturbing the bulb once it is established, as it can take two or more years to flowers after it is transplanted.

Freesia

BLOOM PERIOD: April to May

HEIGHT AND SPREAD: 1 to 1½ ft. tall × 1 ft. wide

GROWS WELL IN: Extreme heat with light shade; cold hardy to 20°F

A favorite cut flower, freesia is also an easily grown garden flower in warm desert areas, but more demanding when grown in pots and overwintered indoors. South African in origin, the grassy leaf blades sprout first, quickly followed by sprawling slender stems that bear the upward-facing tubular flowers. The fragrant sprays can be lavender, pink to wine purple, orange, yellow, or white; new buds unfold for more than a month. Reduce watering and let the leaves dry naturally to restore the corms before dormancy.

Crinum (*Crinum bulbisperum*).

Freesia (*Freesia* cultivar).

Bearded and hybrid iris

BLOOM PERIOD: April and May

HEIGHT AND SPREAD: 18 to 30 in. × 12 in.

GROWS WELL IN: Extreme heat; root hardy to -30°F in dry soil

☀ ☼ 🌡 ⚙ 🐝

Aptly named for the Greek goddess of the rainbow, iris displays large flowers with 3 petals held upward and 3 that drape downward; several elegant blooms gracing each sturdy stem. Boasting easy cultivation and flowers of stately form and brilliant colors, bearded and arilbred irises (and their numerous variations) both originated in Middle Eastern desert areas. They require well-drained soil that is dry in summer when the plants sink into dormancy. Arilbreds tolerate low desert heat the best, but the rhizomes of both are extremely cold hardy. Their blade-like leaves wither by midsummer, so clump them between summer blooming plants like lavender and salvia to fill the gaps after the spring frenzy is over. Siberian irises prefer cooler temperatures or afternoon shade, where they are a good choice for rainwater swales and their slender leaves remain attractive all season.

TOP Siberian iris (*Iris sibirica*). BOTTOM Bearded iris (*Iris germanica* hybrid).

Grape hyacinth

BLOOM PERIOD: March to April

HEIGHT AND SPREAD: 6 to 8 in. × 10 to 12 in.

GROWS WELL IN: Extreme heat in shade; root hardy to -30°F

One of the easiest of the small spring-blooming bulbs, grape hyacinth has grassy leaves that appear in late summer and remain green through winter with occasional watering. Lightly fragrant, small purple flowers are clustered like bunches of tiny grapes at the ends of slender stems, a wash of color early in the season. There are several varieties that are paler blue in color or have larger and double-frilled flowers, but this species is the most resilient and reliable. No need to fix what's already working exceptionally well. Bulbs will multiply and plants also increase by seed, but only where water is available.

Grape hyacinth (*Muscari armeniacum*).

Daffodil

BLOOM PERIOD: **February to April**

HEIGHT AND SPREAD: **8 to 18 in. × 10 to 12 in.**

GROWS WELL IN: **Mild temperatures; avoid heat; needs winter cold to flower**

A popular seasonal cut flower and cheery sign that winter is over, daffodils come in 13 divisions. Criteria for divisions are based on size and number of flowers per stem, flower shapes (such as trumpet, large-cupped, short-cupped, and cyclamineus), and species types that are at least in theory closer to pre-cultivated forms. Many *Narcissus* selections require a period of deep cold to trigger flowering. As a group, the tazetta types are best for the Southwest, as they need less cold. Species types tazetta, triandrus, and jonquilla have clusters of smaller flowers on shorter stems that hold up well in erratic spring weather.

Tulip

BLOOM PERIOD: **March to April**

HEIGHT AND SPREAD: **4 to 24 in. × 4 to 10 in.**

GROWS WELL IN: **Mild temperatures; avoid heat; needs winter cold to flower**

Tulips originated in arid countries surrounding the Mediterranean, a locally favored wildflower. Introduced to Europe, they became the rage, financial as well as horticultural, as family fortunes were traded for single bulbs. The tough little wildflowers became hothouse divas, subject to viruses that weakened the plant, but caused distortions of petal shape and color that made them more valuable than gold. There's a lesson to be learned. For the Southwest, some of the best options are species tulips, including *Tulipa clusiana*, *T. saxatilis*, and *T. sylvestris*, that do quite well in our region, requiring no chilling or other pampering, weathering spring winds and sleeping through summer's heat.

Daffodil (*Narcissus* cultivar). RIGHT Tulip (*Tulipa clusiana* cultivar).

Angelonia angustifolia

Angelonia, summer snapdragon

BLOOM PERIOD: April through October

HEIGHT AND SPREAD: 12 to 18 in. × 10 to 12 in.

GROWS WELL IN: Extreme heat; root hardy to 25°F

☀ ☀ ☀ 🐝▸

This Mexican and Caribbean kin to native penstemon needs heat to bloom well, so it is a good option for large color pots. Spikes of tubular flowers in shades of white, pink, and purple, many lightly fragrant, are nicely balanced by oblong dark green leaves. A summer-long nectar source for hummingbirds, angelonia is remarkably drought tolerant considering its prolific flowering.

Baileya multiradiata

Desert marigold

BLOOM PERIOD: March to November

HEIGHT AND SPREAD: 1 ft. × 1 to 1½ ft.

GROWS WELL IN: Extreme heat; seedlings are cold hardy to -25°F

☀ ☀ ◉ 🐝▸

This is a plant not easy to categorize as annual, biennial, or short-lived perennial. Like many desert survivors, it is an opportunist. After even mediocre summer rains, if you look closely, you'll see tiny clusters of woolly white leaves dotting the ground. Those foliage rosettes of desert marigold must be exposed to enough hours of sunlight or cold to begin forming flower buds. Plants then flower profusely with hundreds of 2-in. yellow daisies if the soil retains a bit of moisture, less so when it is dry. A light layer of stone mulch aids in the yearly process.

Desert marigold (*Baileya multiradiata*). LEFT Angelonia (*Angelonia angustifolia*).

Calibrachoa

BLOOM PERIOD: **May to October**

HEIGHT AND SPREAD: **1 ft. × 2 ft.**

GROWS WELL IN: **Extreme heat; tolerates light frost**

☀ ☀ ☀

If you are a fan of petunias but find them to be more demanding than you'd like, try calibrachoa. It has smaller single and double trumpet-shaped flowers in all the petunia shades, including veined and bicolors, plus terracotta and violet-blue. In flower trials, it blooms longer in the heat, and the 'Million Bells' Series shows exceptional tolerance of alkaline soil. Marketed for hanging baskets (which are really not practical here given the extremely low humidity and strong winds), calibrachoa has similar gorgeous effect cascading over the rim of patio pots and raised beds.

Ornamental pepper

BLOOM PERIOD: **July through October**

HEIGHT AND SPREAD: **1 to 2 ft. × 1 to 2 ft.**

GROWS WELL IN: **Extreme heat; tolerates light frost**

☀ ☀

Maybe it's because we live in the land of salsa, hot food, and festive music that I find ornamental peppers particularly apt here. They grow easily with less water than many annuals do, their rich green leaves are handsome, and though their flowers aren't showy, the clusters of multicolored peppers light up beds and pots, lasting longer than most flowers. 'Basket of Fire' fruits look like red and orange flames and are also fiery on the tongue, but 'Tangerine Dream', 'Sangria', and 'Black Pearl' are mild. Pick young peppers to use as garnish and pickles, and leave others to mature on the plants for show.

Calibrachoa (*Calibrachoa* cultivar).

Ornamental pepper (*Capsicum annuum*).

Blanket flower, firewheel

BLOOM PERIOD: **May through October**

HEIGHT AND SPREAD: **1 to 2 ft. × 1 to 2 ft.**

GROWS WELL IN: **Extreme heat; tolerates frost to 25°F**

The cultivars of gaillardia are bred from western wild-flowers to have increased flower size, a wide range of variations on the natural red and yellow color, and flower forms that are novel. *Gaillardia* ×*grandiflora* and varieties are described as perennial, but tend to be short-lived, especially when the soil is too wet in winter cold or summer heat. Fun new hybrids seem to appear every spring, including 'Fanfare', with fluted ray petals—a ring of little red trumpets with yellow tips; 'Oranges and Lemons' produces flowers that are a rich pumpkin-gold with yellow tips, and 'Summer Kiss' blooms are apricot with a darker center. All give a long season of color when deadheaded and watered occasionally.

Blanket flower (*Gaillardia* hybrid).

Fleabane daisies

BLOOM PERIOD: **Spring and summer**

HEIGHT AND SPREAD: **6 to 12 in. × 10 to 16 in.**

GROWS WELL IN: **Any soil, even sticky clay; tolerates light frost and heat**

There are species of fleabane daisy native to most biomes in the Southwest. Most are similar in appearance and behavior. Plants start as a cluster of small, fuzzy leaves. A bouquet of soft stems emerges, quickly smothered in small white daisies with many fine ray petals surrounding a yellow disc. The petals are typically white, but are sometimes tinged deep pink. Millions of tiny seeds are produced, but since plants are small and seasonal they never become weedy. After a wet winter or generous summer monsoons, plants are abundant. When rain is scant, fleabane daisies may be scarce.

Fleabane daisies (*Erigeron* species).

Gold poppy

BLOOM PERIOD: March to May

HEIGHT AND SPREAD: 4 to 6 in. × 4 to 6 in.

GROWS WELL IN: Moderate heat of springtime; dies out in summer

This is the native cousin of California poppy which is also an excellent spring bloomer, but I prefer the smaller, unimproved gold poppy for a wash of rich color after a wet winter. Wet by our standards is a few good rains or wet snows or irrigations, just enough to tease the seeds out of dormancy. The lacy, pale green, basal leaves appear early, and the satiny cupped flowers soon follow. The show lasts until the soil dries out or triple-digit heat causes plants to set seed and quietly disappear.

Gold poppy (*Eschscholzia mexicana*).

Sunflower

BLOOM PERIOD: July to October

HEIGHT AND SPREAD: 3 to 6 ft. × 2 to 5 ft.

GROWS WELL IN: Extreme heat; seedlings tolerate frost

The Russians first developed the dinner plate–sized, single-flowered form cultivated nearly worldwide for seeds and oil, but the common sunflower has been a food and dye plant in the Southwest since prehistoric times. Whether you simply let the wildflower self-sow in rainwater swales and basins, or cultivate the modern varieties for their beauty in the garden, as a cut flower, or for birdseed, this bold, colorful annual deserves a place in the sun and the modest amount of water required to grow it. Regardless of the selection, the ray flowers—in colors from pale yellow to gold to bronzy orange—track the sun across the sky each day in homage to the source of their energy.

Sunflower (*Helianthus annuus*).

Sweet potato vine

HEIGHT AND SPREAD: **1 ft. × 2 to 3 ft.**

GROWS WELL IN: **Extreme heat; frost tender**

This colorful plant is grown for its foliage, as the ornamental forms rarely flower. Densely leafy on short, vining stems, there are several selections, including 'Illusion Emerald Lace' and 'Sidekick Lime' (with chartreuse leaves), and 'Midnight Lace' and 'Raven' (with deep purple foliage). The lush, bold colors anchor patio pot combinations. The tuberous roots are perennial in mild winter areas, and can be lifted and stored indoors in bags of vermiculite to avoid winter cold and persistent frosts.

Flowering tobacco

BLOOM PERIOD: **June to October**

HEIGHT AND SPREAD: **1 to 2 ft. × 1 ft.**

GROWS WELL IN: **Heat; frost tender**

I confess to a weakness for this plant, as the only gardening I remember my mother doing each spring was planting *Nicotiana* under our bedroom windows for its nighttime fragrance. Its scent is the memory of happy childhood. The broad-leaved rosettes are pale green and fuzzy, like mini tobacco, and the large, star-shaped flowers are available in a rainbow of colors, from white and pale yellow to deep purple. It attracts hummingbirds and sphinx moths, and to avoid hornworm infestations and viruses, keep it away from your tomatoes and eggplants.

Sweet potato vine (*Ipomoea batatas*). RIGHT Flowering tobacco (*Nicotiana alata*).

Desert bluebells

BLOOM PERIOD: **February to April**

HEIGHT AND SPREAD: **8 to 12 in. × 10 to 16 in.**

GROWS WELL IN: **Cooler spring temperatures; well-drained soil**

This showy plant carpets the Sonoran and Mojave deserts at the end of winters with generous rain. Often in close company with Mexican gold poppies, the two make a brilliant display worthy of imitating in our gardens. The intense, bell-shaped, cobalt-blue blossoms stand above a tidy mat of rounded, deep green leaves. Scratching the seeds into loose, sandy, or gritty soil in early winter and following up with a few thorough soakings if rainfall is scant will produce the best results. Once temperatures are consistently above 80°F, desert bluebells stop flowering and ripen seeds for next year's display.

Desert bluebells (*Phacelia campanularia*).

Purslane

BLOOM PERIOD: **May to September**

HEIGHT AND SPREAD: **4 to 6 in. × 12 to 18 in.**

GROWS WELL IN: **Extreme heat; frost tender**

The low, spreading succulent weed that germinates with the first monsoon rains is an unappreciated edible plant—rich in omega-3 fatty acids, vitamins C and A, and known as *verdolaga* in Latin America. It adds tangy flavor, whether the succulent stems and small, plump leaves are stir-fried, steamed, or added to soups and salads as a summer green. Colorful selections may be less nutritious, as they are bred for larger flowers and a wide color range, not for taste, so perhaps the best strategy is to eat your weeds and enjoy the summer color of ornamental selections.

Nasturtium

BLOOM PERIOD: **May to June and October to November in hottest areas; May to October in cooler areas**

HEIGHT AND SPREAD: **1 to 2 ft. × 2 to 4 ft.**

GROWS WELL IN: **Dry heat in part shade, full sun at higher elevations; prefers lean, well-drained soil**

This old garden favorite from the mountains of Central and South America will appeal to you if you love intense flower color, like to graze your flower garden, or want your water use to produce as much as possible. The nearly round, blue-green leaves on trailing stems are peppery tasting in salads, as are the flower buds and open blossoms. The flowers have deep throats and wide ruffled faces in bright colors, from yellow and rusty orange to vermillion and magenta. Float a few blossoms and leaves on gazpacho in summer to spark a heat-dulled appetite. Sow seeds in pots in April or early May.

Purslane (*Portulaca oleracea* cultivar). RIGHT Nasturtium (*Tropaeolum majus*).

GRASSES

Achnatherum hymenoides

Indian ricegrass

BLOOM PERIOD: **February to April**

HEIGHT AND SPREAD: **1 to 2 ft. × 1 ft.**

GROWS WELL IN: **Well-drained soil in extreme heat and cold to -30°F**

☀ ☼ ⚲ ❄ 🐝▸

Indian ricegrass is one of the most desert-adapted grasses, avoiding intense heat by growing, blooming, and seeding in spring, then going dormant through summer. Its wiry leaves are pale sage-green by late January where winter is mild, and by March in the coldest winter areas. It rapidly forms a lacy crown of flowers, and by June or July it has produced its nutritious seeds and turned to pale platinum straw. When late summer rain is abundant, it will green up again in autumn. 'Star Lake' is a cultivar that germinates more easily. Silver spikegrass (*Achnatherum calamagrostis*) is a more robust species from the mountains near the Mediterranean Sea, with showy seed plumes that sway in the breeze. Not as tolerant of low desert heat, it requires watering twice a month, March through October, to thrive.

Bothriochloa barbinoides

Cane beardgrass

BLOOM PERIOD: **July to September**

HEIGHT AND SPREAD: **2 to 3 ft. × 1 ft.**

GROWS WELL IN: **Extreme heat and cold to -20°F**

☀ ☼ ⚲ ⁑ 🐝▸

The glory of cane beardgrass is its fuzzy white seed heads, that glow when backlit by the low-angled sun, late summer through winter. It self-sows readily where soil is disturbed and a bit of moisture is available, an effective component of revegetation seed mixes. It requires warm soil to germinate and root, has stiff vertical stems and fairly coarse blue-green leaves that turn golden-yellow as it goes to seed.

Cane beardgrass (*Bothriochloa barbinoides*). LEFT Indian ricegrass (*Achnatherum hymenoides*).

Bouteloua curtipendula

Sideoats grama

BLOOM PERIOD: **June to September**

HEIGHT AND SPREAD: **2 to 2½ ft. × 1 ft.**

GROWS WELL IN: **Extreme heat and cold to -30°F**

Tiny orange flowers ripen as slender, flat seeds along its upright stems, giving sideoats its common name. A component of desert grasslands throughout the West, it clings to rocky slopes as well as growing in deeper soils on the plains. In landscapes, it helps prevent erosion on slopes and adds subtle vertical texture in sweeps of gaura, penstemon, and salvia. Sideoats grama has somewhat coarse, medium blue-green leaves that dry bronzy tan, in contrast to pale blue grama. 'Vaughn' and 'Niner' are two heat- and drought-adapted selections from New Mexico.

Sideoats grama (*Bouteloua curtipendula*).

Bouteloua dactyloides

Buffalograss

BLOOM PERIOD: **June to September**

HEIGHT AND SPREAD: **6 to 8 in. × 12 to 24 in.**

GROWS WELL IN: **Clay soil in moderate heat; extreme cold to -30°F**

Once cultivated only as shortgrass prairie graze for livestock, cultivars of buffalograss became lawn grass options at least 20 years ago, alternatives for thirsty, cool season bluegrass and fescue. While 'Bison', 'Plains', and 'Texoka' are taller varieties bredto provide more forage in pastures, turfgrass selections such as 'Cody' and 'UC Verde' are shorter, denser, finer-leaved, and richer green. Plug-grown 'Legacy' is the ultimate sod or ground cover, an all-female selection that produces a thick, pollen-free lawn. Weekly watering spring through early autumn is needed to maintain lawn quality.

Buffalograss (*Bouteloua dactyloides*).

Blue grama

BLOOM PERIOD: June through September

HEIGHT AND SPREAD: 1 to 2½ ft. × 1 to 1½ ft.

GROWS WELL IN: Sandy or loamy soil; heat tolerant and cold hardy to -20°F

Blue grama may be the most widespread western range grass, and has been used as a xeric ground cover and lawn grass alternative for several decades. It has eyebrow-like flowers and seed heads that form a fringe above its fine-bladed, soft green leaves. It dries pale platinum when dormant and 'Blonde Ambition' is a cultivar that is both robust and cures to a pale yellow-gold as advertised. While blue grama can be mowed occasionally as a lawn, it is most vigorous and weed resistant when only mowed once in spring to clear the way for new growth. When used as a lawn, it needs water every week or two while actively growing.

Blue grama (*Bouteloua gracilis*).

Berkeley sedge

BLOOM PERIOD: June to August

HEIGHT AND SPREAD: 1½ ft. × 1½ ft.

GROWS WELL IN: Extreme heat in shade; evergreen to 15°F, cold hardy to 10°F

The slender, dark green leaf blades arch to form mounds, with rhizomes slowly filling in gaps between plants. Although it is sometimes mowed, its undulating texture as a ground cover is much more appealing. The brown flowers are not showy and are best removed in wetter areas to curb self-sowing. Sedges are not grasses, having leaves that are triangular in cross-section and a tendency to be evergreen. It is also not a native species, though often mislabeled as such. I include *Carex divulsa* here because it is used as a grass would be, and seems to be better adapted to drier conditions than most sedges. Native meadow sedge (*Carex praegracilis*) is a better option for wetland reclamation.

Berkeley sedge (*Carex divulsa*).

Festuca idahoensis 'Siskiyou Blue'

'Siskiyou Blue' fescue

BLOOM PERIOD: April to June

HEIGHT AND SPREAD: 1 ft. × 1 ft.

GROWS WELL IN: Heat; cold hardy to -30°F

☀ ◑ ☼ 🌡 ❄

Both heat tolerant and drought hardy, 'Siskiyou Blue' fescue is a better alternative to other blue fescues in warm desert gardens. A naturally occurring hybrid of high-elevation blue fescue and Idaho fescue, and native to the Great Basin Desert, it is robust in size and attitude. In spring, slender, silver-blue leaves form graceful mounds, setting off silky, bright green flower heads. It may self-sow a bit in cooler, wetter garden spots, but it is unlikely to run amok when mixed into flowerbeds for soft textural and color accent.

'Siskiyou Blue' fescue (*Festuca idahoensis* 'Siskiyou Blue').

Muhlenbergia asperifolia

Alkali muhly

BLOOM PERIOD: May to September

HEIGHT AND SPREAD: 8 to 10 in. × 24 to 30 in.

GROWS WELL IN: Extreme heat; cold hardy to -20°F, possibly colder

☀ ☼ ☼ 📍 ⚘ 🐝

Alkali muhly has very fine leaves and stems that spread by rhizomes to cover dense patches of ground along streams and in low-lying areas that flood occasionally. Despite its fragile appearance, it is extremely resilient and tolerates strongly alkaline and saline soils. It has a mist-like cover of pale pink seed heads in summer and is a soft alternative to cobblestone for lining rainwater swales and basins that bake in the sun between deluges. Bush muhly (*Muhlenbergia porteri*) is similar in color and texture, but grows in discrete clumps among desert shrubs and succulents.

Alkali muhly (*Muhlenbergia asperifolia*).

Muhlenbergia capillaris

Pink muhly

BLOOM PERIOD: **September to October**

HEIGHT AND SPREAD: **2 to 2½ ft. × 2½ to 3 ft.**

GROWS WELL IN: **Extreme heat with regular watering; cold hardy to -10°F**

In the wetter eastern states where it is native, pink muhly is only found in very sandy soils, which may account for its drought tolerance when grown in heavier soils in the desert Southwest. Its glossy green, fine-textured leaves form large mounds crowned with a haze of deep rose-purple flowers late in the season. The best show is in warmer desert gardens, where frost doesn't abruptly end the season. *Muhlenbergia* 'Pink Flamingos' blooms a month earlier on taller stems standing well above the leaves, and is a good choice for both low and high desert gardens.

Pink muhly (*Muhlenbergia capillaris*).

Muhlenbergia dumosa

Bamboo muhly

BLOOM PERIOD: **January to February**

HEIGHT AND SPREAD: **3 to 5 ft. × 3 to 4 ft.**

GROWS WELL IN: **Extreme heat in afternoon shade; cold hardy to 5°F**

The billowy, soft texture of the slender, bright spring-green leaves on arching, semi-woody stems gives bamboo muhly its unique garden presence. Pale lavender flowers are only noticeable close up. Evergreen in frost-free areas, it cures pale tan where frost is persistent. Thinning out the oldest stems down to the ground and removing winter damage just as plants begin greening up in spring will keep large specimens vigorous. Bamboo muhly rarely self-sows; it slowly spreads by rhizomes to its mature size. Water it deeply every few weeks in summer to keep it green.

Bamboo muhly (*Muhlenbergia dumosa*).

Bull grass

BLOOM PERIOD: September to October

HEIGHT AND SPREAD: 2 to 3 ft. × 2 to 3 ft.

GROWS WELL IN: Extreme, reflected heat; cold hardy to -10°F

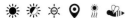

The blue-green leaves of bull grass are wider than most muhlys, giving bull grass a bold look nestled between boulders or clustered for impact. Airy spikes of rose-purple flower heads make plants dominate the autumn garden. After hard freezes, the seed heads turn pale tan and persist through winter. Cut back old leaves and weathered seed stalks close to the ground in spring, before new leaves emerge to keep plants robust. 'El Toro' is a selection with especially colorful flower spikes.

Bull grass (*Muhlenbergia emersleyi*).

Lindheimer muhly

BLOOM PERIOD: September to October

HEIGHT AND SPREAD: 4 to 5 ft. × 3 to 4 ft.

GROWS WELL IN: Extreme reflected heat; cold hardy to -10°F

Slender green leaves arch and mound in contrast to the stiff flower stems that emerge in autumn. The narrow, tapered flower spikes are soft yellow as they open, quickly curing to pale tan, especially in areas experiencing nightly frost. In those locales, the entire plant is platinum by midwinter. 'Autumn Glow' is an aptly named cultivar. Seep muhly (*Muhlenbergia reverchonii*) is a smaller plant overall, and more cold hardy to -20°F. It has shorter, wispier purple flower spikes, floating haze-like above the foliage. Both of these very arid-adapted, resilient grasses can be used in rainwater ponding basins, but are just as happy in drier settings.

Lindheimer muhly (*Muhlenbergia lindheimeri*).

Bush muhly

BLOOM PERIOD: June to October

HEIGHT AND SPREAD: 1 to 2 ft. × 2 to 3 ft.

GROWS WELL IN: Extreme heat; cold hardy to -20°F

The wiry stems of bush muhly are perennial, giving this grass an edge in drought. The leaves are small and pale gray-green, on stems that arch and mound, giving the plant a billowy, soft appearance—especially when covered with fine rose-pink seed heads. Bush muhly glows when backlit by the sun and mixes well with small mounding plants such as damianita, sand penstemon, and mariola.

Bush muhly (*Muhlenbergia porteri*).

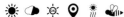

Muhlenbergia rigens

Deer grass

BLOOM PERIOD: **May to September**

HEIGHT AND SPREAD: **3 to 4 ft. × 4 to 5 ft.**

GROWS WELL IN: **Extreme heat; cold hardy to -10°F**

☀ ☁ ☼ 📍 ❄ 🐝

The slender, gray-green leaves of deer grass grow in dense mounds, clustered as accents among lower-growing grasses or as the middle ground between desert trees. The flower stems are narrow spikes that fan out 2 ft. above the foliage. It is valued for its adaptability in gardens and will tolerate periods of drought as well as wet soils in summer. In cold winter areas, the whole plant will cure pale tan, while in warm winter gardens it will remain evergreen. Pine muhly (*Muhlenbergia dubia*) is similar in appearance but much smaller in scale at 30 in. × 30 in. It is cold hardy to 0°F.

Deer grass (*Muhlenbergia rigens*).

Purple muhly

BLOOM PERIOD: **July to September**

HEIGHT AND SPREAD: **2 ft. × 2 ft.**

GROWS WELL IN: **Extreme heat; cold hardy to -10°F**

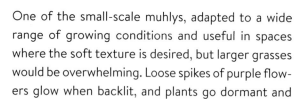

One of the small-scale muhlys, adapted to a wide range of growing conditions and useful in spaces where the soft texture is desired, but larger grasses would be overwhelming. Loose spikes of purple flowers glow when backlit, and plants go dormant and turn pale tan even in warm-winter, low desert gardens. 'Nashville' is the cultivar most widely available.

Purple muhly (*Muhlenbergia rigida*).

Switchgrass

BLOOM PERIOD: **August to October**

HEIGHT AND SPREAD: **3 to 5 ft. × 3 to 4 ft.**

GROWS WELL IN: **Moderate heat; cold hardy to -30°F**

Relatively coarse-leaved with strong upright stems, switchgrass is rhizomatous and will spread into wet soil when used in rainwater basins, or will maintain discrete clumps when drip irrigated. This native of the tallgrass prairie has many selections, with leaves ranging from silver-blue to green, and open sprays of flower heads in varying shades of reddish purple. 'Shenandoah' turns deep red in fall and is more compact than most; 'Alamo' is one of the most heat-tolerant cultivars.

Switchgrass (*Panicum virgatum*).

Little bluestem

BLOOM PERIOD: August to September
HEIGHT AND SPREAD: 1 to 2 ft. × 1 ft.
GROWS WELL IN: Moderate heat; cold hardy to -30°F

☀ ☼ ☀ 🌡 📍 ☀ 🐝▸

The beauty of little bluestem is its ability to wait out summer heat as a tidy clump of innocuous blue-green leaves, quietly making food for a deep and widespread root system. With the first hint of shortening days and cooler nights, it bolts to bloom, limber stems topped with fuzzy purple-bronze flowers that sway in the breeze. Then, instead of sinking back into anonymity, various cultivars display still more color. 'Blaze' turns brilliant scarlet, while 'The Blues' turns pink with the first frosts, before finally fading to russet through winter.

Little bluestem (*Schizachyrium scoparium*).

Indiangrass

BLOOM PERIOD: September to October
HEIGHT AND SPREAD: 3 to 6 ft. × 2 ft.
GROWS WELL IN: Moderate heat; cold hardy to -30°F

☀ ☼ 🌡 📍 ☀ 🐝▸

In desert gardens, Indiangrass is a good option for filling rainwater catchment basins, soaking up storm water, and providing rich wildlife habitat. In spring and summer, it progressively grows a dense cover of coarse blue-green leaves. As nights become cooler, tall flower stems emerge, topped with narrow clusters of yellow flowers and fuzzy bronze seed heads. Although the stems stand strongly upright, they are limber enough to dance in the wind, animating the space they fill. 'Cheyenne' is the most heat-adapted cultivar, readily available and easily grown from seed.

Indiangrass (*Sorghastrum nutans*).

Alkali sacaton

BLOOM PERIOD: **June to October**

HEIGHT AND SPREAD: **2 ft. × 2 ft.**

GROWS WELL IN: **Extreme heat; cold hardy to at least -20°F**

Although the name sacaton comes from the Aztec word *zacatl* (a general reference to grasses), it could easily translate as adaptable, since alkali sacaton grows with as little as 6 in. or as much as 24 in. of rain per year. It produces clumps of fine, pale green leaves crowned with an airy haze of pale gold seed heads. It grows in blazing sun or in the dappled shade of cottonwoods and oaks. It is robust enough to be an excellent choice for erosion control and revegetation projects, and so soft and lustrous in seed, it is planted en masse in gardens where low water, low maintenance cover is needed.

Alkali sacaton (*Sporobolus airoides*).

Giant sacaton

BLOOM PERIOD: **August to October**

HEIGHT AND SPREAD: **3 to 6 ft. × 3 to 6 ft.**

GROWS WELL IN: **Extreme heat; cold hardy to -30°F**

Giant sacaton (*Sporobolus wrighti*).

In floodplains across the Southwest, when you see great sweeps of supersized, pale green grasses topped with open spikes of feathery seed heads, you are looking at a remnant of our desert pampas. Individual plants can be used as you would a shrub; clusters of plants can fill rainwater basins or provide seasonal change, contrasting with large evergreens such as Arizona rosewood, curl-leaf mountain mahogany, or arid-adapted conifers. Groups of giant sacaton accenting a bed of alkali sacaton are particularly dramatic, as layers of airy seed plumes glimmer in the sunlight.

GOOD SOUTHWEST GARDENING PRACTICES

Healthy plants need less care, so matching plants with places and purposes ultimately makes a garden both more inviting and less work. Design and maintenance are the yin and yang of Southwest gardening. The nature of plants and their purpose in the overall plan determine how they are maintained—and the care needed to keep plants healthy and attractive directs how those plants are best used in the garden. Especially in extreme conditions, smart gardening can mean lower maintenance. When hard surfaces are designed to drain rainwater toward green spaces, and compatible combinations of plants are chosen for their fitness to the conditions, the garden will be healthier, less prone to pests. When just enough moisture is available to establish roots and maintain the desired growth, less pruning is needed. When the soil surface is not repeatedly disturbed and perennial plants are mulched and allowed to fill their niches, fewer weeds steal water from garden plants.

A dedicated, organized work space adds to the pleasure of gardening.

SOIL PREPARATION AND PLANTING

Being outside in the garden is the beginning of cultivation in the broadest sense. Whether visualizing the design, digging holes, tracking the progress of new transplants, scouting for pests, cutting a few weeds, or aimlessly surveying, time spent in the garden opens you to the marvels of nature. Simply being in the space often leads to inspiration and epiphanies about how the garden as a whole works—insights that active observation might inhibit.

Encouraging growth is basic to the idea of gardening. Managing growth to produce healthy plants exercises finesse in attaining the results we desire. Forcing growth with fertilizers and water is costly and counterproductive. Added fertilizer and water will not improve conditions for a poorly adapted plant, when heat and low humidity are the problems. Pruning, weeding, pest control, and fertilizing can't fix poor design or planting techniques. Good design and careful planting, including appropriate soil preparation, can reduce the extent of maintenance chores. Because water is the lifeblood of every garden in the Southwest, learning when and how much to water plants given the soil type and ambient weather is the ultimate gardening chore.

There is common ground in the relationship between soil and plants. Soil is the anchor, moisture reservoir, and mineral source for plants worldwide. The soil that best suits individual plants varies greatly and one of the biggest garden myths is that all plants require organic matter to thrive. For example, the roots of arid-adapted plants need abundant oxygen in the soil, thus the frequent mention of well-drained soil.

THE MOST IMPORTANT SOIL IMPROVEMENT: MAKING IT PERVIOUS

In the Southwest (and most places, for that matter), it's very rare to garden in undisturbed soil that is naturally pervious to air, moisture, and roots. By the time a space is ready to plant, it's usually been scraped and driven over repeatedly with heavy construction equipment, until most of the life, the oxygen, and the pore space has been squeezed out. New roots have a difficult time pushing through cement-like soil. Digging large, deep holes and filling them with fluffy potting soil is not a good practice, especially in extreme conditions, because it

OPPOSITE TOP Urban soils have been compacted by heavy equipment. The most important soil improvement is making the soil pervious to air, moisture, and roots. Trenching opens pathways for moisture and roots to follow, helping trees and other large plants establish themselves more quickly. OPPOSITE BOTTOM Compacted soil and shallow watering contribute to poorly rooted trees. The larger a tree manages to grow, the more prone it is to blowing over in strong winds.

creates in-ground "containers" that roots will have a difficult time escaping. Slowly nudging the soil back to life with cover crops and, where winters are persistently cold, watering so freezing and thawing can soften and aerate the surface would be ideal. But homeowner association rules for landscaping and the need for dust control make this slow approach impractical in many gardens.

Plants well-adapted to arid climates will grow well in our low-fertility sand, silt, or rocky soils. Organic soil amendments are generally unnecessary—even counterproductive—as they create a barrier for moisture and roots to breach. But every rule has exceptions: exotics such as fruit trees, berry bushes, and vegetables benefit greatly by improving their soil with copious additions of organic matter. Initially, compost should be worked into an exotic's entire potential root area.

WHAT IS FERTILITY?

Fertile soils are the playground of soil microorganisms, earthworms, and beneficial nematodes that break down redundant roots and fallen leaves. But while soil good for vegetable growing is rich in composted organic matter, it is a poor medium for desert plants that are adapted to lean, fast-draining, mineral-rich soil with little organic matter. Undisturbed desert soils host an abundant and diverse community of microorganisms that partner with the plants, trading increased nutrient availability for more efficient water absorption. These microorganisms languish in soil with alien organic matter. Instead, fibrous mulches such as compost, pecan shells, cotton burrs, and cocoa hulls that release nitrogen and create humus are the best means of maintaining healthy soil for plants adapted to such soils. Arid-adapted plants form alliances with soil microbes already present in aerated native soil, microorganisms that improve plants' ability to

absorb moisture and the minerals they need for growth. Plants anchored in soil that provides the other raw materials they need feed themselves by converting sunlight to energy. Plant care is a bit like good parenting: if you invest in giving plants the tools they need to mature self-sufficiently, the garden will make you proud.

MULCHING AND FERTILIZING

Mulches are materials spread on the soil to keep roots cooler and the soil moist longer. Organic matter feeds the soil and biodegrades quickly, so replenishing the mulch continues to improve conditions from the top down. Mulch also slows the evaporation of moisture from the soil, and suppresses the growth of weeds. Compost, cotton burrs, leaves, and pecan shells are soil building, while bark and shredded wood fiber can slowly deplete the soil as they use nitrogen to decompose. Gravels are usually inert, although some release mineral salts as they weather.

Most trees native to the Southwest grow in places where moisture accumulates. While they do not need amended soil, they do benefit from mulching, and from seasonal pulses of rainwater as part of their water budget. It benefits healthy, large trees to be mulched with their own fallen leaves, recycling resources within the garden. Rather than overflow our landfills with bio-gold, yard waste from healthy plants should remain in the garden. Because of the durability of arid-adapted foliage,

TOP Fallen leaves from healthy plants are an ideal mulch, helping improve soil fertility as they decompose.
BOTTOM Mulches help keep the soil moist and cool. The choice of material depends on the plants being grown. In this garden the most xeric plants are mulched with stone, while the roses are mulched with cocoa hulls and the fruit trees are planted in a living mulch of sheep's fescue.

larger leaves such as those of cottonwoods should be shredded and used as a base for a heavier material, such as shredded bark, to keep the leaf material from blowing away before microorganisms have the opportunity to digest them. In forest areas, conifer needle mulch should be maintained as a fairly thin layer, so that it doesn't pose a fire hazard. Fruit trees should be mulched every year with compost, pecan shells, shredded leaves, clean grass clippings, or cocoa hulls that will continue to feed the soil as they decompose.

Desert shrubs and wildflowers grow well in fine stone mulches, which don't contribute to heating as long as there is enough plant cover to shade much of the surface. A mix of larger-sized stones is the best mulch in rainwater streambeds and basins, as their weight withstands the flow of water that would erode lighter materials. Fibrous materials, including leaves, pecan shells, compost, straw, and bark all have their uses, especially with plants that are less heat loving.

Whatever mulch you use, a 3-in. layer directly on the soil is deep enough to suppress most weed seed germination and to last for a few years before needing to be replenished. Landscape fabrics vary in quality and many types keep light rains from penetrating the soil, so I rarely use them—only as an added preventive measure when trying to suppress persistent perennial weeds (such as bindweed and Bermuda grass).

Arid-adapted plants in loosened native soil rarely need fertilizing. Exotics and lawns usually need supplementing, in part because they have to be watered so much more and in part because they are adapted to soils rich in organic matter. Slow-release balanced nitrogen, phosphorus, and potassium fertilizers such as alfalfa or cottonseed meal, plus micronutrient supplements such as kelp meal, can help new plants when applied just after bud break in spring, when the nighttime temperatures have stabilized. Avoid fertilizing most plants midsummer and wait until late fall, to keep plants from burning in the heat at lower elevations and to help cold-hardy plants ease into dormancy.

TIMING: WHEN TO PLANT

Ideal planting seasons are different in the low desert than at higher elevations, but a general rule is to plant before the temperatures are consistently above 95°F; in colder areas, plant six weeks before temperatures are consistently below freezing. Even in the low desert, December and January days may be too short and temperatures too erratic for setting out small plants, while acclimated woody plants may settle in easily. Likewise in all except areas above 6000 ft. in elevation—much of summer is too hot for large-scale planting. Plants noted as loving heat can be planted as soon as the nighttime temperatures are consistently 50°F, and as long as the daytime temperature stays below 95°F. In summers with good monsoon rains, plant to take advantage of precipitation in intermediate and high desert areas when afternoon cloud cover keeps temperatures a bit lower and humidity high. As long as they have been hardened off, cool season adapted plants can be set out when nighttime temperatures are still hovering around freezing. When daytime temperatures are consistently 85°F, planting can shift to heat-loving species. Above 7000 ft. in elevation, May through August is the best planting time. Below 3000 ft., February, March, October, and November are less stressful for many new transplants.

Part of getting plants off to a good start is setting them out when they are best able to establish themselves quickly. There are the ideal times, and there is the way life actually unfolds. Planting outside the

The hotter the temperature, the more tools such as mulches, shade cloths, automated drip systems, and subsurface rain reservoirs help to offset the heat and keep plants hydrated.

School teachers might tackle major garden projects in summer when they can shift their nurturing from students to transplants. New parents garden at naptime if they have the energy to go outdoors. Ultimately, the best time to garden (besides avoiding peak heat and cold) is when you have time to focus on the task. Understanding the ideal allows you to plan for contingencies. Aids such as shade cloth, automated drip systems, and mulches help to combat the heat. Unless you live in a low desert city where the temperature doesn't cool at night, gardening in the evening gives plants a milder window to settle in. Choosing plants that are adapted to local conditions helps immeasurably in granting gardeners the flexibility to succeed.

SHOPPING FOR THE BEST TREE? GO LOOKING FOR TROUBLE.

When you shop for a new tree, go while you can see the plants in leaf, so that you can compare individuals of the same size and kind. Plants can be lightly stressed for moisture repeatedly without affecting the overall vigor (in fact, a bit of stress strengthens plants), but repeated severe stress can damage a plant for life and there are usually signs in the leaves that it doesn't take a fortune teller to read. Look for plants that have a reasonably dense canopy—plants in containers will never be as leafy as they are when growing in open soil, but if the foliage is sparse, off color, or burnt on the leaf margins, it could be an indication that there's a systemic problem. Examine the bark closely for scrapes, scars, and sunscald. Superficial wounds can heal with little impact on plant health, but deep gashes can allow entry to pathogens and weaken a tree. Sunscald, also called southwest injury, is usually on the southwest side of trees planted in the ground, but could be anyplace on the trunk of trees that are moved around the

least stressful window in your area requires more care; screening new plants with shade cloth and perhaps watering more often and less deeply for a week or two can help reduce transplant shock. Plants need the most consistent care in the first few months after they are transplanted. Until roots begin to develop well, keeping the soil adequately moist is the number one priority. Drip irrigation systems are the most efficient way to provide water, and should be monitored to assure they are working correctly. After the first few weeks, adjust timer schedules to run longer and less frequently. Regular monitoring for pests, from aphids to hungry rabbits to leg-lifting dogs, is advisable while plants are new. Defer structural pruning for at least a year to allow plants to adapt to your garden, fertilizing only to correct obvious deficiencies.

Climate extremes are shifting where plants are best adapted, making it more difficult for new plants to establish, and for gardeners to reconcile the ideal with the reality of when they are able to get the job done. Tax preparers in Phoenix might groan at getting their gardens in order by mid-April.

nursery. Sunscald appears as sunken streaks in the bark, sometimes with frost cracks in the wood, and is caused by the thin bark of young trees warming enough on a warm winter day for sap to flow. Then, when temperatures drop rapidly, the sap freezes and expands in the cells, tearing open cell walls and destroying them. Damage done in winter sometimes doesn't show up until early the next summer. Since most trees adapted to heat are best transplanted while the soil is warm, it's better to not plant them in winter in cold desert areas anyway.

The trunk on a well-grown tree tapers: it is noticeably thicker at soil level than it is 5 ft. above the pot. If there is no taper, it may mean that it was planted too deeply when up-potted or that it was staked so rigidly that it couldn't move at all in the wind.

Think about roots

You generally won't be able to examine the roots until you get the plant home, but sometimes you can see a small root starting to wrap around the base of the trunk. That can be an indication that the plant is pot-bound (it's been kept in an undersized container too long), and the superficial circling root is trying to find room to grow—the poor thing is trying to climb out of the pot. If a tree is wobbly in the container, it may mean that it was recently transplanted from a smaller container, or that it was root-bound when transplanted and its roots haven't been able to escape into the surrounding soil. Moderately root-bound plants can be fixed at transplanting time by washing the soil off the roots and spreading them out in the planting hole, trimming off any dead or damaged sections.

Planting and staking

Given a short timeline and native Southwest soil, the best way to dig holes for trees and large shrubs is with a trencher. In soil that is too rocky to trench, use a jack-hammer. Cut an X at least 5 ft. across and just a few inches deeper than the root ball being planted, then crosscut the X a few more times, so that you have a star that is 5 to 10 ft. in diameter, with 6 or 8 points. Remove the soil from the middle of the star when you plant, and backfill with the loosened native soil. There are then several pathways for roots to take in establishing themselves. The larger the pervious area for trees, the better. Rain and irrigation water will have an easier time penetrating, so roots will grow deeper and spread wider than they would otherwise. Ultimately, your reward will be healthier plants that fill their space in the garden more quickly.

Once you have the hole dug, unpot the tree in the center of the hole, then rinse the soil from the perimeter of the root ball with a strong stream of water in the hole, wetting the soil that the tree is going into while you release it from bondage. The planting hole should be several times wider but only a few inches deeper than the root ball of the transplant, and backfilled, so that the crown—where the roots first emerge from the trunk—is at grade. If the hole is too deep, the tree may sink when you water it thoroughly and be buried too deeply, which can lead to problems in the future.

If you've selected a tree with a burlap and wire- or twine-wrapped root ball, there's less of a possibility that it will have girdling roots, but the trunk of the tree shouldn't shift too much within the soil ball, as that could indicate that the tree has few smaller roots. Once you have the tree centered in the planting hole, cut away the wire, twine, and burlap before backfilling around the root ball. Wire, twine, and burlap are slow to decompose—archaeologists may find them in some future excavation—and will interfere with the tree establishing new roots. Years after a tree is planted, roots encircled with wire or a trunk wrapped with twine (like a tourniquet constricting blood flow), may restrict the sap flow so much that major roots or the trunk itself dies.

After you've filled around the transplanted roots, gently tamp the soil to eliminate large air pockets. Water thoroughly so that the existing roots and soil that the new roots will move into are moistened. If you are going to maintain the tree with drip irrigation, be sure that the emitters are placed at the edge of the root ball, where the existing roots meet the fill soil, so that both are moistened. There should be several emitters at about 12-in. intervals around the root ball perimeter, to allow consistent moisture to begin establishing new roots,plus pockets of irrigated ground cover that will provide moist soil for roots to move into. Better still, plant the new tree where rainwater collects, or divert runoff from gutters and paving to soak in shallow basins. More information can be found on this at http://www.ext. colostate.edu/pubs/garden/02926.html.

Extreme wind can damage plants, but flexing in moderate wind strengthens them. Staking should be done loosely with soft, flexible ties. The professional way is with wide-strap webbing that encircles the trunk loosely and is tied to stakes with cord or wire looped through grommets in the strap. Cut-up sections of pantyhose aren't elegant, but they'll do the job at home. Although it's better than wire alone, the wire-through-a-section-of-garden-hose method doesn't go far enough in spreading the pressure evenly, rather than concentrating the pressure in one spot. Stake from at least two directions and have the ties slack enough that the plant can move in the wind, but not wildly so. Trees shouldn't need to be staked longer than one growing season, until the plants are rooted well enough not to blow over. Rigid ties left on the tree too long can cut into the bark, creating a weak spot. The trunk immediately above the tie can start to thicken—developing the taper that should begin at soil level—making the tree vulnerable to breakage at that point as the limb develops more weight.

Smaller plants may be set out in smaller stars, and ground covers may be planted in the radii of the tree stars.

WATERING

British professor John Adams has a well-known quote about risk management: "It's not rocket science—it's much more complicated." That's sort of how I feel about managing water needs in the Southwest garden, and why I gave it its own chapter. We never stop learning the subtleties of how much and how often plants need water, a study further complicated by climate extremes and the inherent limitations of drip irrigation.

Drip or low-flow irrigation is the best way to get new plants established, and if adjustments are made as the plants grow, also the best way to keep them healthy. Little water is lost to evaporation or run-off, and the soil retains the ebb and flow of aeration and moisture recharge that arid-climate plants seem to prefer. The flexibility with drip irrigation lies in the number and flow rate of emitters per plant, and how often and how long you run the system. All the plants on one valve ultimately need to adapt to the same length of time between irrigations. Observation is the first step toward understanding, and knowledge is power. When first set out, smaller transplants will need more frequent irrigation than larger plants with more roots. A day or two after watering, many plants may be drooping on a sunny afternoon in June—but go out in the garden early the next morning, and you'll see how well they've recovered overnight. A serious student of watering efficiency might keep a calendar of temperatures,

Vitex, hesperaloe, and lavender are complementary in color and balanced in proportion. Just as important, they are compatible in how often they need water.

as well as when and how much water was applied. If only one or two plants show signs of stress, give them a bit more water by hand and adjust your timer to add 15 minutes or a half hour to the drip's run time. Assess the effect of deeper watering before opting to water more often. If the same plants continue to droop sooner than the others, try replacing their emitters with ones with higher flow rates. Desert plants are adapted to pulses of water followed by periods of drying, so allowing them to endure moderate levels of stress keeps them better adapted, a "no pain, no gain" regimen familiar to athletes—especially those who play the extreme sport of gardening in the desert. Within three generations, plants can become better suited to changes in their environment—or less so, if arid-adapted plants are watered and fertilized to the point they become less resilient.

WAYS TO APPLY WATER

There are many ways to apply water: a hose left to trickle, sprinklers of all kinds (including shrub sprays and microsprays), bubblers that flood small areas, a myriad of drip irrigation equipment, and traditional

When water is applied shallowly with sprinklers, roots remain superficial and more vulnerable to heat, cold, and drought.

To be most efficient, acequia irrigation requires precise grading to level the soil, and careful control by the irrigator to stop the flow in good time.

agricultural flood irrigation through a system of canals called acequias. Sprinklers of all kinds are the most wasteful method, since even when run at night, a portion of the water evaporates without much benefit to the plants. Microsprays tend to clog easily and apply water unevenly, as minerals salt up the orifices. Low-spray-angle sprinklers that deliver water in droplets are the best way to water lawns and native grasses used as prairie ground cover. Warm season grasses take less water because they are dormant longer than cool season grasses. Careful soil preparation—tilling large amounts of compost into the soil as uniformly as possible—creates a surface that retains water better. Still, lawns will take three to ten times the water that arid-adapted plants do.

Hose watering by hand (managed by an attentive gardener with time to water slowly) can be very satisfying and productive, as it allows observation of growth and insect activity, as well as a bit of bird-watching. But laying a hose on the ground even when just trickling and forgetting it for hours is wasteful. Bubblers are relatively expensive, but can require less maintenance and operate effectively longer without modification. They can be an ideal way to water large, long-lived plants, but distributing water evenly to lots of small plants from bubblers can be difficult. Acequia irrigation, an ancient and much more extensive flood method, requires precise grading to level the soil, so that water flows across a broad surface relatively uniformly. It also requires careful control by the irrigator to stop the flow in good time. It can be as water intensive as sprinklers in evaporating surface water, but since the excess percolates to the shallow water table, it can also be a means of maintaining subsurface connectivity with the river that is the source of the acequia.

Rainwater Harvesting

Storm cells grow more potent, stall over an area, and drop a tremendous amount of water in a short period of time, often on powder-dry soil that repels water until the surface tension is broken. The rain that should be cause to celebrate becomes a threat to property, and a surprising amount of rainwater is rushed curbside to storm drains—while trees in the garden suffer drought. There are easy and more complex remedies for this situation. Contoured, shallow streambeds that direct water from rooftop gutters to planted basins should be part of every new garden design. When the garden slate is clean, no obstacles such as pavement or existing large tree or shrub roots bar the flow of water. Pavement can become part of the means of diverting flow to plants. It is a simple matter to dig swales 8 in. deep and of varying widths, depending on the anticipated flow (every inch of rainfall delivers up to 600 gallons of water from 1000 sq. ft. of roof surface) that drains to shallow basins, where trees can soak it up. In record-breaking storm events, the excess can overflow to storm drains. Channeling rainwater on the surface is considered passive rainwater harvesting.

A somewhat more complex harvesting technique is to install a series of trenches or pits, filled with pervious rock such as pumice or scoria, or large-diameter perforated pipes, in gravel-filled trenches, as underground storage. Trenches should be placed where the largest plants will have access to stored moisture. This is a variation on the theme of French drains, but the purpose is not simply to prevent ponding. It is to get the water into underground storage, where plant roots can use it before it evaporates. In permaculture parlance, porous, rock-filled trenches are called pumice wicks. Because pumice

This galvanized steel cistern is set in concrete and sealed to prevent leakage; it is painted to match the trim on the house and, accented by the plants it sustains, is a feature in the garden. The cistern has a 1000-gallon capacity and overflows during most monsoon seasons.

and scoria are light, they will float unless weighed down on the surface by heavier stone, large flagstone slabs as pathways, or the like.

Active rainwater harvesting is collecting storm water in tanks large enough to capture most of the water, with the passive system of swales and basins handling any excess. The water can then be drained as needed through drip irrigation tubing, to supply plants during the long periods between rain events. While rain barrels are inadequate for capturing significant amounts of rainfall, they are (as an astute rainwater harvesting pro has said) a gateway drug to capturing the rain. Once gardeners see the barrels overflowing, they go shopping for bigger tanks. Storage capacity is matched to maximum input during average rain events (depending on the roof area), annual rainfall, and area on the ground to place the tanks. It's much easier to design cisterns into the architecture of the building than to retrofit.

Passive rainwater harvesting is the most effective flood irrigation technique, channeling rain from rooftops and pavement through shallow streambeds toward plants. It uses no potable water and maintains the pulses of deep watering to which native plants are adapted. The limitations are a quite obvious lack of rain, sometimes for a year or more, and the less diverse number of plants that will thrive without any other supplemental water. If the choices are no extra water to garden or a garden of plants adapted to rainfall only, a beautiful garden is still quite possible, given the garden is filled with resilient plants that will adapt to rainfall alone once they are well-rooted. Rainwater harvesting always should be designed into gardens, as it would be foolish to forego a free source of high-quality water. The network of swales and basins are beautiful landforms

Perforated drainpipe is wrapped in landscape filter fabric; an outer layer contains scoria or pumice above and below the drainpipe in the trench, to prevent large roots from infiltrating.

when dry, and when the streambeds fill with rainwater and flow in to the garden, it is cause to celebrate.

Gray water systems recycle water, and when designed and maintained well, they can be an excellent alternative to potable water for irrigation. Rainwater stored in cisterns and gray water systems can both be supply sources for drip irrigation, and there are several excellent manuals in the Recommended Reading that detail both. Drip irrigation is the most efficient way to dole out water, especially when a controller is set to a conservative schedule and compensates for ambient weather conditions. In smaller gardens, drip systems can be easily maintained if they are designed and installed well and the equipment used is good quality. In very large gardens, a hybrid of bubblers on trees and shrubs and drip within the smaller areas may be the best option. Drip systems require monitoring and adjusting—at the very least, flushing as often as needed given the water quality. Flow rates of emitters may need to be changed as plants mature. While automated systems are easy, they depend on the efficiency of the controller. Even the newest so-called smart controllers are only as smart as the person programming and monitoring them.

Trenching can also be done to install drainpipes a few feet below the surface, to improve drainage and aerate compacted soil.

WHEN TO WATER

Different soils absorb and hold water at different rates. Clay and clay loam absorb water slowly, but also hold more and release it more slowly. Water filters through sand quickly, leaving it dry sooner. Well-watered soil absorbs more sunlight during the day and releases more heat at night, oxygenating and cooling plant roots in summer. Keeping the soil saturated, especially in cold weather, can lead to root rot. Heat and drought-loving desert natives are particularly vulnerable to excess winter moisture, but excess watering while plants are metabolizing very slowly in the heat of summer can have a similar effect. In all desert areas, there are two active growing seasons and two periods of rest: high spring in the low desert peaks in March, while in the high desert the surge of new growth and blooming is usually early in May. Persistent 100°F heat induces somnolence; plants siesta through the hottest part of summer and awaken to a new season of growth and flowering as temperatures cool, especially if summer monsoons are generous.

It is amazing how much impact even a mediocre rainy season can have on desert plants, so it's no wonder gardeners are tempted to keep the water flowing. As counterintuitive as it is to limit watering in the sizzling summer heat, allowing arid-adapted plants recovery time keeps them healthier. Reduce irrigation late in summer as daylight decreases, to help concentrate sugars in plant sap that act as antifreeze, giving plants more cold resistance. Even low desert plants that bloom throughout winter need less water November through February than they do when temperatures begin their upward spiral. Smaller transplants will need water more frequently until they have established roots. Larger transplants will need watering more deeply than their smaller companions at first. Succulent plants need water more frequently when they are first planted, but can be weaned more quickly.

HOW MUCH TO WATER

Drip irrigation is a wonderfully efficient tool, but only works well if it meets the needs of all the individual plants, large and small, xeric and less so. Irrigation zones should be based on how frequently plants will need water. Individual plant needs in a zone can be met by varying the emitter flow rate and number of emitters per plant. A tree may have four 2-gallon-per-hour (gph) emitters spaced evenly where the transplanted root ball meets the native soil backfill, while a smaller desert shrub or succulent might have one 2-gph emitter placed a few inches from the stems, and a desert wildflower one 1-gph emitter. The initial run time for the zone might be an hour once a week when planting is done in April, or forty minutes twice a week when plants are set out in late May. After several years, the tree should have eight or more 2-gph emitters at the edge of the branch canopy, or have a ground cover planted with the tree that has the emitters already in place, to serve the tree as it grows.

As the plants root out, increase the run time to 2 hours, but cut back on the frequency to every ten days or two weeks. Fruit-producing plants such as figs or pomegranates and less xeric shrubs and perennial flowers may need a separate zone, so they can be watered more often in shorter cycles, perhaps never less than weekly while plants are blooming and setting fruit. Run times should be less frequent and somewhat longer in autumn through winter, to wash any accumulating salts below the root zone and allow for the root growth that will support new top growth and flowering in spring. These are general examples, better suited to desert plants than the short daily cycles often recommended for drip irrigating agricultural crops. Ultimately, the best results will come with watching the plants and tweaking the emitter flow rates and timer schedule in response to how plants react.

When a tree is first planted, it may need watering once a week in summer, the water soaking in deeply enough that it penetrates 6 or 8 in. deeper and at least a foot or so wider than the original root ball. As time passes, especially as temperatures cool in autumn, water every two weeks—but increase the length of time and amount of water applied. In winter, most evergreen trees can be watered once a month when the soil is not frozen, and every few months if they are heat-loving; just often enough to keep the soil from drying to the point that it repels water. A soil probe is the best way to gain an understanding of how water permeates your soil. Commercial probes are expensive and often too short to probe deeply enough. You can have a simple one made at a shop that does wrought iron work: cut a 4-ft. section of ¼-in. solid rod, sharpen one end, and bend 4 in. of the other end at a right angle to use as a handle. Mark the rod at 1-ft. intervals from the bottom. After you've watered, wait several hours to push the probe into the soil where the fill soil meets the transplanted roots. The probe will sink into moist soil fairly easily and become hard to push in where the soil is dry or where caliche interferes with root growth.

If you're using drip irrigation and you ran the system for an hour, you'll know how long to program the timer to get water to the desired depth. No matter what type of soil you have, it's a good idea to probe in several places to get an overall idea of how consistently water moves downward. After a tree has been in the garden for a few years, its roots should extend beyond the edge of the branch canopy by at least a few feet. Watering near the trunk of established trees is counterproductive because those woody, corky roots don't absorb water well and keeping the trunk of a mature tree too wet can lead to disease problems. It can take three or four days for new roots to sprout in response to precipitation, but it only takes soil microorganisms active in and around the fine root hairs a few hours to respond to rain. Simulate rain, watering at the edge of the canopy where the plants can make best use of it. Planting ground covers a few feet from the tree trunk and other plants farther away creates moist soil areas for trees to root into. In time, healthy large trees may share water with all the plants within 40 ft. of the trunk.

PRIMING PLANTS FOR ERRATIC WINTERS

Plant damage inevitably follows mild winters interrupted by severe deep-freeze events. The new phenomenon is that plants known to be cold hardy to -25°F are dying, while plants thought to be much less cold tolerant survive, largely unaffected. It seems that the condition of the plants when the temperature plummets has much to do with the damage that occurs. Plants that are heat adapted and fully dormant when subject to cold often fare better than plants actively metabolizing and full of moisture when temperatures dive. Gardening rules are often refined by their exceptions, so while delaying the onset of growth in spring is not a universal proscription, its benefits outweigh its disadvantages consistently enough to use it as a fundamental coping strategy for dealing with extremes. We are in strange new territory here, forced to reassess how we garden in order to adapt to twists in climate patterns. Dryland gardeners are only beginning to understand the nuances of drought stress. We also need to factor in the effects of temperature stresses on both the low and high end of the scale, and how water applied or withheld influences plant resilience.

In extreme climates, the mature size of plants partly depends on the resources available. A large shrub may assume the proportions of a small tree if it finds a sweet spot where extra water is available, but it may remain smaller than its potential size if it is growing at the limits of its adaptation to drought, heat, or cold. Desert willows, mesquites, palo verdes, ironwoods, and acacias are among the most arid-adapted tree-shrubs, growing as large as the extremes allow. When cold shortens their period of active growth or repeatedly nips their new shoots, or when heat shortens the growing season, or drought minimizes new growth, these desert trees may never grow larger than 6 or 8 ft. tall. Likewise, large xeric shrubs such as Apache plume and fernbush—that under harsh conditions grow only 4 to 6 ft. tall—may double that size in your garden with time and favorable conditions. Being generous with water in the short term can fill space more quickly. Being conservative with water long-term can save you pruning time and ultimately produce stronger plants. Like the man said, it's not rocket science . . .

PEST AND WEED CONTROL

Climate extremes are affecting pests, too. Unfortunately, because insects are some of the most adaptable organisms on the planet, they seem to have the upper hand when it comes to surviving extreme conditions. When plants are stressed, they release pheromones that literally sing to insects to end their misery.

Forced to grow luxuriantly with nitrogen fertilizer and frequent watering, plants are beacons in the desert—Vegas-style, flashing-neon, "eat-me" lures for every pest in the neighborhood, including the four-legged furry ones. Integrated Pest Management (IPM) is a practical approach to establishing and maintaining a natural balance in the garden based on observation first, action only after the extent of the problem is understood, and intervention only when absolutely necessary. In order to act effectively and responsibly, we need to understand the problem. How bad are the insect infestation or disease symptoms? Are they damaging to the plant or just cosmetic? Is there a beneficial insect or microbe likely to find the pest a dietary bonanza? Is the problem environmental: Not enough or too much water? Withering heat? Is there too much or not enough light? Is herbicide or deicing salt causing the symptoms? When weighing whether cosmetic damage is great enough to treat, consider whether the problem plant is where people or pets play, or where birds, bees, or butterflies feed.

Once the problem is identified and deemed severe enough to need intervention, start with the least toxic remedy. Removing insects by hand takes effort to get past the yuck factor, but squishing a few hornworms underfoot can be surprisingly satisfying. Vacuuming up or washing away the problem with a pressurized hose nozzle can also provide some control. A few repeat visits will insure that pests have been reduced to non-threatening numbers. Learn to recognize predatory insects that may occur naturally as pest populations flourish. The life cycle of beneficial bugs is timed to allow their food source a head start, so pest populations always boom first.

Beneficial organisms may also be purchased and introduced. Most require specific temperatures to thrive, and understanding those conditions is critical to their effectiveness. Finally, insecticidal soaps and biological sprays may be used to restore balance. While some (such as neem oil) are plant derived, they are broadly effective and benign to humans and animals, but toxic to beneficial insects as well as pests—so their use should always be targeted.

Cross vine (*Bignonia capreolata*) smothers most weeds within its canopy by depriving potential competitors the light and moisture needed to get started. Hummingbirds benefit from abundant nectar produced by the thriving vine.

Aphids are a ubiquitous early-season pest.

Hawk wasps are elegant insects that vacuum up aphids with gusto.

Even plants that have adequate moisture available will reduce their evaporative surfaces in the midday heat by wilting temporarily, recovering as the evening cools. Watering assessments are best done in the evening or early morning, so this heat adaptation is not mistaken for a need to irrigate. Conveniently, as summer heats up, dusk and dawn are when it is most pleasant for us to be meandering through the garden. It is also when many pests are foraging, so garden observations early or late in the day offer the most information regarding water needs and insect activity. Now that every mobile device has a camera, and many universities have extensive insect identification sites, learning what's bugging you has never been easier. You can also e-mail photos to your local extension service entomologist, who probably appreciates a few good photos more than live bugs crawling across the desk. Many pests are either specific to certain plants or likely to be present at certain times of year. This can aid in making a positive identification and intervening effectively when necessary.

People living in or near forest land in the West are painfully aware of the link between beetle-ravaged trees and fire. Several species of bark beetle found the increased heat, longer frost-free stretches, and especially the increasing drought stress of the early 2000s ideal conditions to increase their populations to plague-like numbers. More information on the impact this infestation has caused can be found at http://www.fs.fed.us/ccrc/topics/bark-beetles.shtml.

Ideal conditions for insects include a large number of plants of the same species and age, too many plants sharing limited space, and too little water to support the number of plants. In naturally occurring and still-healthy pine and juniper woods, thinning out weaker plants and watering those that remain and are near a house may help save them. In urban gardens, where increasing warmth and reduced rainfall have caused soils to dry out beyond previous norms, supplying enough water to help plants resist borers has become critical. Cottonwoods, junipers, ash trees, lilacs, and many other trees and shrubs are vulnerable. Removing failing trees can reduce the spread of pests. When renovating older landscapes, assess the value of existing plants and preserve healthy trees and larger shrubs that provide shade, food, or habitat. Eliminate the clutter and competition for resources of redundant plants. Antoine de Saint-Exupery could have been describing gardening in extremes when he wrote, "Perfection is achieved not when there is nothing more to add, but when there is nothing left to take away."

SEASONAL PESTS AND THEIR HOSTS

Whole books and university-linked websites are available on pests and possible interventions, so I will focus on some of the most common in the Southwest, beginning in spring. Aphids appear as soon as plant sap begins to flow and new growth emerges. They are everywhere on almost all new growth, and are usually a short-lived problem. Their numbers decline dramatically as heat and wind make growth less succulent, and as the many aphid predators hatch and begin to feast. Fertilizer and water will keep plants soft longer, so less new growth is the trade-off for fewer insects. The many species of psyllids akin to aphids are specific to single plant families, including acacia, sumac, eucalyptus, and manzanita, but rarely occur in numbers great enough to cause more than cosmetic damage on plants that are well-adapted to the Southwest. When psyllids attack tomatoes, potatoes, and citrus, controls may be necessary. Leaf beetle larvae skeletonize cottonwood leaves, turning them brown; later

the adults eat holes in leaves. On established trees the problem is usually cosmetic, but an infestation can defoliate and weaken new transplants. *Bacillus thuringiensis* (Bt) ssp. *kurstaki* controls the larvae until plants outgrow the threat.

Spring webworm on *Sophora* is also controlled with Bt, as are elm leaf beetle larvae on susceptible species. The new elm hybrids of *Ulmus parvifolia* seem immune; the hybrids of *Ulmus pumila* parentage are vulnerable. The early-stage, small black and yellow larvae of grape leaf skeletonizer are also controlled with Bt; later stages succumb to parasitic *Apanteles harrisinae* and *Amedoria misella* insects. There are several strains of Bt recommended for various larvae, including the flea beetles that can reduce evening primroses, sundrops, and gaura to skeletons. Bt is most effective when applied in the evening, as soon as you notice larvae. Target only the larvae you recognize as pests. Bt will kill the caterpillars that morph into butterflies as well. You can diversify your controls by drenching the soil around evening primroses and related genera with beneficial nematodes, to control the pupal stage.

Horticultural oil can be used early in spring to smother scale insects. Various oil formulas are available, and temperature range specifics are given on the labels of these products. The intensity of sunlight in the Southwest can result in leaf burn if the recommendations are ignored. Sycamores and pines are two of the many plants vulnerable to scale. Beginning in March in the hottest areas, April or May in cooler places, mealy bugs are a scourge of succulents. Freshly squeezed lime juice is a very effective control on potted plants. Cochineal, found on prickly pears, resembles mealy bugs, but exudes a brilliant wine-red fluid when scraped away, a prized source of red dye when grown for that purpose, but a pest in the garden. Washing it off limits its spread; neem

Cochineal is common on prickly pear.

and chlorosis. Pines are dying in unprecedented wildfires. Even when well cared for in gardens, increasing heat is making them fall prey to bark beetles, pine tip moth, needle scale, and pine blight, this last malady a blanket term for "I just can't live here anymore." Cypress bark beetle and cedar borer have begun killing native junipers, an indicator that warming has reached another level in drying the soil beyond the point where conifers can thrive in low and intermediate deserts. For more information on these pests and their management, visit http://www.ipm.ucdavis.edu/PMG/menu.invertebrate.html; http://www.wripmc.org/; and http://aces.nmsu.edu/ces/plantclinic/related-links.html.

RECOGNIZING THE BENEFICIAL INSECTS

Listing all the garden pests is paranoia inducing. Rest assured that there are many more beneficial insects than there are garden pests, and many of them are already in your garden. When faced with an obvious infestation, it's tempting to call out a SWAT team. Establishing a balance takes time, understanding, and most importantly, an attitude adjustment. If you're planting nectar-rich flowers for seasonal color and to attract pollinators, growing culinary herbs to spice up your menus, and including a wide variety of plants in your garden because there are just so many beautiful plants to try, you're already aiding and abetting the beneficial insects. You may rarely see them, or sometimes see them actively feeding on pests. Just as you learned to distinguish penstemon from salvia, and how to identify lady bugs and praying mantis by sight, you can also learn about garden friends such as aphid midges, assassin bugs, collops beetles, damsel bugs, minute pirate bugs, hover flies, and big-eyed bugs. Songbirds and hummingbirds get in the act, too. Your pests are

oil will kill it—eventually. Some insects rarely cause damage to plants, but their sheer numbers make gardeners queasy. Red and black rain tree bugs that feed on the seeds of golden rain tree and annoyingly gather around doors and windows can be vacuumed up. Spittle bug, a pest occurring on many different kinds of plants, resembles white foam and sometimes proliferates to unsightly numbers, but is easy to wash off. Spider mite is a summer pest with many predators. Foliage may look faded (in fact, sucked dry) by these tiny pests that prefer dusty foliage. Wash the plants with a strong stream of water to reduce the mite population to non-threatening numbers.

Some plants are under siege with such intensity that not planting them where they will be perennially stressed seems the best recourse. Agave snout weevil will destroy plants before you realize they're at work inside the plant. Healthy plants produce acidic sap that repels them, but agaves and yuccas in slow-draining soil or frequently watered garden beds are vulnerable. Remove infested plants and the soil immediately around them. While velvet ash is native in the Southwest, some commonly sold cultivars are vulnerable to lilac borer, ash bark beetles,

Spiders are unsung heroes among beneficial insects, as common as the multitude of pests they help control. Orb weavers wrap up grasshoppers in their silken shrouds for later consumption.

Common to southwestern gardens, voracious praying mantis is opportunistic and (like non-selective pesticides), kills beneficial insects as well as pests.

their gourmet dining. When you forego the poisons, you soon learn just how many friends a gardener can have. An online pocket guide to beneficial insects of New Mexico can be found at www.nrcs.usda.gov/Internet/FSE_PLANTMATERIALS/publications/nmpmcbr10943.pdf.

PLANT DISEASES

Whether fatal or mostly cosmetic, prevention is the best strategy for dealing with plant diseases.

Verticillium wilt is a fungus that infiltrates the plant's vascular system, causing dry, sometimes reddened, distorted smaller leaves, and reduced tip growth. Sometimes single branches die back; sometimes most of the plant is affected. Pruning out infected areas, disinfecting tools after each cut, and creating better growing conditions can prolong the life of plants. The fungus remains in the soil for years even without a host, so don't replant susceptible species where others have been infected. Chronic infections can be made milder by keeping plants well watered, or in the case of Chinese pistache in lawn areas, by removing the lawn so the tree can be watered deeply and less often. Generally it is not a good idea to feed struggling plants, but very low doses of fertilizers applied to wilt-affected plants sometimes delays the inevitable. Remove and destroy infected branches; clean up and trash leaves to limit the spread. Pistache, ash, maple, elm, and roses are vulnerable; oak, mulberry, sycamore, poplar, and walnut are resistant.

Anthracnose is another systemic fungal infection affecting sycamores. It presents as browning leaf veins extending into much of the leaf. Otherwise healthy, well-watered sycamores can live many years with the infection.

Powdery mildew is a widespread fungal problem. Spread by wind and rarely fatal, it starts as sooty white patches on the leaves; if unchecked by mid-summer, it gives a hoary cast to the whole plant, limiting photosynthesis by shading the leaf surfaces. It is most likely to occur on plants that are crowded and planted in low, shaded areas, and when plants are watered with overhead spray. Open up spacing to improve air circulation (especially in the shade), use low-flow irrigation to put water into the soil rather than using sprinklers that may spread spores through their spray, and clean up infected leaves and dispose of them. Sulfur dust and horticultural oil sprays are good low toxicity controls but must be used when temperatures are below 90°F to avoid burning. More information can be found at http://ag.arizona.edu/pubs/diseases/az1124/#vfw.

WEEDS

Weeds are pests. Like insects, they tend to be seasonal, assisted in their quest to take over the garden by repeated soil disturbance, excess watering, and fertilizing. The best annual weed deterrents include using low-flow spot irrigation; applying mulches deeply enough to smother weed seedlings or deprive them of the light they need to sprout; and only fertilizing to treat deficiencies. Disturbing the soil mechanically exposes seeds in the soil to the light and air they need to sprout. Cutting annual weeds close to the ground before they set seeds, and mulching over the tops are much more effective controls. Perennial weeds need persistent weeding efforts or repeated spot treatment with herbicides to remove the top growth and starve out the roots. Removing regrowth quickly (before it can photosynthesize enough to restore energy) weakens and finally kills perennials. Smothering persistent weeds such as bindweed and bermuda

Purslane is an edible summer weed that germinates with abandon after a soaking monsoon rain, shades and stabilizes open soil, then disappears with the first frost.

grass never works—there are few things in life I am absolutely certain of, but that unfortunately is one of them. Choose the least-toxic effective control and resort to herbicides only as a last resort, reading labels carefully and avoiding products that persist in the soil, could run off into watershed, or could contaminate groundwater. For more information on bio-control of bindweed, visit www.wci.colostate.edu/Assets/pdf/bindweed.mites.wci.pdf.

SEASONAL PRUNING AND CLEANUP

Plants are often undermined by pruning too much too soon after planting. Removing a few broken branches damaged while transporting or transplanting is the only pruning that should be done on new trees and shrubs for a year or longer.

The small side-branches that grow from the main trunks not only help shade tender bark, but also photosynthesize, making food for new roots and thickening the trunks of young trees. Wait until the bark begins to get corky before you remove those shoots. In extreme climates with little cloud cover and erratic temperatures, the shading and insulation of the main trunks by smaller, leafy stems helps to prevent sunscald of thin bark. Auxins needed to produce new roots are synthesized in the growing tips of branches. Pruning tips to stimulate growth has the opposite effect. Thinning is usually not needed unless the branches are extremely leafy—which may be the result of too much fertilizer—and the plant will self-prune, shedding some of the oldest, least-productive leaves to balance water uptake with transpiration. Once plants have rooted out and begin to claim their space, consider pruning only if and when plants will benefit from the effort.

Misunderstanding what plants are intended to do in a space leads to trouble. Holding back large shrubs that are intended to act as small trees; weeding out unrecognized wildflower seedlings; watering or fertilizing plants in late summer, leading to vulnerability

Sunscald is an unintended but all-too-common consequence of exposing tender bark to intense sunlight, especially when temperatures fluctuate wildly. OPPOSITE Small branches photosynthesize food for new roots.

Thoughtful placement of plants avoids later shrink-to-fit pruning that destroys the natural shapes of plants.

Misunderstanding the purpose of plants in the garden can result in pruning that undermines that function.

and freeze damage—the list of unintended consequences is long and unproductive. When plants are young, they will outgrow the damage. Older trees that are topped become a liability in the landscape.

The best management practices for a plant can be different, depending on how the plant is used. A large shrub may be meant to buffer wind, shade the soil, or be trimmed regularly as a formal hedge. Pruning is an opportunity to look at plants closely and to understand where buds originate and how they develop into branches, leaves, or flowers. It is an opportunity to notice the scent of the leaves or twigs; how light filters through the stems; whether bugs are present, and if their presence is beneficial or causing trouble. With both feet firmly planted on the ground and shears in hand, the best frame of mind to have for pruning might be that of an 8- or 10-year-old climbing trees and plunging headlong into shrub thickets or tall bunchgrass, single-mindedly present in the moment.

Well-shaped desert trees make streets cooler. LEFT When branches are pruned properly, the cells of the branch collar will grow over the cut and protect the cambium from pathogens.

TIMING: WHEN TO PRUNE

As temperature plunges increase the potential for winter injury to plants, there will likely be a need for more remedial pruning. Those first balmy spring days, the same warmth that teases apricots to bud prematurely pulls gardeners out into the garden, shears drawn like high-noon pistols at the O.K. Corral. Stop yourself. Spend those days finding the first green shoots pushing through the mulch. Even if you know that the winter-burnt foliage is truly dead, it acts as a buffer for the live tissue below it and shades the soil, helping keep plants dormant. Removing that insulation in January or February makes plants more vulnerable. Wait until the spring weather roller coaster is over before you get into full gardening mode.

Structural pruning of trees is usually done while plants are dormant and the form is easy to see. Topping trees, lopping off the ends of large branches to reduce the tree's overall size, and lion-tailing (removing most of the lateral branches, leaving tufts of green at the very ends of large limbs) are bad practices anywhere, at all times. They are especially hazardous in extreme climates, where unfettered access for pathogens, sunscald, and wind breakage are added stresses on trees that may already be on the edge of viability. Lion-tailing also reduces a tree's ability to photosynthesize, as interior branches may continue to produce food after the exterior canopy closes stomates to conserve water. Such mutilation reduces healthy trees to liabilities and drops property values.

For summer-blooming plants, pruning to stimulate new growth and to encourage the strongest show of flowers is done in late winter or spring. Wait until after spring-blooming plants flower, pruning to encourage their next season's bud formation. To keep shrubs young and vigorous, thin out a few of their oldest stems each year. In all these instances, as little as 10 percent and no more than 20 percent of plant mass should be removed at one time to prevent sunscald of newly exposed growth. Light pruning also avoids stimulating a surge of new growth that could attract aphids and require more moisture to sustain.

The exception to this rule is the need to prune shrubs adapted to fire—forest and chaparral natives such as oak and sumac—much more severely, to simulate the effect of fire. Each winter, thin out the tallest, oldest stems down close to the ground, so that within 5 to 7 years, most of the stems have been replaced. Shrub oak understory may be pruned down to the ground every 4 or 5 years. It will grow slowly from the root mass as a low ground cover, and not allow fire to ladder up into trees. New growth holds more moisture and is less flammable. Ornamental grasses are the other exception. They should be shaved off as close to the ground as possible right before active growth begins. Leaving too much stubble for the new leaves to push through eventually weakens grasses and looks terrible as plants decline.

Cacti and succulents are best pruned during warm weather to prevent rotting. Dead branches, leaves, and pads can be removed anytime, but to avoid sunburning surfaces that have been shaded by each other, avoid removing more live material than is necessary. When the goal is to emphasize sculptural forms, early summer in intermediate and higher elevation gardens is also the best time to prune small trees and shrubs. Unlike late winter or spring pruning, the increasing heat will suppress sprouting of axillary buds. In the low desert, heat builds earlier, so sculptural pruning should be done in late spring. No pruning should be done August through early October, as it is likely to stimulate frost-tender new shoots too late in the season.

While thinning invigorates plants, shearing is a poor pruning practice in extreme climates. There seems to be no good time to do it. Shearing in early spring produces soft tips that are vulnerable to roller coaster temperatures and abrasive spring winds. In summer, unprotected new tips are likely to sunburn and encourage infestation of psyllids, an otherwise innocuous pest. Topiary is an art form rarely practiced in the Southwest, but the random box and gumball shapes imposed on plants (obliterating their beautiful natural forms) is all too common, and takes time to repair. So-called maintenance professionals who mutilate plants to prove they've been on the job (and to insure ongoing work) need educating—or to be replaced by pruners who understand plants and care about their well-being. Well-pruned plants don't appear barbered; they just look like extremely fine examples of their kind.

When grown with minimal irrigation once they are well-established, desert plants grow at a modest rate and have naturally compact shapes that require little pruning. That "old saw" of carpentry—measure twice, cut once—seems to apply to any sport involving sharp tools. While these plants are often resilient enough to recover from an overly enthusiastic pruning session and other gardening misadventures, when in doubt, it's usually best to do less and observe more. The likelihood that you'll learn something new every time you step out into your garden is one of the joys of gardening in the arid Southwest.

TOP Shear ornamental grasses close to the ground before growth starts. BOTTOM Many arid-adapted plants are naturally mounded in shape and require only infrequent thinning to rejuvenate them. This rosemary was mutilated by unskilled pruning.

Acknowledgments

Thanks to Scott Calhoun, Ron Gass, Janet Rademacher, Judy Mielke, and Marcus White for their always interesting conversations about plants and for helping me gain a better understanding of their hotter climate. Thanks to Will Pockman and Dave Gutzler for helping me better understand the impact of climate extremes on plants in the Southwest. Thanks to Allison Abraham, Karyn DeBont, Tracy Neal, Katherine Peel, and Jay Rice for their help in honing my writing and design ideas.

Thanks to those who lovingly care for the gardens gracing these pages and their willingness to share their experience with the rest of us: Kathy Brown and Jami Porter Lara, Paula Dorris-Osborn, Fred and Sandy Gale, Verne and Laurie Loose, Macon McCrossen, the Rembe family and staff at Los Poblanos Inn and Cultural Center, Doreen Radcliff, Beth Richards and Joe Hardesty, the staff of the Rio Grande Botanic Gardens, the staff and volunteers at Santa Fe Botanical Garden, the staff at Tohono Chul Park, Howard and Virginia Stephens, Susan Stinchcomb, and Wa-ki and Juan Zambrano. It has been a pleasure to spend time in their gardens; always new lessons to learn.

Thanks to all the people already named and all those lifelong learners who garden on the edge, acknowledge the extremes of climate, and find ways of making beautiful spaces with only a little extra water but buckets of enthusiasm.

And thanks to Julie Talbot, Tom Fischer, Andrew Beckman, Laken Wright, and Sarah Milhollin at Timber Press for their help in turning gardening ideas into pages of books.

Gopher spurge (*Euphorbia rigida*) prefers loose, gritty soil, and needs only occasional watering.

Recommended Reading

Much of the information and many of the ideas in these pages had their beginnings as personal experience, or observation supported by a body of research and hard data that quantifies or clarifies many of the concepts. Since this book is intended as a practical working guide and not a scholarly dissertation, I tried to minimize jargon and did not cite specific research in footnotes. Anyone wishing to know the science applied to my experience and conjecture may find the following sources as interesting and thought provoking as I do. Most of this work is far from extreme in the scholarly sense, as scientists are (as a rule) quick to observe and document, but slow to speculate or prognosticate.

PLANT DESCRIPTIONS

Busco, Janice, and Nancy R. Morin. 2003. *Native Plants for High-Elevation Western Gardens*. Golden, Colorado: Fulcrum Publishing.

Carter, Jack L. 2013.*Trees and Shrubs of New Mexico, Revised and Expanded*. Silver City, New Mexico: Mimbres Publishing.

Cartron, Jean-Luc E., David C Lightfoot,Jane E. Mygatt, Sandra L. Brantley and Timothy K. Lowrey. 2008. *A Field Guide to the Plants and Animals of the Rio Grande Bosque*. Albuquerque, New Mexico: University of New Mexico Press.

Dodson, Carolyn and William W. Dunmire. 2007. *Mountain Wildflowers of the Southern Rockies*. Albuquerque, New Mexico: University of New Mexico Press.

Dodson, Carolyn. 2012. *Guide to Plants of the Northern Chihuahuan Desert*. Albuquerque, New Mexico: University of New Mexico Press.

Epple, Anne O. Revised 2012. *A Field Guide to the Plants of Arizona*. Guilford, Connecticut: The Globe Pequot Press.

Ivey, Robert DeWitt. 2013. *Flowering Plants of New Mexico, 5th edition*. Albuquerque, New Mexico: www. lulu.com.

Martin, William C. and Charles R. Hutchins. 2001. *Flora of New Mexico Volumes 1 and 2*. Koenigstein, Germany: Koeltz Scientific Books.

Mielke, Judy. 1993. *Native Plants for Southwestern Landscapes*. Austin, Texas: University of Texas Press.

Phillips, Judith. 1995. *Natural By Design*. Santa Fe, New Mexico: Museum Of New Mexico Press.

———.1995. *Plants for Natural Gardens*. Santa Fe, New Mexico: Museum Of New Mexico Press.

———. 1987. *Southwestern Landscaping with Native Plants*. Santa Fe, New Mexico: Museum Of New Mexico Press.

Vines, Robert A. 1976. *Trees, Shrubs and Woody Vines of the Southwest*. Austin: University of Texas Press.

PLANT PESTS

Books

Western Society of Weed Science and Cooperative Extension Service. 1991. *Weeds of the West*. Jackson, Wyoming: University of Wyoming.

Websites

Fact sheet: Healthy Roots and Healthy Trees
http://www.ext.colostate.edu/pubs/garden/02926.html

Information on verticillium and fusarium wilts
http://ag.arizona.edu/pubs/diseases/az1124/#vfw

Traditional architecture and contemporary climate-adapted plants blend seamlessly under the southwestern sun.

SPECIFIC PLANT FOCUS

Books

Allred, Kelly. 1995. *A Field Guide to the Grasses of New Mexico*. Las Cruces, New Mexico: New Mexico State University.

Clebsch, Betsy. 1997. *A Book of Salvias: Sages for Every Garden*. Portland, Oregon: Timber Press.

Gould, Frank C. 1951.*Grasses of the Southwestern United States*. Tucson: University of Arizona Press.

Haukos, David A. and Loren M. Smith. 1997. *Common Flora of the Playa Lakes*. Lubbock, Texas: Texas Tech University Press.

Irish, Mary. 2000. *Agaves, Yuccas, and Related Plants*. Portland, Oregon: Timber Press.

Nold, Robert. 1999. *Penstemons*. Portland, Oregon: Timber Press.

——.2008. *High and Dry: Gardening with Cold-Hardy Dryland Plants*. Portland, Oregon: Timber Press.

Websites

Maps and fact sheets by state or region http://plants.usda.gov for extensive.

Plant database, Ladybird Johnson Wildflower Center, Austin, Texas www.wildflower.org/plants/

NMSU SW Plants app can be downloaded from iTunes. A link is also available at www.xericenter.com/swplants

https://pollinator.org/PDFs/AmericanSemiDesert.rx8.pdf

Excellent low desert information from the Desert Botanical Garden in Phoenix http://www.dbg.org/gardening-horticulture and http://www.dbg.org/research-conservation

Forum on types of plants www.biology-online.org/biology-forum/about459.html

NATIVE PLANT SOCIETIES

Arizona: http://aznps.org

Colorado: http://conps.org

Nevada: http://heritage.nv.gov for maps and fact sheets

New Mexico: http://npsnm.unm.edu; also: http://nmrareplants.unm.edu for maps and fact sheets

Utah: http://unps.org

ECOLOGICAL LANDSCAPE CONTEXT

Books

Alexander, Christopher, Sara Ishikawa, and Murray Silverstein. 1977. *A Pattern Language*. New York, New York: Oxford University Press.

Basso, Keith. *Wisdom Sits In Places*. 1996. Albuquerque, New Mexico: University of New Mexico Press.

Brown, David E., ed. 1982. *Biotic Communities of the American Southwest United States and Mexico.*

Desert Plants: Vol. 4, No. P1-4. Tucson, Arizona: University of Arizona Press.

deBuys, William. 2011. *A Great Aridness: Climate Change and the Future of the American Southwest*. New York, New York: Oxford University Press.

Lopez, Barry, ed. 2006. *Home Ground—Language for an American Landscape*. San Antonio, Texas: Trinity University Press.

McAuliffe, Joseph R., Louis A. Scuderi, and Leslie D. McFadden. *Tree-ring record of hillslope erosion and valley floor dynamics: Landscape responses to climate variation during the last 400 years in the Colorado Plateau, northeastern Arizona.* Available online @ www.sciencedirect.com.

McClaran, Michael P. and Thomas R. Van Devender. 1995. *The Desert Grassland*. Tucson, Arizona: University of Arizona Press.

Nassaur, Joan Iverson, ed. 1997. *Placing Nature, Culture and Landscape Ecology*. Washington, DC: Island Press.

Phillips, Steven J. and Patricia Wentworth Comus, eds. 2000. *A Natural History of the Sonoran Desert*. Tucson, Arizona: Desert Museum Press.

Scurlock, Dan. 1998. *From the Rio to the Sierra: An Environmental History of the Middle Rio Grande Basin*. Fort Collins, Colorado: USDA Rocky Mountain Research Station, General Technical Report 5. (www.fs.fed.us/rm/pubs/rmrs_gtr005.pdf)

Silvertown, Jonathan. 2008. *Demons in Eden: The Paradox of Plant Diversity*. Chicago: University of Chicago Press.

Thompson, J. William and Kim Sorvig. 2007. *Sustainable Landscape Construction, 2nd Edition.* Washington DC: Island Press.

Waring, Gwendolyn L. 2011. *A Natural History of the Intermountain West.* Salt Lake City, Utah: University of Utah Press.

Woodward, Joan. 2000. *Waterstained Landscapes: Seeing and Shaping Regionally Distinctive Places.* Baltimore: The Johns Hopkins University Press.

Websites

Climate change favors C4 plants
www.biology-online.org/biology-forum/about459.html

Climate change in the Southwest
http://www.southwestclimate
change.org/

PLANT CONSERVATION

Documenting/quantifying the value of trees
www.naturewithin.info/new.html

Center for Plant Conservation
www.centerforplantconservation.
org

Plant Conservation Alliance
www.nps.gov/plants

WATER

Books

Barnett, Cynthia. 2011. *Blue Revolution—Unmaking America's Water Crisis.* Boston: Beacon Press.

Fishman, Charles. 2011. *The Big Thirst—the Secret Life and Turbulent Future of Water.* New York: Free Press.

Lancaster, Brad. 2006, 2008. *Rainwater Harvesting for Drylands and Beyond, Volumes 1 and 2.* Tucson, Arizona: Rainsource Press.

Miller, Char, ed. 2000. *Water In the West: A High Country News Reader.* Corvallis, Oregon: Oregon State University Press.

Postel, Sandra. 1999. *Pillar of Sand: Can the Irrigation Miracle Last?* New York: W.W. Norton and Company for Worldwatch Institute.

Reiser, Marc. 1986. *Cadillac Desert: The American West and Its Disappearing Water.* New York: Viking Penguin.

Zeedyke, Bill and Van Clothier. 2009. *Let Water Do the Work: Induced Meandering, an Evolving Method for Restoring Incised Channels.* Santa Fe: Quivira Coalition.

Websites

U.S. Drought Monitor
http://droughtmonitor.unl.edu/
home/regionaldroughtmonitor.
aspx?west

Arizona Water Conservation
http://www.azwater.gov/azdwr/
StatewidePlanning/Conservation2/
default.htm

http://water.tucsonaz.gov/water/
conservation

http://www.glendaleaz.com/
waterconservation/

http://watershedmg.org/

New Mexico water conservation
www.cabq.gov/waterconservation

http://www.santafenm.gov/
water_conservation

http://www.ci.rio-rancho.nm.us/
index.aspx?nid=178

http://www.las-cruces.org/Departments/Utilities/Services/Water%20
Conservation/Resources.aspx

Southern Colorado water conservation
http://www.secwcdxeriscape.org/

Texas water conservation
http://texaslivingwaters.org/
water-conservation/

Utah water conservation
http://www.conservewater.utah.
gov/

Abstract on controlled alternate partial root-zone irrigation
http://jxb.oxfordjournals.org/content/55/407/2437.long

http://xeriscapenm.com/wp-content/uploads/Resources.pdf

"The Last Drop: Climate Change and the Southwest Water Crisis"
www.sei-us.org/publications/id/371

Metric Conversions

INCHES	CENTIMETERS
¼	0.6
½	1.3
¾	1.9
1	2.5
2	5.1
3	7.6
4	10
5	13
6	15
7	18
8	20
9	23
10	25
20	51
30	76
40	100
50	130
60	150
70	180
80	200
90	230
100	250

FEET	METERS
1	0.3
2	0.6
3	0.9
4	1.2
5	1.5
6	1.8
7	2.1
8	2.4
9	2.7
10	3
20	6
30	9
40	12
50	15
60	18
70	21
80	24
90	27
100	30

TEMPERATURES

$$°C = \tfrac{5}{9} \times (°F - 32)$$

$$°F = (\tfrac{9}{5} \times °C) + 32$$

Credits

PHOTOGRAPHY

Eric Bernard: 22, 24, 270 top, 282, 283
Scott Calhoun: 5, 6, 73, 78, 79, 88, 89, 99, 104 left, 107 right, 118, 119, 125 left, 142
    left, 152 left, 159 right, 161 left, 163 right, 165 left, 167, 170, 172, 175 right, 181
    right, 183 right, 185 left, 189 right, 192 right, 193 left, 194 right, 197, 202 right,
    209 left, 216 left, 235 right, 240 right, 244 right, 260 left, 302
Eloise Colocho: 245 left
Noelle Johnson: 108 left
Dr. Alan Lipkin/Shutterstock: 224 left
NeilStanners/iStock: 113 right
peganum/Flickr: 188 left
Stickpen/Wikimedia: 181 left
Hunter Ten Broeck: 38, 64 top, 69 right, 85, 107 left, 109 left, 111 top, 127 left, 130
    left, 139 left, 141 left, 144, 157 right, 159 left, 169 right, 171, 176, 178 left, 184
    right, 220 right, 235 left, 237 left, 247, 248 left, 257 left
Janice Tucker: 92, 95 top, 227 right
Juan Zambrano: 236 left

All other photographs are by the author

GARDEN DESIGN

Allison Abraham: 54
Scott Calhoun: 73, 78, 79, 88, 89, 99, 125 left, 302
David Cristiani: 66 bottom
Jami Porter Lara and Kathy Brown: 61
Judith Phillips: 32, 62 right, 64 bottom, 67, 69 left, 74–77, 80–87, 97, 98
Hunter Ten Broeck: 64 top, 66 top, 69 right, 71 left, 90, 91, 268
Sites Southwest: 62 bottom left
W. Gary Smith: 56, 92–95, 273
University of New Mexico Planning and Landscape Architecture students: 96

Index

About the Author

Allison Abraham

Judith Phillips has spent more than forty years gardening in the Southwest and is still adapting. She is the owner of Judith Phillips Design Oasis, an ecosystem-inspired garden design and consulting service. She has designed thousands of residential gardens in New Mexico, Colorado, and Arizona and has been fortunate to be involved in diverse public projects from habitat gardens at wildlife refuges and parks, to healing gardens at hospitals, and outdoor classrooms for elementary schools. The common ground is luring people outdoors to spend time with plants. As a part-time faculty member at the University of New Mexico, she focuses on native and climate-adapted plants for arid landscapes. She has contributed to many books, and is the sole author of *New Mexico Gardener's Guide*, *Southwestern Landscaping with Native Plants*, *Natural by Design*, and *Plants for Natural Gardens*.